Brit,
  I hope you enjoy my uncle's
book.
          Happy Holidays,
             Susan

ANOTHER *fine* MESS

you've gotten us into

The Life and Adventures of a Quad

ROBERT PRONDZINSKI

Nasus Publishing

Bloomington, Minnesota

Published by
Nasus Publishing
Bloomington, MN • 952.484.4262
nasuspublishing@successideas.com

Jacket Illustration and Design by
Anthony Alex Le Tourneau, www.anthonyletourneau.com

ORDERING INFORMATION
QUANTITY SALES: Special discounts are available on quantity purchases by corporations, associations, and others as arranged directly with the publisher. Please use contact information stated above.
BOOKSTORE ORDERS: Available through Baker & Taylor Books.
INDIVIDUAL SALES: Available at www.finemessadventure.com and Amazon.com

Printed in the United States of America

Library of Congress Control Number: 2008927036

ISBN 9780967029122

Dedication

This book is dedicated to my parents, John and Stella Prondzinski, and brother, Bill, whose love and support got me through the tough times, and to Mr. Louis Winokur, whose intervention provided me with the opportunity to really make something out of my life.

I also extend a special dedication to my good friend Edward Weishaar. Edward and I have experienced together much of what you will read about in this book. He has been with me during the best of times and worst of times and has always been there for me when I needed him. We have been friends for forty years and he hasn't killed me yet. "Thank you, Edward, for everything."

And, finally, I'd like to thank my loving wife, Diane, for her continued support, and for living with my craziness.

CONTENTS

An Introduction You Must Read!

Why I started writing this book.

My friends have been telling me for years that I should write a brief account of all the strange and unusual situations I got them – and myself – into over the last forty-four years of living my life as a quadriplegic. I was repeatedly told, *"Well, this is another fine mess you've gotten us into"* – hence the title of this book.

As with most good stories and anecdotes, the situations weren't always so funny during the time my friends and I were going through them. Yet, putting years between the actual events and the telling of them helps to find new perspective on how truly comical some of them were.

Now, when various friends and I get together, we often reflect back on these predicaments and laugh. After being continually pressured by the people who hear them, I decided to take the time to put my favorite stories down on paper.

Lost in translation?

When I have occasion to tell a story, it's nearly always in a social setting with a group of friends or family, and we are typically gathered around a table for dinner. In the course of normal dinner conversation someone makes a comment that triggers one of the stories that fits the topic. A friend might turn to me and say, "Bob, tell them about the time we…" Or, if no one at the table was a part of the story, I'll simply launch into the tale myself.

After deciding to document my stories, I soon realized that verbally recounting a short anecdote is a lot different from writing it. When telling the story I'm enthusiastic. My body language and voice inflection help me and others relate to what I am saying. Those things don't carry over into the written word.

Yet, despite the potential for some of the nuances to be "lost in translation," the advantage to writing the story down is that I get to include relevant details in the story and in the context that surrounds it. Hopefully, as you read them, you'll laugh along with the rest of us.

I get by with a little help from my friends.

I have been fortunate to make many good friends at different stages of my life who make up the cast of characters you are about to meet in my many stories. Without setting out on these adventures together, and often getting them in trouble – or at the very least, a little harmless mischief – this book could never have been written.

I would like to say to all of my friends right now how much their friendships meant and still mean to me. Thank you all for putting up with my weirdness and for being passengers in one heck of a journey. Since our adventures together caused me to spend so much time writing this manuscript, it's my turn to say to you, *"This is another fine mess you've gotten **me** into."*

What this book turned into.

No one is more surprised than I am to say that this book has four parts. Part 1 gives the background of my accident, rehabilitation, schooling, job hunting, and some information that I hope answers questions people may have about what it is like to be a quadriplegic. Part 2 is my favorite part – the stories and anecdotes that were the catalyst for this book. Part 3 also includes stories but they detail some of the serious medical issues I've encountered. Part 4 is a reflection, looking back on what my life has been like and how things have changed for disabled people over the years. I've also included an addendum that outlines many of the technologies, products and equipment I use to make my life easier, in the hopes that it may help others bypass a lot of trial and error if they have similar needs to my own.

While I started this book with the intent to simply document my stories, I realized that the stories needed to be put in some sort of context relating to my life as a quadriplegic in general. My friends and the people who know me will understand the stories and relate to the strange and unusual situations a quadriplegic can get into and find humor in them, but the general reader might view the stories differently.

For those of you who do not know me, I felt the entire sequence of events in my life – both good times and bad – is just as important to document. I hope that Part 1 of this book provides some insight about what it has been like to go through most of my life as a quadriplegic. Perhaps then you will be able to see the humor that my friends and I found in the stories contained in Part 2 of this book. Many are definitely not situations that most of you will ever encounter in your lifetime.

Working through the good, the bad, and the ugly.

Writing this book brought back a lot of my life's history that I almost forgot about. In remembering the many situations and events throughout my life, a lot of thoughts and emotions I had during the time the events actually happened became as vivid to me now as they were then.

Like any of you, I've had my ups and downs. Life has been good. Life has been bad. And sometimes life would deliver a little bit of ugly. My original intent for this book has not changed, yet it has been expanded to show life from my perspective: a quadriplegic struggling to become a benefit – rather than a detriment – to society.

Family and friends had curiosities and questions that they often did not ask. People who do not know me do not know how – or if – to approach me. I now have the opportunity to answer some of those questions.

The serious side of this book.

Every forty-one minutes another person is added to the list of more than 250,000 Americans living with spinal cord injuries. A broken neck can leave you a quadriplegic or a broken back can leave you a paraplegic. Both injuries will more than likely leave you confined to a wheelchair for the rest of your life. Those of us with spinal cord injuries were all ordinary people living ordinary lives and in one split second our lives were changed forever.

Picture yourself as a typical healthy and active teenager one minute, and a minute later being confined to a bed or wheelchair for the rest of your life. Or picture yourself as a parent who has just been told by a doctor that your son or daughter will never walk again.

*Close your eyes and take five minutes to imagine what the rest of **your** life would be like.*

I don't have to imagine it. I know what life would be like because, for the last forty-four years, I have lived it. I have been a quadriplegic as a result of crushing my neck in a freak swimming accident. I know the emotional pain and suffering of my parents and brother trying to cope with the situation.

This story is as real as it gets but it's not as bad as you might think. The good news is there is life after a spinal cord injury.

In the following pages I try to convey what it was like trying to adjust to the new reality of being a quadriplegic and how the trip through life can still be successful. Many realities of being a quadriplegic were very hard for me to put into this book. I felt I was exposing the last little part of my private life and thoughts. It was extremely difficult for me to write about my daily hygiene needs and sex life, but without doing so I don't think you can come close to understanding what it really means to be a quadriplegic.

Christopher Reeve experienced a spinal cord injury that left him a quadriplegic after he gained notoriety as an actor. Because he was a well-known celebrity, his contribution to making the general public aware of what it means to be a quadriplegic was inspiring. Only when the public becomes aware of the issues involved with spinal cord injuries can there be sufficient support for increasing medical research in this field. Public awareness also contributes to broadening career opportunities available to the quadriplegic by providing an understanding that this disability does not prevent one from leading a successful and fulfilling life in business.

At the time of this writing, more than 29,000 US soldiers have been wounded in Iraq since 2003. They suffer from all kinds of injuries, including spinal injuries and amputations. If this book can help just one person or family through some of their questions and concerns about the future, then it will have been worth the writing.

I have seen many changes in the last forty-four years. I know firsthand that someone currently suffering from a spinal cord injury or amputation can not only make it in this world, but can excel in this world. You can live an exceptional life. To paraphrase a current political slogan of optimism for America's future, "Yes you can! Yes you can! Yes you can!"

Part 1: My New Journey Begins

For seventeen years I lived my life like any other typical kid growing up in the Midwest. But in the blink of an eye my life changed forever. Part 1 documents the accident, the realizations, and the adjustments I had to make as I started an unplanned journey through life as a quadriplegic. This section also gives me an opportunity to answer many unasked questions by friends and family, and explain as best I can what it is physically like to be me.

Since Part 1 serves as background, it has a serious tone as I describe how I learned to live in my new reality. If, after reading a few of the chapters, you decide this section is more serious than you like and does not hold your interest, feel free to move on to the more humorous stories and anecdotes in Part 2.

CHAPTER 1

The Accident

It was June of 1964. I was three months from my eighteenth birthday, attending Stout State University in Menominee, Wisconsin, prior to the start of the regular fall term.

It was a beautiful summer day. My friend, Rick Winokur, and I decided we should get a few couples together and go to the lake for an evening beach party. We managed to get four couples together and headed down to the beach during late afternoon for a great little picnic lunch. After lunch, we decided we would swim to the raft located about 200 feet from shore.

We all started running on the beach and into the water. I was running so fast that when my feet entered the water I lost my balance and went flying head over heels. I landed on the top of my head about ten feet from shore in about a foot and half of water. My head was pushed into the bottom of the lake with such force that it crushed the fifth cervical vertebrae in my neck. This one brief, defining moment changed my life forever.

And a new quadriplegic entered this world.

With my head face down and under water but still conscious, I knew that something was drastically wrong. I was a lifeguard for many years and earned my high school letters by competing on the high school swimming team. As I held my breath, Rick came to see why I was not moving and discovered there was a lot of blood in the water around my head. I hit with such force that I lacerated my scalp, causing it to bleed.

Rick quickly turned me over and dragged me to shore. I was completely paralyzed and had absolutely no feeling anywhere in my body from the neck down, but at least I was still conscious. As Rick was about to lift me farther up the beach, I managed to tell him to stop and just let me lie on the shoreline while he called for help.

When the ambulance arrived, I asked the ambulance driver not to pick me up but, instead, move me to a stretcher for the trip to the hospital. The hospital in Menominee, Wisconsin, is very small. After taking a couple of x-rays, the physicians determined that they could not handle such a damaging spinal cord injury.

The hospital personnel made me as comfortable as they could but wanted me to stay conscious, so they didn't give me any medications. I couldn't feel anything, so I guess it really didn't matter. They positioned and provided support around my neck to prevent it from moving around too much. They then made arrangements for an ambulance to take me to Miller Hospital in St. Paul, Minnesota, which was approximately sixty-five miles away.

The Midnight Ride

It was close to midnight when the ambulance arrived to transport me to Miller Hospital. During the ride I remember staring up at the ceiling of the ambulance and hearing sirens in the distance. But, for the most part, my mind was focused on my physical condition.

I tried moving my arms, but no part of them would move and I wondered how long this would last. When people touched me I couldn't feel anything and I wondered how long that would last. I hoped that when I finally got to the hospital in St. Paul they would figure out what was wrong, fix me up, and have me out of there and back to college in Menominee in a few days.

Since I didn't remember anything else about the ambulance ride from Menominee to Miller Hospital in St. Paul, Rick later filled me in on what we went through.

The Menominee Hospital called a locally available ambulance to transport me to Miller Hospital in St. Paul. The ambulance was an old-style Cadillac vehicle that probably did double duty as both a hearse and an ambulance. I was later told that this was commonplace in rural areas.

During the 1960s, ambulances were not outfitted with high-tech medical gear, nor were there any paramedics with extensive medical training to accompany patients. So when I was placed in the back of the ambulance, there were only two people who would accompany me to St. Paul and neither of them had any medical experience. Rick said they were dressed in normal street clothes and the driver either owned the ambulance or was an employee of the company that did. The second person was the driver's son.

After assessing the situation, Rick intervened and insisted that he travel with us so he could be by my side. Although my neck and head had already been placed in protective supports at the Menominee hospital, once in the ambulance, the driver told Rick to help keep my head still to prevent any jarring movement while on the road. Concerned that he might hurt me further, Rick was hesitant, but given the alternative of leaving me in the hands of the driver's son, he agreed and we left Menominee to begin the sixty-five mile trip to St. Paul.

When the ambulance pulled onto the main highway we were met by two Wisconsin State Patrol vehicles assigned to escort us to the Wisconsin border. At the border we were to be met by two Minnesota State Patrol vehicles that would escort us the rest of the way to Miller Hospital.

As we caravanned along the highway, Rick realized that what started out as a light rain earlier in the evening had now turned into a raging thunderstorm and the rain was pouring down nonstop. Visibility was poor and the ambulance occasionally fishtailed on the slick roads as it sped along the highway.

Rick thought we would all be killed if the ambulance swerved off the road so he asked the driver if he could slow down. The driver told Rick that he needed to keep up with the police escort – which was traveling in excess of 100 miles per hour – and that there was no way for him to communicate directly with the State Patrol vehicles to ask them to slow down. He began to flash his headlights on and off for about a minute until the State Patrol vehicles noticed and finally slowed down.

As we neared the Minnesota border, the thunderstorm eased up and the police escort sped up again. At the border the Minnesota State Patrol took over the escort to Miller Hospital.

I never realized what a commotion I caused until Rick told me the whole story. I guess our "midnight ride" was the first time after my accident that my friend could have said, *This is a fine mess you've gotten me into.*

Quite frankly, after hearing the entire story about the ambulance ride, I'm surprised that either of us was still alive.

I Must Have Holes in My Head

When the ambulance arrived at Miller Hospital, I was immediately taken out of the ambulance, put on a hospital gurney, and wheeled into the emergency room. Because they were expecting me, I was in the emergency room only a couple of minutes before they took me for surgery.

One of my first thoughts as I was being wheeled into the surgical area was, "Am I wearing clean underwear?"

Yes, it's a strange thing to think of while lying paralyzed on a gurney. But, growing up, my mother had always been adamant about our wearing clean underwear. If something were to happen, you didn't want others to think you never changed them.

Of course, I wasn't wearing underwear at all – I was wearing bathing trunks. I hoped at least those were clean.

Once in the operating room, I was asked a constant stream of questions about the accident while the surgeons prepared to set my neck in traction. I was conscious for the entire surgical procedure. I heard the doctors talking about what they were going to do that weekend at the same time they were drilling holes in the sides of my skull. They used a small hand drill like the one I used when building model airplanes. I listened to the sound of the drill, thinking it was like putting your ear to a wooden board or desk and then knocking on the wood. It amplifies the sound and you think it is coming from inside your head.

With all the talking and drilling, I listened anxiously, wondering if I was also going to hear the surgeon say, "Oops."

Luckily that never happened.

The Circle Bed

Once a hole was drilled into each side of my skull, a clamp was placed over my head and the ends of the clamp were inserted into the two newly drilled holes. About twenty pounds of traction was placed on a pulley that was connected to the clamp in order to keep my head in a straight and level position. Then I was wheeled to a hospital room and transferred into a circle bed.

I remember my experience in the circle bed as if it were yesterday.

A circle bed is a strange device (see the photos in the Addendum). If you view it from the side, it is actually a circular frame about seven feet in diameter with a narrow board-like device placed along the diameter, cutting the circle in half. This whole circular device sits on a rectangular frame that stands about a foot above the floor. My body was placed on the board-like device.

When I was on my back and staring at the ceiling, the board would be under me. When I needed to be turned to prevent pressure areas from developing on my backside, they clamped another board to the front of my body and strapped the two boards together to prevent me from sliding out sideways during the turn. A good analogy might be to picture a sandwich. The two boards would be the bread and I would be the meat.

Once strapped in, the bed can be rotated in either a clockwise or counterclockwise direction in order to turn me over. Once my body was horizontal, face up or face down, the board closest to the ceiling was removed. During the turning process, the traction adjusted itself so there wasn't extra pressure on the neck. Usually I was turned at least once an hour to prevent pressure sores from forming and damaging the skin.

After the first few days, as your body acclimates to lying in a horizontal position, the turning process can be quite interesting. Using a clock analogy, when I was in a prone position, my head would be at three o'clock and my feet at nine o'clock. Once the boards were inserted and I was strapped in, the circle would be turned in a counterclockwise direction. My head would go from the three o'clock position to two, one, twelve, eleven, ten, and nine before the bed is stopped. I would then once again be horizontal only, this time, face down.

Life in the circle bed is extremely boring since there is literally nothing else to do during the day except wait to be turned every hour. But I did discover one happy distraction.

When the body is in a constant prone position it does not respond normally to being upright. When I would reach the vertical position

10

during the turning process, the blood would drain from my head and I would momentarily pass out.

I loved passing out. It was a great feeling and I looked forward to it during every turn. Every once in awhile when I started to regain consciousness I would pretend I was still unconscious so that the people turning the bed would start to get concerned. Ah, yes, sometimes it's the little distractions that help you get through the bigger challenges.

My stay in the circle bed lasted over six weeks while the traction was slowly lessened and eventually eliminated. Once I was able to use a neck brace, the traction was removed altogether and the circle bed and I were finally free of each other.

Gravitational Pull

One time, while in the circle bed, things went drastically wrong in the middle of the night. After being sandwiched between the two boards in preparation to turn me over, the hospital staff either forgot to strap the boards together or the strap wasn't secured. As the rotation approached the vertical position, I slipped out the side of the sandwich, ripped off my traction, and my limp body fell eight feet down to the floor. I lay there for quite awhile until the hospital staff and doctors decided how best to get me back in the circle bed. Once back in the bed my rotation regimen returned to normal.

At the very least, this incident further broke up the monotony of my confinement.

CHAPTER 2

Contemplation

D octors at Miller Hospital told me that I would never walk again. Some doctors even indicated I would be bedridden for the rest of my life and incapable of using a wheelchair. During my two months there I had a lot of time to contemplate how my life would have to change.

What Now?

One of the surgeons who set my neck in traction when I first arrived at Miller later told me I was very lucky that, at the time of the accident, I was conscious and able to tell my friend not to carry me to higher ground. He said that if my neck had been moved any more there was a good chance I would have been dead because additional displacement could have affected my ability to breathe.

A teenager at the time of my accident, I never seriously reflected on my own mortality – actually, I never considered it at all. But as I lay on the beach with a broken neck, this near-death experience gave me plenty of time to think about it. Death was no longer frightening to me. If it happens it happens. Don't get me wrong, I was ready to live and cope with any challenges I would now face, but I no longer had to dwell on or spend more than two brief seconds contemplating death.

I had always been very carefree and lived for the moment. But the accident had a chilling effect on me. I now had to consider various scenarios of my future, most of them not very pleasant. No more living moment to moment. I had to grow up fast and plan out small, achievable goals. During my stay at Miller Hospital, I matured very quickly.

In my pre-quad life I was very athletically active. I played organized baseball, basketball, and lettered on the swimming team. My parents used to take our family on vacation trips to northern Minnesota and Wisconsin where we would spend a lot of time hiking in the woods and fishing. My dad later bought a small little house trailer on a lake that we would go to most weekends, even during the winter. It was a great little place for both summer fishing and winter ice fishing and we fondly referred to it as our "cottage" up north. Located in Nicolet National Forest, there were plenty of places to hike and hunt. I now saw this previous life being denied to me because of my inability to walk.

My parents and I were very close. I knew that my accident was going to affect their lives tremendously. They both thought they would have to take care of me at home for the rest of their lives and were very worried that, when they died, I would become a ward of the state and be institutionalized. I admit that I occasionally had similar thoughts and was frightened about what the future really had in store for me.

I knew I had to put a plan together so that I would not become a burden to my parents or society. I didn't know how I was going to accomplish this, but I was determined to find a way to turn my life around and make as many positive things happen as I could.

Choosing "Can" Over "Can't"

Many people have asked me how I felt once I knew I would never walk again. My usual answer was that I was devastated. And unless you've gone through it yourself, I don't think anyone could really understand the range of feelings I had immediately after my accident. Sure, I wondered, "Why me?" What had I done to deserve this fate? And for a while I convinced myself the doctors were surely wrong and that after a few weeks I would be back to normal.

As the weeks went on I finally came to realize that I would never be normal again. From that point on my life as I knew it was over. All my dreams for the future were dead. No longer would I be able to do the things that made me happy like going out with my girlfriend to enjoy a day or evening. No longer would I be able to just go out and party with my friends. No longer would I be able to actively participate in my favorite sports like swimming or playing basketball and baseball. No longer would I be able to enjoy fishing trips on some north Wisconsin lake. No longer would I be able to walk out by myself through the tranquil forests of northern Wisconsin. I was devastated, depressed, and angry. But after a little while I came to acknowledge that there was nothing I could do to change what physically happened to me and I had a choice: I could wallow in self-pity and do nothing the rest of my life feeling angry at the whole world because life is unfair, or I could accept my redefined abilities, move on and plan to make this new life of mine the best life I could.

To this day I cringe when somebody says life is unfair. There are no rules that guide fairness or unfairness in this world. And there are no promises made that bad things won't happen. You have to take what life throws at you and deal with it as best you can.

I have always been told that I am an optimist, searching for and finding the silver lining in any bad situation. That might be true but that's not something I work at, it's just the way I am. I also enjoy challenges and, whenever I am told I can't do something, I strive to show others that I can... and often succeed.

Brain Versus Brawn

I was realistic enough to understand that in the short term I needed as much help and support as I could get. And one thing was blatantly clear: I would need to get a college education to even have a chance at earning a living. While lying flat on my back and motionless in a hospital bed, I decided that my first goal would be getting a college degree.

Unfortunately, I had pretty mediocre grades throughout high school. I needed to change my mindset and start using my brain to reach the potential others always told me I had. At the time I had no clue how to start this process but I knew it had to be done. I was a typical kid just getting out of high school, so I really didn't have any idea what areas of study I wanted to pursue in college. All I knew is that I enjoyed the sciences and was very interested in astronomy when I was growing up.

My teachers always told me I was an underachiever. Looking back, I can see it was true. I kept my grades up just enough to stay on the swimming team. I was the kind of guy who would borrow somebody's book report so that I could trade that one for one more, and then I would have two to trade for two more, which would get me four to trade for four more until I had a surplus of book reports to hand in.

I would ace classes that I liked, like Earth Sciences, with hardly any work at all. But my biggest downfall was that I didn't apply myself to English and language courses. To get into a quality college, I knew I would have to take some remedial courses to get my grade point average back into shape. In this new world of mine I would have to use my brain more than my physical abilities to get me through life.

I also realized that I would have to be twice as good as other candidates to successfully compete for a job. Scholastically, I felt I would need a master's degree to compete with somebody who has a bachelor's degree. During my initial days in Miller Hospital, I didn't realize how accurate this assessment would prove to be.

CHAPTER 3

Rehabilitation

After a two-month stay at Miller Hospital, I was sent to the Sister Kenny Rehabilitation Institute in Minneapolis for physical and occupational therapy. The Sister Kenny Institute was well known during the 1950s for treating polio patients; however, after the polio epidemic was controlled, the Institute changed its focus to spinal cord injuries and stroke victims. When I arrived in 1964 there were approximately twenty quadriplegics and paraplegics who had broken their necks or backs in various accidents.

I was surprised at how many people survived with a broken neck. Before I had my accident I thought that anybody with a broken neck would be dead and that I was a very lucky survivor. It also amazed me how many people break their necks in freak accidents. There was a quadriplegic at the Institute who had a fifty-pound sack of grain fall on his head while touring a warehouse. Another one fell off of a sled while going down a snowy hill. Even my accident of tripping while running fast from the beach into the water was pretty freakish. I would expect most broken necks to occur in car crashes or diving accidents, but that didn't seem to be the case.

Therapy

During my nine months at the Sister Kenny Institute I spent a lot of time in physical therapy (PT) and occupational therapy (OT). Every Monday through Friday we would have a session of each therapy type in the morning and then again in the afternoon.

Physical therapy

PT activities not only involved exercises that helped strengthen all the muscles I could still control but also helped me to regain better balance with my body and keep my joints limber. The regimen of exercises included things like:

- Lifting weights: To build and strengthen muscles that still worked, gloves were put on my hands and fastened with Velcro strips. Various weights would then be strapped to the gloves so that I could lift the weights myself. This greatly improved my bicep and shoulder strength.

- Mat exercises: I would be placed on a large mat that was on a table about two feet off the ground. I would then be taught how to move the muscles I still had in order to turn myself over from my stomach to my back and to my stomach again. The therapist would also get me into a sitting position with my legs hanging over the table and then little by little release me until I was balancing myself in a sitting position. This greatly improved my body balance.

- Range of motion: Numerous range of motion exercises were used to stretch and move each joint as far as possible in all directions. Because I could not move various parts of my body such as my fingers and legs, the physical therapist would perform passive range-of-motion exercises on them. Although these exercises do not build up muscles or make them stronger, they keep the joint areas flexible. This is important because, without these exercises, blood flow and flexibility in moving and bending of your joints can decrease. Joints, such as your knees and elbows, could become stiff and locked without range of motion exercises.

Occupational therapy

I first believed that occupational therapy would be of little interest to me. I didn't see myself making breadboards, bird feeders, or weaving baskets for the rest of my life. But I soon found out that OT provided many more benefits than I originally thought.

- **Sanding wood:** Two projects that increased my arm and hand coordination as well as strengthening my muscles involved sanding a lot of wood. For one project I sanded and painted a breadboard for my mother (although she'd never used one). The other project involved sawing, shaving, sanding, varnishing, and polishing a transfer (sliding) board. I actually used that item for a few years to transfer from my wheelchair to a hospital bed or car seat.

- **Standing frames:** OT had a standing frame that I used regularly. While sitting in a wheelchair, long leg braces were attached to my legs. The occupational therapists would then lift me into a standing position and secure me to a standing frame. This was to prevent secondary complications that often result from prolonged use of a wheelchair. The medical benefits are: Develop and improve upper body balance and strength, improve range of motion in spine, hips, knees, and ankles, decrease abnormal muscle tone and reflexes such as leg spasms, improve bladder, digestive, respiratory and circulatory functions, lessen progressive scoliosis and assist with skeletal development, stabilize and prevent loss of bone mineral density which would lead to weakened brittle bones that can fracture easily. I was also told it would help prevent the formation of kidney stones.

- **Tenodesis Splint:** This is a device used to grasp objects. It helps quadriplegics who lack finger movement but retain the ability to extend their wrist. My occupational therapist and the biomechanical engineer in Sister Kenny's adaptive equipment department custom-made a device like this for me. Although I had very limited wrist movement, this tenodesis splint allowed me to grasp a fork and spoon so that I could feed myself for the first time since my accident. I was also able to hold a pencil so I could start writing again. The device strapped onto my forearm, hand, and fingers. When I extend my wrist (back of hand toward forearm), my thumb and next two fingers were pushed together in a pinching position allowing me to grasp small items. The engineer later added a small electric motor that I could control by moving my shoulder up and down that assisted me with my wrist movement. This provided me with a much stronger grasp so I could lift heavier objects. (Photograph included in the Addendum.)

- **Hygiene techniques:** I learned how to shave myself with an electric razor, brush my teeth, comb my hair, and wash my face and arms. This might sound easy, but try it without using your fingers or wrists. You will soon see that simple things you take for granted are very difficult without the use of your fingers or hands. I also learned to use some devices to help me feed myself. When I didn't use the tenodesis splint mentioned above, I used forks and spoons that had egg crate type foam taped around their handles so I could grip them in my normally contracted hand. Again, feeding yourself is a normal activity that others take for granted and may be hard to conceive how difficult it is for me.

Vocational Training

A company that had plans to transition from the typewriter market to computers offered vocational training. That growing company was IBM, now a giant in the industry. In the 1960s, computers were still very much in their infancy and programming the machines consisted of placing jumper wires into different locations on a pegboard.

The reading materials described how to program IBM's new computers and included end of chapter tests to determine if you understood the materials. But after a few chapters I lost interest. Although computers later became a big part of my life, at the time my primary focus was to leave this facility, get home, and get into college.

Life at the Institute

We lived four patients to a room in the patients' side of the Institute. There was also an outpatient services department in addition to the doctors' offices, administrative, staff, therapies, recreation and kitchen areas. Two of the people in my room arrived and left around the same time I did and we became good friends while we were at Sister Kenny Institute. The other bed seemed to have revolving patients who would come to the Institute for two or three weeks at a time and then leave.

We had a lot of free time after finishing physical and occupational therapy each day and amused ourselves by playing board and card games. Sometimes we even managed to smuggle in liquor to party with during the weekends. And occasionally we made arrangements with one of the orderlies to go out on the town with him on a weekend. There was security in numbers and going out as group of people in various stages of rehabilitation was easy and comfortable. I remember once going to a Minneapolis car show, and also seeing Louis Armstrong perform for about an hour.

Culture Shock

I quickly realized what a culturally sheltered life I lived prior to my stay in Minneapolis.

I grew up in the small town of South Milwaukee, Wisconsin, and was raised as a Roman Catholic during the time when the Mass was said in Latin. I attended a Catholic grade school with very strict policies about inter-faith relations. In fact, the elderly priest who taught our daily religion classes said it was a sin to even talk with Protestants and Lutherans.

The Catholic Church has changed many of its ultraconservative views over the years. Yet, being so young and impressionable at the time, there are things that I do today that I sometimes feel guilty about – for no reason other than what we were taught in Catholic grade school.

After eight grades of what I now consider to have been more brainwashing than teaching, I attended a public high school where there were students with all kinds of religious backgrounds. Once I met students who were not brought up Catholic, I was surprised to find that that they were not weird or any different than me. We had common interests, similar likes and dislikes, and we were all just trying to get through high school.

My high school had a little over one thousand students and more than one quarter of us were Polish. In our community, if you weren't Polish you were most likely German. As kids we used to tell Polish jokes all the time. Until I got out of the city, I didn't realize how negative they were until others told them with an underlying connotation and disdain.

Since we grow up to live what we learn – from family, school, and the communities we are raised in – I came to be thankful that my parents taught my brother and me to always treat people with respect and not to judge anyone based on stereotypes associated with race or religion. It took getting out of South Milwaukee before I realized that others weren't brought up the same way.

One of the orderlies at Sister Kenny Institute and I became very close friends. His name was Ralph and he was the first African-American friend I ever had. Ralph was a huge and muscular black man about six feet four inches tall. He was a very intelligent individual with a fantastic upbeat and positive personality. He used to bring me food on weekends from some of the area restaurants, and occasionally we would go out on a weekend evening to various places in Minneapolis.

I remember the first time Ralph met my parents when they came to visit me over the weekend. Ralph immediately went up to my dad and shook his hand saying how wonderful I was. He then went over to my mother and hugged her tightly. Wrapped in Ralph's arms, you could barely see my mother who was a rather thin and small woman. I could see from the startled look on her face that my mother didn't quite know what to do or say, and I believe that was the first time she ever met and talked with a black person.

Ralph worked hard and saved enough money to buy a house in one of the better areas of Minneapolis. Unfortunately, during the mid-1960s people became fearful when a black family moved into their neighborhood. He came to work late one afternoon and told me how when no one was home somebody came in to his home, clogged up all of the water drains, and turned on all the faucets in the house. There was a lot of damage to repair, items to replace, and cleanup to do.

I was astonished. In my naïve and unworldly life at the time, I couldn't believe people could treat other people that way just for being a different race.

I guess I learned a lot more about life at the Sister Kenny Institute than just participating in physical and occupational therapy.

Note: I still have some good friends from those days more than forty-four years ago. I talk with or see one of my roommates, Jim Trueman, and two of the occupational therapists, Nancy McCracken and Kathy Laughlin, who were there during my stay.

Home on Christmas Holiday – A Glimpse of Things to Come

About five months before I left the Sister Kenny Institute for good I had my first experience flying on an airplane by myself. One of my second cousins who lived in Minneapolis picked me up at the Institute and drove me to the airport. I was scheduled on a flight from Minneapolis to Milwaukee for the Christmas holiday.

The people from the airline boarded me on the airplane without incident and we took off on schedule. However, as we neared Milwaukee we were informed that the city was experiencing a snowstorm and we were rerouted to the Detroit airport.

At the time, I used a Texas catheter, which is an external urinary catheter that is held in place with some adhesive and stretchy elastic tape. Since two or three people had to lift me out of my wheelchair, into the portable aisle seat, and then from the portable seat to the airplane seat, the catheter loosened. Every time I urinated, it leaked onto the seat under me so by the time we got to Detroit both my pants and the airline seat were completely drenched. I was taken off the airplane and placed back into my wheelchair in the Detroit terminal feeling totally embarrassed. Not only did these people have to lift me on and off an airplane with my soaking wet pants, I knew they would also need to replace the urine soaked airline seat.

Once in Detroit it was unclear whether or not the airline would have a flight back to Milwaukee. One of the possibilities being discussed was to hire taxicabs to drive some of the passengers back.

I started to panic. Taxi rides might be a good solution for some passengers, but what were they going to do with *me?*

After a few hours the snowstorm in Milwaukee subsided and I was rescheduled onto a flight headed west with a stop in Milwaukee. Once again, I was carried – wet pants and all – into the plane. Luckily, airline personnel had put a protective plastic cover on the seat I would be sitting in.

When the plane landed in Milwaukee I was lifted from the plane one last time, placed in my wheelchair and taken into the terminal where my parents were waiting. My father was extremely nervous and my mother was crying. They had no idea what had happened to me. All they knew was that I was somewhere in Detroit. While this was a harrowing experience for me, I realized that it was equally as harrowing for them. This really started me thinking about how my life would be completely different from that point on.

This was the first time I was home since my accident nearly six months earlier. My old bedroom was on the second floor of my parents' two-story house, but they rearranged a room on the main level to be used as my new bedroom. My Uncle Kelly constructed a ramp for me to be able to get in and out of the house.

During that brief Christmas holiday I had a constant stream of people coming to visit with me so I didn't have a lot of time to dwell on what it would be like once I was home for good.

Luckily, my flight back to Minneapolis was uneventful. However, the flight between Minneapolis and Milwaukee via Detroit really opened my eyes to what the real world had in store for me. My stay at Sister Kenny Rehabilitation Institute reaffirmed my previous commitment to get a decent education so that I would not be a burden to my parents or anyone else if I could help it.

What's a Bagel?

When growing up Catholic in the 1950s and 1960s we were discouraged from socializing with people of other faiths. But once out of the confines of parochial schools and teachings, this "rule" made little sense. In fact, one of my best friends, Rick Winokur, is Jewish.

Rick lived in the dormitory room next to mine at Stout State in Menominee. And even though we'd known each other only a week before I broke my neck, it seemed like we had known each other all our lives and became fast friends with plans to be roommates when the fall semester began. I had never met a Jewish person before and, once I found out he was, I wondered what all the commotion was about being a friend of a Jew. To me he was just a friend and a great one at that.

The first weekend I was hospitalized after the accident, Rick drove back from the hospital to the dormitory with my parents. Since my plans to attend college were now put on hold, my parents needed to get into my room to clean it out and pack up my things. With no room key to be found or anyone around to let them in, Rick took matters into his own hands and "broke in" through the window to unlock the door.

To hear Rick describe it, my room wasn't just a place to sleep and study – it was more like a general store with stacks of ready-to-eat canned food and piles of bagged snacks stored in a half dozen places throughout the room – not to mention the three or four sticks of sausage hanging in my closet. Rick could hardly believe how much food they packed up that day. My mom gave a whole new dimension to the idea of sending your kids "care packages" while at school and she made darn sure that I wouldn't starve.

With Rick and I being such close friends and my parents traveling to see me every weekend, they had the occasion to meet and spend time with Rick's parents, too. And his parents and my parents became friends for life.

When I got out of rehabilitation and lived at home, Rick and his parents, who lived in Chicago, would come and visit. Most of the time we sat around the kitchen table during the afternoon and visited over lunch. One time they brought with them a large bag of bagels, lox, cream cheese, very thinly sliced corned beef, and a few other items from the Jewish delicatessen they frequented in Chicago. This was the first time anyone in my family ever saw a bagel much less eaten one. My entire family and I thought everything tasted great so every time they came up to South Milwaukee we had them bring lunch from their favorite delicatessen.

I can't believe I went eighteen years without knowing what a bagel looked or tasted like!

CHAPTER 4

Adjustments

I arrived home from the Sister Kenny Institute for good in May of 1965 and was fortunate to have a family support system. Both of my parents worked full time jobs, but my grandmother and Uncle Adam lived with us so, while my parents were at work, my grandmother was available to help take care of me. Also, my Aunt Phyllis, Uncle John, and two cousins, Jack and Barbara, lived next door to us. My Aunt Phyllis was available if I needed any additional help during the day, and Barbara often came over after school to see if she could help me with anything or just to visit. Barbara was always willing to help me then, as she is always willing to help me now.

Friendships, however, were another story. With a handicap like mine, I quickly found out who my real friends were. Except for one, the closest friends I had growing up in South Milwaukee I practically never saw again. I hoped it was just because they felt uncomfortable being around me and didn't know what to do. To be honest, when I tried to imagine myself in their shoes I don't know how I would have reacted to me, either.

In fact, while at the Sister Kenny Institute I took a number of psychological tests. One was a booklet with literally hundreds of questions in it. One of the multiple-choice questions that kept popping up in a variety of ways went something like this:

If you are walking down the sidewalk and a handicapped person in a wheelchair is ahead of you, would you:

a) Walk up to the handicapped individual and ask if he/she needed assistance?

b) Say "Hi" to the handicapped individual as you walk by?

c) Walk by without looking at him/her directly?

d) Immediately walk across the street to avoid him/her at all costs?

Well, my answer to the half-dozen or more questions of this sort was always (d).

I guess that shows you where my head was at when I thought about handicapped people even though I myself was extremely handicapped. In some respect I'm glad my mind did not allow me to view myself as extremely handicapped. Yet, remembering my own answers to these questions helped me to better understand how some of my old friends might have felt.

First Outing

Once home, it took about a month to settle into a routine and during that time I never left the house to go anywhere. The first time I did go out I really felt awkward.

My parents put me in the car and we drove to a shopping mall. I felt like everybody was staring at me as though I were on display. After a short time, a little kid who was unattended by his parents came over to the wheelchair and asked me why I was sitting in it. What do you say to a six or seven-year-old?

I said, "I can't walk."

He asked, "Why?"

I didn't know what to say next and I was grateful when his parents quickly came over and grabbed him away. Yet, believe it or not, similar incidents with small children happened two more times before we finally left the mall about an hour and a half later.

As we moved through the mall I could see that people were staring at me, and when I looked at them directly their eyes would shift elsewhere. I had never encountered stares like that in my entire life. I just wanted to hide somewhere. I knew from that point on that whenever I went out in public little kids would ask me the same questions and I would have to endure a lifetime of people staring at me.

I was devastated.

Going out in public while at the rehabilitation institute was a completely different experience than going out in public once I moved back home. At the institute I lived and associated with other spinal cord injury patients, and a group of us would go places together accompanied by an orderly. Living and going out in that environment was fairly comfortable. But being home for good and going out to a public place where children ask questions of you while others stare at you – and you alone – was something that I was not mentally prepared for.

I immediately realized that, among normal people, I was the center of attention. I felt that I was somewhat less than human and was to be pitied. It was probably the darkest day in my entire life. Even now I cannot adequately put into words how I felt. Saying I was "devastated" is the closest I can come to describe my emotions on that day.

For several days after our trip to the mall I withdrew into myself, like a turtle retreating into its shell. I couldn't eat and I wanted to stay in bed under the covers. My parents had no training for dealing with me in that state of mind and became very worried. No amount of coaxing or encouragement could make me feel differently. After about a week I finally snapped out of it. Yet, even though I began to feel more like myself, I refused to leave the house.

New Perspective

That summer, my parents were very concerned that I would never want to leave the house. My dad confided his concerns to Louis Winokur, my good friend, Rick's, dad who took immediate action.

Mr. Winokur was a corporate patent lawyer in Chicago who had a great number of connections. He arranged, unbeknownst to me, a trip to visit James Graaskamp who was a professor at the University of Wisconsin in Madison. James was stricken with polio in 1950 and had many of the same physical problems I had as a quadriplegic.

One day Mr. Winokur arrived at my parents' house and told me the two of us were taking a day trip. He didn't explain where we were going or why until we were well on our way. When he finally told me what he had planned it was too late to protest. I had no choice but to go along for the ride.

James had his own four-bedroom house off-campus. He provided room and board to two or three students who lived at the house and took care of him.

I thought this was a very unique living situation and it certainly showed me how a quadriplegic could be fairly independent. Seeing how James set up the living arrangements for multiple students to take care of him was very eye opening for me. He was very gracious and generous with his time, talking to me for a few hours on the ups and downs he had living there.

When James first started living on his own he had only one student to help out. Eventually he discovered that it took too much of the student's time to be available at the different hours James might need him. He then decided to find two or three students who could fill in for one another to cover all the times he needed assistance.

James talked about how difficult it was to make sure that no one student was relied upon for the majority of duties necessary to help out. He eventually developed a weekly schedule of daily duties and spread the workload as evenly as possible between the students. When setting the schedule there was a lot to take into consideration, such as getting to and from class and attending various functions and meetings.

James shared his philosophy on life and filled me in on the problems a severely handicapped person can have when living alone, as well as solutions for working around some of those problems. He was very up-beat and had a great attitude. By the time I left James' place, what I originally thought was such a unique situation was fast becoming something I thought I might be able to do if I had enough perseverance.

I was extremely grateful for Mr. Winokur's intervention. He gave me the opportunity to see someone who was as handicapped as I am, yet able to live on his own. I knew then that living on my own could and would become a reality for me. All I had to do was focus on an outcome and make sure I did not let disappointments I was sure to encounter get in the way of reaching my final goal: to be as independent as was reasonably possible.

I don't know how my life would have ever turned out without the help Mr. Winokur gave me.

In fact, Mr. Winokur intervened one more time – despite many protests from my mother. He drove Rick and me to my parents' cottage in northern Wisconsin to spend the entire weekend without my parents around to assist. He got right down to the dirty work of getting me dressed and undressed as well as taking care of my personal hygiene. He was determined to prove to my parents – and to me – that I would be able to leave the house without depending on them twenty-four hours a day, seven days a week.

After my visit with James and the trip to northern Wisconsin, I decided in my own mind that I was not going to feel funny or apologetic about how others saw me. I cannot change being handicapped and in a wheelchair with the inability to use my hands. If people felt nervous or uncomfortable around me, it was something they would have to deal with.

Admittedly, even with this new perspective and conviction, to this day it is still hard for me to meet new people or get involved in public situations. But I just keep reminding myself that this is who I am and if the other person doesn't like it, too bad.

People have to take me as I am.

School

Soon after my trip to the University of Wisconsin in Madison, I started enrolling in courses from the University of Wisconsin in Milwaukee. The courses I took were correspondence courses that I could complete from home. Online courses were nonexistent at that time and assignments would be sent back and forth through the mail. The first courses I took were in English composition and algebra.

With all the time I had since my accident I started reading quite a bit and came to enjoy it. In fact, I became a reading fool! I could knock out at least one paperback a day and sometimes be halfway into my second. I particularly liked science fiction, spy novels, and adult fantasy novels. At that time, Ian Fleming's James Bond series of books were extremely popular, and books like J. R. R. Tolkien's *The Hobbit,* and *The Lord of the Rings* trilogy took me into worlds that were very different from my reality – worlds that I felt very comfortable imagining myself in.

As I was taking the correspondence courses I contacted my former English teacher, Mrs. Muldoon, to ask if she would come over and tutor me. As I mentioned in an earlier chapter, as a teenager I excelled at the subjects I was interested in but was always placed in what they considered the "slow learners" class in English.

Mrs. Muldoon came to the house and read some of my current English compositions. Based on her previous experience with me, she was astounded at the clarity of my papers. Never in her life did she expect to see me write anything but disjointed prose. I guess all of that reading increased my vocabulary as well as contributing to a better writing style – even if most of it was science fiction, spy novels, and adult fantasy books. I was doing so well that she only came back once or twice after that to check on how things were going.

After completing the coursework for the correspondence courses, students were required to go to one of the University of Wisconsin's affiliated sites to take the final exam, which I did. I'm proud to say that I passed with A's.

The correspondence courses gave me enough positive reinforcement to actually enroll at the Milwaukee Institute of Technology junior college. I knew I would have to keep my grades up for a couple of years before I could even consider enrolling in a major university and this was a good place to challenge myself to do it.

Within two years I received an associate degree from the Milwaukee Institute of Technology with a 3.5 average, the equivalent of a B+ average. My only stumbling block to that elusive 4.0 was the language requirement. I chose Russian because I knew that I wanted to major in physics or astrophysics and this was a time of the early manned space programs and the Cold War. I thought it would be very beneficial to be able to read and translate Russian. Despite my valiant attempts to learn the language, I was unable to ace the course. To this day, I have a mental block toward learning languages.

During this time I began getting out and doing things with some newly found friends I had in South Milwaukee and a few new friends I made at the Milwaukee Institute of Technology. We frequented our favorite bars and enjoyed listening to live music. Occasionally we would go up north to spend weekends at my parents' cottage just to fish and enjoy the north woods. I would do this without thinking twice about leaving my parents at home.

After all my worrying about how people would react to me, the greatest compliment I continue to receive over and over again since my accident is when my friends tell me they don't think of me as being in a wheelchair. They just think of me as being one of the gang.

I now felt I was ready to move out of South Milwaukee and get out on my own. I applied to three of the schools in the Midwest that have special programs set up for the disabled. This usually meant special dormitory facilities and scheduled buses between the dormitories and academic buildings on campus. The three colleges were the University of Illinois in Champaign, the University of Southern Illinois in Carbondale, and the University of Missouri in Columbia, Missouri.

All three universities accepted my enrollment application. But before I determined which college I would attend, I visited each campus to see their facilities. After spending a day or two at each one I decided that I felt most comfortable at the University of Missouri in Columbia. It was a little farther south than the Illinois schools, but I liked the atmosphere of the campus in Columbia and hoped that the winters in Missouri might not be quite as bad as those in Illinois.

The dark cloud that hung over me when I thought I would be a burden to my parents was quickly dissipating. I knew now that I could make it in the real world if I stayed focused on getting my bachelor and master's degrees in the sciences. At last I was starting to feel like a normal human being again. It was a feeling that was unknown to and forgotten by me since my accident.

I finally had my life back on track.

CHAPTER 5

That Elusive First Job

I made it through college and received my Bachelor of Science and Master of Science degrees from the University of Missouri in physics. I was now set to tackle the world. During college I became quite good at programming computers using the Fortran and Basic computing languages. Fortran was the scientific programming language at the time. I also learned how to program a graphics plotting machine that has its own special computer language called Focal. I loved programming computers and actually earned a few dollars while in school working for a couple of the professors doing their computer work for them.

Pre-Grad Interviews

Just prior to graduation I mailed out more than one hundred résumés in hope of finding a computer position that would allow me to program in the sciences. I received only one invitation to interview and that was from the University of Arizona. They needed a scientific computer programmer to do data analysis of data collected at its Kitt Peak Observatory. I traveled to Tucson, Arizona, for an interview only to find out that the position I applied for was put on hold because of cost overruns on new hardware they were installing at the observatory.

I received one more opportunity to interview for a potential position as director of a city planetarium located in the Midwest. I was told there were over three hundred candidates who originally applied for the position. From those applicants only ten were called to meet and interview with a panel of top university administrators and city officials. I believe there were six people on the panel. I felt that my interview went exceedingly well and found out later that I was third on the list for the position. The person that was first on the list accepted the job offer.

I later learned that a couple of the people on the panel were not receptive to the idea of a quadriplegic representing the planetarium. As director, part of the job included getting out into the community and talking to schoolchildren about astronomy and the planetarium. There was concern that the schoolchildren would focus more on my disability and less on what I had to say. They also had reservations about the image I would project on television and when speaking at other public gatherings.

In reality, I understood the concerns of the panel members and can see how I might have presented a problem for them. I don't really blame them for making their decision based on my mobility limitations and appearance as a public figure. Yet this was the first inkling of things to come, and I realized I was going to have a major problem securing a job.

In the early 1970s, it was extremely rare to see a quadriplegic in a highly visible position and I don't ever remember a quadriplegic person being in the public eye during that time. In fact, it was 1995 before I first saw a spokesperson for spinal cord injuries. Well known for his role as Superman, actor Christopher Reeve was thrown from his horse and suffered a spinal cord injury that left him a quadriplegic. His notoriety and the formation of the Christopher Reeve Foundation has since brought visibility and accelerated funding for spinal cord injury research.

More Rejections

After graduating, I returned to South Milwaukee and began my job search near my hometown. Milwaukee was a large manufacturing city so many of the newspaper ads were from companies seeking qualified computer programmers. Unfortunately most of the ads were looking for people who could program in the COBOL business language. Although I have an aptitude for learning computer languages and believed I could learn COBOL in a relatively short period of time, I didn't have a computer available to me like those at the University for writing and testing COBOL programs. Unable to meet COBOL requirements, I focused on newspaper ads that were geared toward engineering applications.

I answered every newspaper ad from companies that were looking for computer programmers in engineering areas. At the time I thought that my scientific computer programming skills would be extremely valuable because Fortran programmers were very hard to come by in this relatively new field of computer programming.

After receiving a couple dozen automatic rejections by mail, I was getting very discouraged. I wasn't even being asked to come in for an interview. I revised my résumé and removed the reference to my being a quadriplegic to see if that would make a difference in response. It did and I began receiving invitations to come in for interviews. However, when I arrived at the human resource offices I was given a few minutes of their time and told that they would get back to me. And they always did get back to me… with a rejection letter.

At the time there were no job discrimination laws like the American Disabilities Act of 1990 for the disabled, but I held a Master of Science degree in physics with more than three years of intensive scientific computer programming under my belt and I thought that might count for something.

It didn't.

Some of the excuses I heard for not wanting to hire me were just plain bizarre. For example:

- I was rejected for one job because I couldn't carry twenty pounds across the room. *I always wondered what that had to do with programming computers.*

- Another company was concerned that I might not be able to operate an elevator button and therefore might get caught in one. *If I can program a computer, I think it's pretty safe to say I can push an elevator button.*

- A third company decided that, since I did not drive a car, they were not sure I could make it to work every day and needed somebody they could count on to show up. *Let's see, I made it to classes every day in school and somehow managed to get to the interview… I never before heard that driving a car was a requirement to get a computer programming position.*

I heard excuses like this over and over.

I spent about nine months applying to more than a hundred companies around the Milwaukee area. With both of my folks working, my friend Roman would drive me to two or three companies in the Milwaukee area each day. I eventually stopped sending out my résumé. Instead I would check the ads for computer programmers in the morning paper and go directly to each company to fill out an application form in person.

The rejections kept coming and I became very depressed. I did everything I could think of to be seen as a viable candidate and didn't have a game plan for what to do next.

Chicago – the Land of Opportunity

Rick, the friend who pulled me out of the water when I had my accident, was working in Chicago at a company called G.D. Searle pharmaceutical. I gave him my résumé and he took it to Searle's human resources department, telling them straight out that they would miss a great opportunity if they did not hire me.

Rick was either very influential in the company or very convincing when he told them about me and I was set up to interview for a job that sounded perfect for me. The position would be working with a small group in the company's computer department that programmed in Fortran for the scientific areas in the pharmaceutical laboratories. My dad agreed to drive me to Chicago for the interview but, after seeing me rejected for job after job in the past months, he had little hope that something would come from it.

I interviewed with the manager of the department, Edward Walsh, and we talked for more than an hour. He was impressed with my background in computer programming to help analyze data for a couple of the physics laboratories at the University of Missouri. I also had programming experience in the specific Fortran programming language he needed for his open position so, as I left his office, I felt very good about the interview. Dad had a few words with him alone before we left the building to go to the car.

Dad helped me into the passenger seat, loaded my wheelchair into the trunk, and then got into the driver's seat – but he didn't start the car. As we were sitting in the parking lot he broke down and cried. This was the only time in my life I ever saw my dad cry. In the few moments that my dad had alone with Mr. Walsh, Mr. Walsh told my dad that he was going to talk with the human resources department and offer me a position to work for him.

That was the start of my computer career and I am forever grateful to Mr. Walsh for giving me the opportunity to show him what I could do. I excelled in the position I was hired for and was quickly promoted to a systems analyst. The company then needed some additional help in the business area of the computer department and asked if I would like to move to this other area. I did, and excelled in that area as well.

All I needed was a chance to prove myself and now people were actually asking me to join their business group. How great was that?

One day I received a call from a computer headhunter who told me that somebody at Baxter Laboratories had heard about me and wanted me to come for an interview. I was very satisfied with the people and position I had at G. D. Searle and had no intention of leaving the company but I was curious, flattered, and thought it would be a good chance to polish my interview skills. I thought, "What harm would there be to go to this interview?" So, on a whim, I said, "Yes."

One night after work I met with the manager of the Technical Services area of the computer department at Baxter Laboratories, later to be called Baxter Healthcare. Evidently this manager was one of the rising stars in the company's computer department and was going to be starting a small group that would be working closely with their scientific laboratories. This was in addition to his also being the manager of Technical Services.

We talked for almost two hours and as we were finishing he asked me what it would take to get me to move to his organization. I was astonished and completely taken aback. Since I hadn't given any serious thought to leaving my current position, I also hadn't given any serious thought to what compensation it would take to get me to leave it. Not knowing what to say, I stated an outrageous salary along with three weeks of vacation, which was unheard of at that time. He thanked me for my time and I left the meeting figuring that things went well until I told him what I wanted.

To my amazement I received a call the next day and was offered a position at Baxter. Not only was the company willing to pay the outrageous salary I had asked for, but increased the amount by a couple of thousand dollars. I asked for some time to think about it and a couple days later decided it was an amazing opportunity and I would make the move. That was the start of my twenty years with Baxter Healthcare and its joint ventures.

I worked my way up through many positions in that organization over a twenty-year time span. As my career moved more toward business management, I decided to get an MBA and enrolled in the executive program at the Lake Forest School of Management. Lake Forest has a fantastic executive MBA program. Many of its teachers are top executives in Chicago area companies with expert credentials in the specific courses they teach.

I spent two years attending classes at Lake Forest every Saturday from eight o'clock in the morning until five o'clock in the afternoon and graduated with a Masters of Business Administration degree. It was a grueling two years of class work and assignments that would take up many of my evenings during the week and most Sundays. Looking back, I don't know how I survived the schedule to make it through this program while working full time.

As tough as it was to get through, earning my MBA degree furthered my career path. Eventually Baxter and Nestlé formed a joint venture company called Clintec Clinical Nutrition, which lasted around ten years. I transferred to Clintec Clinical Nutrition, as its director of information technology in what I believe was its fourth year in existence. A few years later I was promoted to a corporate vice president of Information Technology for both Europe and the United States. After a couple of years in that position, Baxter and Nestlé dissolved their joint venture and I had a choice to stay with either company. I decided to stay with the Nestlé organization. Nestlé renamed its new company Nestlé Clinical Nutrition and I was with the company for two more years before retiring from the corporate world.

My parents and family were very proud of me. There was a time they thought they would be taking care of me for the rest of their lives and here I was, able to work and live on my own. I was also very proud of myself. I feel I accomplished more than I could ever have hoped for in both my education and career. And I continue to be ever grateful to Mr. Edward Walsh for giving me the opportunity to show that I could make it in the workplace.

CHAPTER | 6

Living Independently

During my college years at University of Missouri, I hired students to take care of my daily needs. There were always students around campus looking for part-time jobs to help pay for their schooling. For their assistance, I gave them room and board and paid a stipend of a hundred dollars a month. I needed help each morning to take care of my daily personal hygiene, get dressed, and transfer from bed into the wheelchair. Every evening I needed help to get back in bed and undressed. I also needed help preparing my meals and once a week I would need help with a shower or bath.

Once I got to know a few students at the University, I managed to have a couple who would be on standby if my standard caregiver needed to be elsewhere during the times I needed him. They would also fill in when my caregiver needed a break. This arrangement worked out pretty well both while I was living in the dormitory, and after I moved off campus into an apartment.

Living in Chicago proved to be an entirely different experience. Since I was living close to work and nowhere near a campus I flooded the surrounding campuses with five-inch by six-inch cards offering the same compensation as I did at school: free room and board and a stipend of a hundred dollars a month for their assistance in taking care of me. I received quite a few replies but had difficulty finding anybody of the same quality of the students that I had at the University of Missouri. Living in a city as big as Chicago, I thought it would be a piece of cake to find and hire qualified individuals. I was wrong.

The first interview I held was with a person who told me he was going to cure me and I would be standing and running around the block in a couple days. I explained to him that I broke my neck in a swimming accident and the nerves in my spinal column were severed, leaving me paralyzed. He said that was irrelevant. Curious as to where this guy was coming from, I asked how he planned to cure me. "Easy," he said. "All I have to do is physically lift you out of your wheelchair, stand you up, and then let you go." The remainder of the plan was for my subconscious to kick in and my mind would force me to stand up by myself because I would have no other choice but to fall.

I bid him a good day and thought, "Oh my God, what am I about to venture into?"

I soon found out.

Roger

The first person I hired I'll refer to as Roger. Roger was just starting college after recently returning from Vietnam. He appeared to be a very mature individual and I needed someone to start quickly so I hired him. His experiences in Vietnam must have really messed with his mind, though, because at night I could hear him having nightmares in his bedroom. I also noticed after a few weeks that my liquor cabinet was dry, leading me to assess that he was also an alcoholic.

One day after putting me to bed, I heard Roger ranting and raving in the living room. I also realized that he must have turned the temperature up to about ninety degrees and it was hotter than hell in the apartment. When I called him in to my room to ask about the drastic change in temperature his demeanor was strange and he seemed really out of it.

Without saying a word Roger picked up my portable wheelchair, lifted it over his head, and then threw it across the room. The wheelchair hit the opposite wall and put a hole in the plaster. Roger then started screaming over and over, "I'll kill them all. I'll kill them all." I knew I was in deep trouble.

Roger left my room and I managed to reach the phone that was on a table next to my bed. I dialed the operator and asked her to call Rick, who lived about eight miles from me. After I told Rick what was happening, he immediately called the police and then rushed over to my apartment, arriving just before the police. He tried to calm Roger down, but it didn't work. When the police arrived, it took four of them to hold him down and keep him from injuring anyone. They managed to get Roger under control and took him off to the police station.

When Roger went to court to be arraigned his mother begged me not to press charges. She told me some of the horrifying stories that he witnessed and took part in while in Vietnam. I told her I wouldn't press charges as long as he would not come back to my apartment or attempt to see me. She agreed and later came by the apartment to pick up his things. When cleaning out his room to prepare for the next attendant, we discovered that he evidently would often get out of bed at night and urinate on the walls.

From that point on, I knew I had to develop a better method of screening the people I hired.

While I looked for my next caregiver, Rick or my mom would fill in to get me through my daily routine. With little experience at interviewing people, I tended to take them at their word, but after my experience with Roger I thought I'd better start checking applicants' credentials and asking for references. I also asked Rick to sit in on as many interviews with potential caregivers as he could, thinking that between the two of us we could better assess the capabilities – or at least the sanity – of potential applicants.

You might think that taking extra precautionary steps to choose the next caregiver might help. They didn't.

CT

The next person I hired asked me to call him by his initials so, for this story, I'll call him CT. CT was a very personable African-American who said that he was an orderly at one of the local nursing homes. This sounded like a great match since he already had some medical training and, if he could take care of somebody in a nursing home, he could certainly take care of me. Doing my due diligence, I verified his employment with the nursing home and it checked out. I hired him and remember always seeing him leave and come home in a white orderly's uniform.

CT took great care of me and was always around when I needed him. Whenever my friends came to the apartment it wasn't long before they became CT's friends, too. Although CT was a great companion, he had some weird quirks.

One time a representative from Pitney Bowes came to see him at our apartment. Pitney Bowes is a company that makes postage machines that are typically found in the mail rooms of large companies. The postage machines stamp legal U.S. postage directly onto envelopes so you didn't have to buy individual stamps. I thought this was kind of weird, but maybe he was in the habit of writing a lot of letters. His personal life was none of my business so I didn't question him on why he needed a U.S. postage stamp machine.

A day or two later another weird thing happened. A box arrived for CT that looked like it had been stuck in storage for an awfully long time. It was dusty, musty, and dented. When he opened it, dozens of cockroaches scurried out of the box and I actually had to call the exterminator a couple of days later. Not only was my apartment infested with cockroaches, but all of the apartments down the hall from me were, too.

After the cockroaches escaped and scattered, CT proceeded to take a check-printing machine out of the box. Again, it's the kind of machine that is most likely used in a company or a bank. You type in a dollar amount and the machine writes out what looks like a cashier's check.

By this time I was wondering what CT was up to, so I asked him. He simply said he had a small side business to earn some extra cash. This sounded plausible and he took good care of me, so I didn't pursue this line of discussion any further.

Something else CT did was to call a taxicab service and have the driver go to McDonald's and pick him up a couple of hamburgers to be delivered to the apartment. He would pay the taxicab driver for the hamburgers and whatever the meter fare was, and then give the driver a significant tip. Actually, I thought this was pretty cool and thought I might try it myself sometime if I got hungry for food from a restaurant that didn't have a regular delivery service.

As the holiday season approached, I told CT that I would be spending a few days over Christmas break with my family in South Milwaukee, and let him know when I would be back. The night I was leaving I noticed a wad of cash lying on my work desk in the living room. I asked him where all that money came from. He told me it was cash tips he received from the relatives of some of his patients at the nursing home for taking such good care of them. It was Christmas time so I thought that was a valid answer. Besides, it was really not my business to question him about it. We wished each other a happy holiday and I left for South Milwaukee to spend Christmas with my parents and brother.

After having a great holiday with my family, I arrived back at my apartment and found a big surprise waiting for me. A Christmas card from CT was on my work desk. I opened it and found ten dollars enclosed with a note. He wished me a Merry Christmas and said that he had left town and would not be returning. He also said he enjoyed his time living here and wished me the best.

CT had been with me for about a year. I really enjoyed his company and what I thought was his friendship, but his leaving without notice really put me in a bad situation. When I read the note to my parents, none of us could believe it. I considered myself lucky that my mother offered to take care of me until I could find another attendant.

A good-bye and good luck note wasn't all that CT left behind.

For the next eight months, I received phone calls from all kinds of bill collectors and creditors. Evidently CT was a pretty slick con man and took a great many people for a lot of money. I literally received about thirty phone calls that started as soon as I came home from work and continued until six o'clock the following morning. It seemed like it took forever to convince these companies that I had nothing to do with CT's activities and had no knowledge of where he went from here. They certainly were tenacious and it took many months before the bill collector and creditor calls dwindled to zero. To this day, I still wonder what kind of con game CT was involved in.

So much for feeling more secure in my choices by relying on references!

Helen

The next person hired was a woman I'll refer to as Helen. When I met with Helen she told me she was a retired nurse and seemed like a nice, capable, elderly lady. She gave me references that I was unable to get in touch with, but Helen kept calling and saying how great she thought this job was and would like a chance to live with and take care of me. After a couple of days I finally agreed and Helen moved in.

Helen actually knew how to take care of somebody like me. And besides taking care of all of my daily needs she was a great cook, which

I felt was a real bonus. From time to time she would wear her nurse's uniform and cap around the apartment. Yes, it was a little strange but if it made her feel more professional and she continued to take good care of me, I didn't care.

After Helen was with me for a couple of months I noticed that it was very hard for me to get her up in the morning so that I could get dressed for work. I eventually found out that she was an alcoholic and would pass out in the evenings after she put me to bed. I had some serious talks with her and tried getting her professional help. A friend of mine recommended a place that could help her so I called and arranged for Helen to talk with someone about her alcoholism. She told me that she went and was getting help, but I don't really know whether she went or not. She was better for a few weeks but after a few more she again began to drink heavily.

One weekend my brother, mother, and aunt came to visit me. Helen was so intoxicated that she fell on the living room floor and my brother had to help her up. My folks told me I had to get rid of her but I said I wanted to try and make the situation better. When Helen was not drinking she was great to have around and I really did not want to see her go.

About a week after the incident, I awoke in the middle of the night – around three o'clock in the morning – and Helen was standing over my bed just staring at me. She was dressed in her nurse's uniform, complete with cap perched atop her head. I spoke to her but she just continued to stare at me without any response. This scared me a little and I didn't know what to do so I just kept quiet. After about ten minutes she turned around and walked out of my room. I don't know if she did this a lot or if this was the first night it happened. But after that night I decided that things were getting too weird and I would have to ask her to leave.

Helen often spoke of her son and I was hoping he would be willing to come to get her. She told the same stories about him over and over and more than once I asked her to invite him over for dinner someday so we could meet. She always had some reason to put it off. Helen also told me that she called her son often but claimed to always use a public pay phone. Several times I tried to get her to tell me his phone number, hoping to talk to him about what was happening, but I was never able to get the phone number out of her. By the time I decided it was time to ask her to leave, I really didn't know if her son was alive or dead – or if he even existed.

One of my friends helped her get all her belongings packed and into her car. I thought she would go to stay with her son but for the next couple of days I saw her out in the parking lot in front of my apartment building, sleeping in the front seat of her car. I sincerely felt bad about letting her go, but, for my own personal safety, I don't think I could have done anything else. A couple friends of mine went over to her car a few times to ask if she needed help or assistance. She always told them, "No." After three or four days I did not see her or her car again.

Even now, I feel guilty about having to let Helen go; yet I know that I really had no other choice at the time. She was a very good person and I often wonder what happened to her.

Frank

The next caregiver was Frank. He proved to be a breath of fresh air after the last few caregivers I had hired. Finally I had a normal person living with me from start to finish.

Frank happened to be a younger brother of Rick Winokur's wife, Pat. He had come to start work in Chicago after graduating from high school in Iowa so he needed a place to stay and I needed a caregiver. Living with Frank reminded me of my days in college.

Frank had no trouble learning what needed to be done and we had a good relationship until he decided that the big city wasn't for him. Frank went back to Iowa to seek other employment and I really missed him when he left.

Paul

My next roommate and caregiver, who I'll call Paul, lived with me for quite a few years. Paul was pretty young and, like Frank, had just graduated high school. Paul had recently moved to Chicago from California and, being as idealistic as people his age are, had big plans to start and run a business of his own. He spent a lot of time developing business ideas and put many different plans together while he was working at a pet shop.

Paul used to bring different pets from the shop home for the evening and I enjoyed playing with most of the animals he brought home. One of my favorite furry guests was a ferret. Being small and curious it got between the front buttons on my shirt, crawled up my chest, burrowed through the armpit of my shirt, and exited out my sleeve. I thought it was great and ever since then I have wanted a pet ferret. Besides being fun to play with (if you can ever find them), they can be litter box trained.

Owning a ferret was not feasible at the time so, instead, Paul set up a twenty-nine gallon freshwater fish tank that we both enjoyed. I find aquarium fish to be soothing to watch.

The first hint of a problem started when Paul brought home a bird that he purchased while he was back home in California for a visit. It was a lesser sulfur crested cockatoo and stood about a foot or more tall. When I was home Paul always kept the bird in a cage, which was fine with me and actually my preference. When I was not home, however, Paul would let it have free rein throughout the apartment. I returned home from work one day to see the bird perched on our sofa with half of the sofa stuffing strewn around the floor. And all too often there were bird droppings all over the living room carpet.

Paul also often kept the bird in the bathroom. It would perch on top of the shower curtain rod and literally scare the crap out of anyone who went in to sit on the toilet. The bird and its habits got to be a real bone of contention between Paul and me. But a turn of events caused us both to believe we could end the standoff.

I received a notice from my landlords announcing that they were turning the apartments into condos and that I had the first option to buy it. The price was exorbitant for an apartment with paper-thin walls. I remember sharing a wall with a neighbor who thought he was God's gift to women (and maybe he was). His bedroom was on the opposite side of my living room wall and there were many nights when my friends and I could provide play-by-play commentary about the moaning and creaking of bedsprings on the other side of the wall. If I was going to invest in property ownership, it certainly wasn't going to be this apartment-turned-condo.

My parents and my Aunt Susie began looking for an affordable house located closer to where I worked. Thirty houses later we found one in Northbrook, Illinois, and I was on my way to owning a real home of my own. It was a small ranch-style house with a furnished basement that I never saw. I really liked the room that was to become my office because it had a cathedral ceiling, a large fireplace, and a large nine-foot glass sliding door that led to a concrete patio with a decorative brick privacy wall. It was perfect for me. My parents and aunt loaned me the money to purchase the house and set up an equitable repayment schedule.

By getting out of the apartment and moving into this larger house there was more room for Paul to keep his bird in its own area so it wouldn't damage anymore furnishing or leave droppings all over the place.

Now that our issues over the bird were resolved we decided that, with a bigger house, we could get a bigger aquarium. Paul brought home a previously owned 125-gallon aquarium to put next to the television in the living room. This time instead of a freshwater aquarium we set up a saltwater tank and stocked it with saltwater fish, anemones, shrimp, and eels. The new aquarium was expensive to populate but very beautiful. It also required occasionally exchanging part of the water with new salt-water to maintain a better environment for the fish.

One day I came home from work and noticed that there was only about three inches of water in the aquarium. Assuming that Paul was in the middle of exchanging the water, I called out to see where Paul was and to let him know I was home.

Paul didn't answer.

As I proceeded to go from the living room area toward my back bedroom I noticed that my wheelchair wheels made kind of a squishing sound on the carpet. A sinking feeling came over me as I realized that Paul wasn't doing a water change – our "previously owned" 125-gallon aquarium had a leak.

With only about three to four inches of water left in the tank, I quick-ly concluded that more than 110 gallons of salt water had soaked into my living room carpet, and down to the wooden floors. Putting it mildly, I was not a happy camper when Paul came home.

Although clean up, repair and putting in new carpet was expensive, I still wanted to have an aquarium so we replaced the tank, refilled and restocked it.

Despite our isolated pet-related experiences, Paul and I got along great for the following years that he was with me.

Frick and Frack

When Paul left, I found a recently married couple to help take care of me who I'll refer to as Frick and Frack. They answered an ad that I had placed at a Bible school in downtown Chicago. They both attended this Bible school and were enrolling in Trinity, a religious college in the northern suburbs. After explaining my needs to them, they both said they had no problem with what needed to be done and that both of them would be able to help out. I hired them. What could possibly go wrong while being cared for by people who were so dedicated to religion?

Whenever I saw one of them I usually saw the other. In the four months that they lived with me I don't believe I ever saw one of them alone for more than two minutes. They would actually go into the bathroom and do their thing together but, what the heck, who was I to judge? They were there to care for me when I needed it and their personal lives were their own.

Before long, living with Frick and Frack started getting a little weird. When attending to my personal care, like changing my catheter, they were continuously laughing together. At first I thought it might be nervous laughter since this was new for them. But when they started telling me to be wary of people whose eyes glowed, I began to have strong misgivings about hiring them. They went on to tell me in all seriousness that there were a lot of these glowing-eyed people in my neighborhood and that they came out of the Jesuit monastery located just up the street.

I always considered myself pretty open-minded and respecting others' beliefs, but this was getting far too strange. Based on previous experiences I knew that I might have bigger problems with these two in the future.

By that time my girlfriend, Diane, was spending most weekends with me and admitted that she also was concerned about Frick and Frack's bizarre behavior. With a little encouragement from Diane, I let them go. When I sat them down to tell them of my decision, I found out that they, too, were looking for a way out of the situation. I don't know if they were pretending to be weird so that I would ask them to leave or if they really believed everything they told me. I guess that's something I'll never know. I'm just glad they left.

When Frick and Frack left, Diane said she would like to take care of me for a while. By this time our relationship had grown considerably and we were together most of the time, so I agreed.

Looking Back

As you can see, I've had an eclectic array of caregivers over the years. Today there are many placement agencies that help to find and prescreen live-in aides and assistants, but during the time I needed them those agencies did not exist. I can't believe how difficult it was to get hired help to live in and it never did get easier.

As I look back at the various caregivers I hired in order to live independently, sometimes I wonder how I ever got through it without one of them seriously hurting me – or me wanting to seriously hurt one of them. I guess that's just been part of my series of adventures – and my life.

CHAPTER 7

What Sex Life?

As a quadriplegic, my physical sex life was pretty much over when I had my accident. Not being able to feel the bottom three-quarters of your body, nor be able to control it, pretty much puts a damper on the physical aspects of sex. Emotionally, however, your mind still persists with sexual thoughts and urges from time to time. It is extremely frustrating to have these urges and not be able to do anything about them. They don't even go away as you enter those golden years. At least now, for me, they rarely occur anymore.

Just Friends

When I first had my accident I told myself that I wanted to stay away from ever getting deeply involved in a relationship with a woman. I felt extremely inadequate and did not feel any woman could have intimate feelings for me. After all, what could I physically offer a woman?

As I do in many situations, I tried to put myself in the other person's shoes to determine how they might perceive me. Once I did this, I felt there was no way that I would want a relationship with anybody as disabled as me. And, in some ways, an intimate relationship actually sounded perverted to me. I built some extremely high emotional walls to make sure that I stayed away from any potential serious relationship.

Don't get me wrong – I don't avoid women. As a matter of fact, I have many great female friendships. I just didn't want to give anyone the impression that I would try and make it anything other than a friendship. In the last forty-four years there are only three females that I wished I had the nerve to tell how much I liked them and how much they really

49

meant to me. But I always stopped short of expressing my feelings. I don't know if this was a good thing or bad thing. I just know that, at the time, I thought it was the correct thing to do.

Breaking Through the Walls

I met my wife, Diane, while working at Baxter and from the start we had a great friendly relationship. Diane and I hung out a lot with my social group of friends and after awhile I felt very comfortable talking to her about things I never spoke of to others.

Little by little, Diane started tearing down some of the protective walls I built around myself. And as our friendship turned into something greater, I realized that a relationship is not just about sex; it's more about a mental and emotional closeness with one another. Although I could not fulfill any of my sexual desires, I wanted to provide Diane with whatever I was physically able to provide for her. After over a year and a half I finally worked up the nerve to propose to her, believing that by this time she knew what she would be getting into by marrying a disabled person like me.

I decided to propose to Diane at a Japanese restaurant I especially liked and on that night tucked an engagement ring inside my suit coat pocket. Typically at a Japanese restaurant a table seats about eight and it is designed in a half-circle around an open grill so that the chef prepares and serves the meal while you watch. If there are just two of you, you will be seated with up to six other people at the table.

I had asked the person taking reservations if we could be seated at a table alone. He was kind enough to escort us to a table that holds eight but he sat only Diane and me. If Diane actually accepted my proposal, we would have a great restaurant to go back to on our anniversary every year. I don't know if that was really forethought on my part, or if I just had a hidden agenda that would be a great bonus if she said, "Yes."

I presented the ring, asked the question, and she said…

"It's about time you asked me to marry you!"

With that happy response, I realized that it had taken a long time for her to break through that final wall.

Relations and Reservations

As the relationship between Diane and I grew I did have some reservations that were beyond just the two of us. Diane had a lovely daughter from a previous marriage and I wondered what she would think of her mother marrying a quadriplegic. I also had the same reservations and questions when it came to Diane's parents. What would they think about their daughter marrying me? I was sure they thought that she could do much better than someone like me.

When I broached the subject with Diane she told me not to be concerned about those matters – and she was right. When I met Diane's daughter, Sandy, and her parents for the first time they really put me at ease and didn't seem to have any problems with my situation. Over the years I have grown to love Sandy and her family and I truly consider her as my own daughter, and her two kids, Eric and Lauren, as my grandchildren. And I can't even image having better in-laws.

"I Do!"

We had a very small wedding ceremony in the family room of my home, with the atmosphere set by the fireplace burning in the background. The entire guest list consisted of our immediate families and my best friend living in Chicago at that time, Ray, who was my best man.

Since we didn't have a rehearsal for the ceremony, I kept looking at the minister for my cue to say, "I do." He nodded his head and I said, "I do." But it wasn't the right time so he pretended not to hear me and continued with the ceremony.

Another nod and I said, "I do," again. But it still wasn't the right time for me to speak.

The third time his nod was very distinct. "I do," said I. Nope. Wrong time again.

Finally, the minister paused, looked right at me, and nodded. "I do," I said again. I'd finally gotten it right on the fourth try.

Whenever we talk about that day, it seems that all Diane remembers is how I agreed to marry her over and over again. But I guess things worked out just fine – we recently celebrated our twenty-second wedding anniversary.

CHAPTER 8

Quadriplegic: What It's Physically Like to Be One

In addition to the emotional problems that come with being quadriplegic, there are some very specific physical problems that one has to be constantly aware of. Some people have asked me what it's like to be a quadriplegic. I'm sure there are other friends of mine who would like to know but don't really want to ask. I will attempt to describe as best I can what it physically feels like – or doesn't feel like – to be a C5 partial quadriplegic.

When I crushed my fifth cervical vertebrae I essentially severed all of the nerves in the vertebrae. After many months, there was some nerve regeneration, but it was minimal. A neck injury affects all four limbs of your body, thus the word "quad" or quadriplegic.

I have no feeling in my body from the upper chest down to my toes. People wonder what it's like to have no feeling. I've thought about this a lot, but when I try to explain it, I'm at a loss for words trying to convey the feeling to someone who has never experienced it.

When I close my eyes I still picture my body as having legs, feet, and toes. My mind tells me that they are there and in good shape and functional. If I really concentrate on moving a finger or toe, my neck muscles tighten and after awhile I am physically exhausted. The feeling is difficult to describe but it is a little like sitting on the toilet seat and pushing hard to try and relieve yourself, but nothing happens.

When I see someone touch an area on my body that has no feeling, my mind is ready to place the anticipated touch at that location, but when the area is actually touched I feel nothing.

You might think an advantage to not being able to feel anything is that I cannot feel pain. Yet, the seemingly biggest upside to not having any feeling in my lower body is also my biggest downside. I have had elastic bandages wrapped around my legs and fastened with a safety pin that actually went through a quarter inch of skin without my knowing it until the bandage was removed. Without the ability to sense hot or cold, it can be dangerous if I'm exposed to either extreme. I have touched a coffee cup that had just been filled with hot coffee from the stove and didn't realize I burned my fingers until after they blistered.

The Butt, Bowels and Bladder

I wish at some point in time I could feel pain because it would've helped prevent pressure sores from developing. Pressure sores are the bane of most quadriplegics. As you sit or lie in bed the pressure on certain areas of your body can stop the blood from flowing to those areas and the cell tissue around those areas dies.

Most pressure sores occur by sitting on a wheelchair cushion that is too hard or too soft. I now use a seat cushion that is filled with air. Trying to keep the right amount of air pressure in a seat cushion is a delicate balance. An under-inflated seat cushion is just as bad as an over-inflated seat cushion.

It really helps to prevent pressure sores if you are able to shift your body around a little bit while sitting to keep your blood flowing through the different pressure areas. This has to be in the back of my mind constantly while sitting in a wheelchair. Forgetting to shift – even for ten minutes – can have disastrous consequences. For something that can occur in less than a half hour, I can end up spending many weeks or even months healing.

Anyone – even you – could get a pressure sore in less than a half-hour just by sitting in the same spot and not moving your body in any way. Fortunately as a normal person sits they unconsciously shift their weight if their body senses discomfort.

I have had many pressure sores in the past twenty-five years and, as I get older, they occur more frequently and my skin becomes less durable.

On the other hand, not feeling parts of your body can sometimes be beneficial. Recently, I broke my femur right in the middle of the bone and did not feel a thing. Although the bone did not come through the skin, I knew that something happened because I heard a crack and could see that my thigh was bent at a funny angle.

Surgeons inserted a titanium rod in the femur. Because I have no feeling in that area I did not need to take painkillers in the hospital after the operation. In this case, I guess I'm glad I didn't feel anything. However, the benefits of not feeling anything are inconsequential compared to the negatives. I continually get myself in trouble by not being able to feel pain or discomfort.

Pain can be beautiful.

There are some quadriplegics who experience phantom pain whereby they seem to feel their extremities in pain but the pain is not really there. Fortunately I do not have these phantom pains.

In my lower body, I don't have any control over my bowels or bladder.

The bowels are usually not much of a problem except for occasional bouts of diarrhea. Diarrhea, which I sometimes refer to as the "Big D", is not a good thing to have happen when you're sitting in a wheelchair. I watch what I eat or drink because there are certain foods and alcohol that can bring on diarrhea very quickly. For better bowel control, I usually try to keep myself just a little constipated. I need assistance from my caregiver each morning to clear out my bowels. Emotionally, having to rely on someone else to assist me with this is hard to reconcile and I often feel guilty about it.

In quadriplegics, the bladder is a major concern because it is prone to frequent urinary tract infections. Probably the two most dangerous medical problems that can happen to a quadriplegic are:

- A blood clot that travels through your arteries until it reaches your heart and stops it.
- A urinary tract infection that enters the bloodstream (goes septic).

I believe statistically that these are the two most frequent killers of quadriplegics and, as you will read later in one of my anecdotes, I almost died from a urinary tract infection.

At one time doctors believed that giving a small amount of antibiotics would prevent major urinary tract infections and I was prescribed a daily dose. However, the adverse effects of continually taking antibiotics were still unknown. As I took low doses of various antibiotics every day for almost a year, even the weakest bacteria built up immunity toward everything I was taking. I was soon in dire straits because if I were to get a high-grade bladder infection the only way to kill these bacteria was with very strong IV antibiotics, administered during a week long stay in the hospital.

I was lucky that, at about the same time the bacteria built up immunity to all of my oral medications, the drug industry finally came out with a new class of antibiotics that I am now able to take occasionally without having to worry about urinary tract infections going septic. There's nothing like good timing.

I still have to carefully monitor my urine by periodically taking small samples and dipping a diagnostic test strip into them to make sure that my infections are low-grade. If I do show signs of the onset of a bad urinary tract infection I have to make sure that, when the hospital labs conduct their usual standard tests, they also do a sensitivity analysis on my urine at the same time.

There were a couple of times when the hospital lab did not do sensitivity cultures. They thought that the specific bacteria they identified could be killed with a very commonly used antibiotic. Normally they could. Unfortunately for me, those specific bacteria were already resistant to that commonly used antibiotic.

Results for a standard urine culture takes more than forty-eight hours, and a second test for sensitivity takes an additional forty-eight hours. Unless the tests are conducted simultaneously, I would not know for four days what antibiotic would kill the bacteria. Waiting four short days could make my infection go septic if not treated with the appropriate antibiotic and I could be dead.

I recommend to anyone that if the hospital is going to take a urine sample for analysis, you should stress to the person sending the sample to the labs for analysis how important it is that the lab makes sure a sensitivity analysis is also conducted.

Most, if not all, quadriplegics require some means of catheterization. Catheterization can take three forms: external, indwelling, and intermittent. The Texas catheter is an external method of catheterization that is less prone to infections if you can get your bladder to empty out completely. A Foley catheter is an internal method of catheterization where a tube is inserted in the bladder and this usually results in having a low-grade infection at all times. A urine collection device is generally worn attached to the side of the leg when using a Texas or Foley catheter.

The third method is straight catheterization, which is intermittent. Periodically, usually every three or four hours, a straight piece of sterile tubing is inserted in the bladder in order for it to be emptied. When the bladder is emptied the tubing is then removed and thrown away.

Although I do not have any feeling from the chest down, I am able to tell if I need to have a bowel movement or if my bladder is full and needs to be emptied. In either case, I get a kind of chill up and down my spine. It's a little different for each so that I am able to distinguish whether I need to concentrate on my bowels or bladder.

If the bowel is impacted or the bladder stretches because it is blocked in some way, a condition called *autonomic dysreflexia* can occur. Autonomic dysreflexia occurs when the blood pressure fluctuates radically. It commonly happens to people with spinal cord injuries. One minute the blood pressure could be 90/70, the next minute it could be 180/120, and the next minute it could be back down to 90/70. Other symptoms include migraine-type headaches and body sweats. I have experienced autonomic dysreflexia episodes a few times and I hope I never have another one. They are not at all pleasant to go through.

Form and Function

In my upper extremities, I have feeling in the top parts of my hands, arms, and shoulders, but very limited feeling in the palms of my hands and inside areas of my arms, with no feeling in my armpits. I have extremely strong shoulders and biceps but virtually no use of my wrists and absolutely no ability to move my triceps or fingers.

When seated in a wheelchair, I can usually move my arms and hands around to different positions by using my biceps, along with gravity. In this way, I am able to type on a computer keyboard using a pen or pencil wedged between my fingers. As a matter of fact I have gotten so good at it, that I can out-type many able-bodied people using the computer keyboard. I can feed myself if my food is cut up, and wash myself if I have a pan of water in front of me with a washcloth. One uses what one can. The parts that do work can compensate for some of the ones that don't and it's amazing how one's body can adapt to abnormal situations.

Because of the limited use of my arms and hands, I cannot dress or undress myself. This was always a significant problem when I used to travel alone by airplane. If something happened between destinations to delay or reroute the flight, I might be forced to stay in a hotel and I would be lost without any help. Where would I even begin to search for someone in a strange town to help get me dressed and undressed and into and out of bed? Who would change my catheter? Who would assist me in my bowel regimen? Who would know how to get me in and out of bed and into a wheelchair without hurting me? Who would take on and volunteer for these sorts of activities? In one of the anecdotes later in this book, I recount how very close I was to actually having to address this major problem.

Temperature Control

When I severed the nerves in my spinal column, I screwed up my temperature regulating system. If I am in a cold environment, my temperature drops a couple degrees below normal. If I am in a hot environment, my temperature is a few degrees above normal. Whenever I'm admitted for hospital care, this fluctuation in temperature drives the nurses nuts. And no matter how I try to explain this little quirk in the rise and fall of my temperature, they only seem to be willing to accept that if my temperature isn't exactly 98.6 degrees I have a problem.

I love sitting out in the sun during the summer months, but when the temperature gets into the 90s my normal body temperature can rise to almost 101 degrees. The solution is to get into an air-conditioned environment every half hour or so to bring my temperature down. After about fifteen minutes in air-conditioning I can then go back out into the sun at which point my temperature rises again. Sometimes I go back and forth five or six times in an afternoon. It sounds stupid, but I like being outdoors so it's something I need to do if I want to enjoy the summer sun. My family and friends think I'm nuts to constantly monitor time and temperature to be outside. Why would I expose myself to such craziness?

I have had to give up many things in my life because of my accident, but I have always enjoyed sitting and reading a book in the sunshine and I am not going to sacrifice that enjoyment. I choose doing what others see as a bit crazy over giving up a simple pleasure.

In addition to an irregular body temperature, another thing that drives the doctors and nurses nuts are blood pressure fluctuations caused by autonomic dysreflexia. More than once I've gotten into trouble with doctors who want to treat a high blood pressure symptom, not realizing that two minutes later I will experience very low blood pressure. After the first high blood pressure reading, they always try to give me medicine to lower my blood pressure. Telling them of my varying blood pressure readings from minute to minute does not seem to make much of an impression. During one hospital stay I was nearly killed by a resident's orders to treat my high blood pressure reading.

It was about eleven o'clock in the evening and the regular nursing staff conducted routine vitals. This consists of having your temperature, pulse, and blood pressure taken. My blood pressure was 189/115. The nurse mentioned it was high and I told her not to worry about it because it was a common occurrence for me and an hour later it would likely be low. Evidently she decided to report it to the resident on night duty. Without even stopping to see me to discuss it, and obviously having no clue about the medical differences between a normal able-bodied patient and a quadriplegic, this resident ordered medication to lower my blood pressure.

About three hours after my blood pressure was originally taken, a nurse woke me up from a deep sleep and told me to take some pills that were in a cup she was holding. I was awake enough to ask what they were for and was told it was to bring my blood pressure down. I said there was no way I was going to take them, and this did not sit well with the nurse. After arguing back and forth and repeatedly telling her that my blood pressure fluctuates radically at times but is usually pretty low, I finally convinced her to take my blood pressure again before I would take the pills. When she took my blood pressure it was 85/60.

Amazingly, the nurse still thought I should take the pills because the doctor prescribed them. I'd had enough. After explaining what a Patient's Bill of Rights was and that I could – and would – refuse this medication, she abruptly turned on her heel and stormed off. I shudder to think what taking medication to lower my blood pressure would have done to my already low blood pressure. Even after this first incident, medicine to lower my blood pressure was prescribed and brought to me every day until I was released from the hospital. Evidently they never updated the records. So every time a nurse brought the medication, I refused to take it. My conclusion? Hospitals are scary places to be.

Back and Forth Forever

I have had many problems with pressure sores over the past fifteen years and have had numerous operations to repair the damage caused by them. I have even had the inner thigh muscles from each leg moved up and placed into my butt area for additional padding in what is called skin flap surgery.

Because of all the problems and repercussions that pressure sores can cause, I now use a wheelchair that tilts back and forth so that my back and head can tilt to a prone position. This is different from the reclining wheelchair I once owned that fully reclined so my entire body was prone. My current wheelchair is analogous to sitting in a regular chair and having the whole chair tilt backwards and forwards.

This tilting motion relieves the pressure on my butt to minimize the chance of getting pressure sores. Unfortunately, I have to tilt my wheelchair back every four or five minutes and keep it there for a minute or two.

Yes, that's right; I need to tilt my wheelchair back every four or five minutes.

Tilting the chair every few minutes is critical to my being able to sit for any length of time. If I forget to do this just once and stay upright too long I can develop a pressure sore that requires a long hospital stay and many months of recuperation.

Tilting my chair back and forth is just one more thing I have to remember to do every time I sit in my wheelchair. I sometimes feel a little funny tilting my wheelchair back every couple of minutes when I'm at a shopping mall or in a restaurant, but by now I realize that my health comes first and if that's what it takes, then that's what I'll continue to do.

Summary

Every day I wake up, I need to be aware of and prepared to deal with all the issues described above. If I forget to pay attention to any one of them I could quickly jeopardize my physical health, and I need to keep all of these factors in the back of my mind as I go through my regular daily activities.

Having to constantly be aware of my physical condition can be very draining while I try to lead as normal a life as I can. But after all is said and done, this is my life. And these are the things I must do to be able to live it to its fullest.

Part 2: Anecdotes

The many anecdotes and stories that I've told over the years recount things that have happened to me, with me, and because of me. Some of the situations could happen to anyone, and some could only happen to someone confined to a wheelchair. Yet it is because of stories like these that friends encouraged me to start writing them down. While the year indicated on each anecdote may not be exact, it is very close to the time the story happened. Some are funny, some are serious, and some are a mix of both. Some might even be hard to read if you're a little squeamish, but the facts are the facts when describing my physical vulnerabilities.

As I mentioned in the Introduction, these anecdotes were the catalyst for the title, "Another Fine Mess You've Gotten Us Into," because that's the phrase my friends repeatedly used whenever we found ourselves in situations with unanticipated outcomes.

As this book was being developed, a comment received early on from someone who read a few of the following stories was, "Some of these stories read like nothing more than frat house follies." Although the person making the comment might have thought that was a criticism, to me it was a great compliment. It once again confirmed to me that, even though I was quadriplegic, to my friends and family I was "just one of the guys."

And that, in fact, is the point of this entire book.

CHAPTER 9

Into the Twilight Zone (1966)

Although my original home was in South Milwaukee, Wisconsin, my brother, Bill, and I had a second home in Winona, Minnesota, where we visited during most summers while school was out. Winona is a beautiful town located on the Minnesota side of the Mississippi River about thirty miles north of La Crosse, Wisconsin, and about two hours south of Minneapolis. It's an extremely beautiful area located in a valley with bluffs overlooking the Mississippi.

My dad's family originally came from Winona and I have many relatives there. When Bill and I would go to Winona we always stayed at my Uncle Louie's house. Uncle Louie's family and my brother and I are actually doubly related. Uncle Louie is my dad's cousin and my Uncle Louie's wife, Aunt Florence, is my mother's sister. So my three cousins in that family are also my second cousins. I always thought that was pretty weird.

My three cousins are very close in age to my brother and me. Sharon, the oldest is one year younger than me. Jim, the second oldest, is the same age as my brother. Susan is two years younger than Bill and Jim. Being so close in age, my brother and I used to spend two or three weeks during the summer in Winona and then he and I and our cousins would all go back to South Milwaukee to spend another two or three weeks together. We were a very close-knit family group.

After my accident, I was in rehabilitation in Minneapolis for over nine months. Winona was a good spot for my parents to stay overnight when traveling from Milwaukee to Minneapolis to visit me, as they did almost every weekend while I recovered from my accident.

A Night for Music

After I moved back home to South Milwaukee following my accident, we would still visit my cousins in Winona. During one of those visits, I suggested to Sharon that the two of us take a ride around town to see if we could find a bar with a live band to listen to and then afterward stop somewhere to have a pizza.

Sharon and I borrowed my father's car and, at that time, I would get in and out of the car by placing one end of a sliding board under my thigh and lay the other end across the front passenger seat. I would then slide over and Sharon would lift my ankles into the car, remove the sliding board and close the door. At this time I didn't travel with an electric wheelchair because it was too cumbersome to handle. Instead I used a lightweight collapsible wheelchair that was easy to push around. After getting in the car, Sharon lifted the wheelchair into the trunk and we went on our way to places unknown.

Winona was home to three colleges so I figured there were probably plenty of bars in the area that had live music. Sharon said she didn't know of any so we drove around the city and looked for bars that might advertise live bands. After about an hour of cruising around the city, we decided that there were none to be found in Winona. Realizing that La Crosse, Wisconsin, was only thirty miles south of Winona and also a college town, we thought we'd drive down there and see what we could find.

It only takes about thirty minutes to get to La Crosse from Winona and as you cross the Mississippi you also cross French Island, an old logging town that's only about five miles long and two miles wide. When we arrived in La Crosse we drove around most of the downtown area to try to find a bar with a live band. Sharon even went into two bars and inquired if there was any live music in the area. Nobody she talked to was aware of any place we could go for live music.

I thought, "So much for that," and told Sharon to just drive back to Winona. We could go to one of her favorite pizza parlors and grab something to eat. As we began crossing back over the Mississippi at French Island, I noticed a sign above a place call the Twilight Zone that indicated it had nightly entertainment. I thought, "How serendipitous, this is just what we were looking for." The sign said entertainment started at nine o'clock and I was glad we were there early. It was only about eight o'clock and I figured we were early enough to get a good table in front of the stage area where the band would play.

Sharon took the wheelchair out of the trunk, I slid into it, and she pushed me into the bar. Sure enough the place was still relatively empty and we got a great table right in front of the stage. It didn't look like there would be much of a band because at the back of the stage was one guitar, a very small drum set, and a very small electric piano keyboard. But what the hell – beggars can't be choosers. At least we would accomplish our mission to hear some live music that night.

We ordered a couple of beers and sipped them slowly. I couldn't drink much alcohol without experiencing bouts of the Big "D", and Sharon was not a drinker either, but she would socially have a beer or two with me during the course of the evening.

As we sat across from each other at the small table, I noticed Sharon had kind of a quizzical look on her face. She whispered to me that there was a woman sitting at the bar oddly dressed and donning what she described as a feathery pink shawl. I repositioned my wheelchair around a little bit so I could get a glimpse at this unusual woman. Once I saw the woman in her 8-foot long pink feather boa, I thought, "Oh, my God."

The entertainment we were patiently waiting for was going to be a strip show.

A Slow Retreat

I should have realized that something was amiss when Sharon was one of only two females in the bar. The lady sitting at the bar with two-thirds of her breasts falling out of the front of her dress had enough make-up on to apply to a whole troupe of circus clowns. Sharon's entire family is pretty conservative and I am sure she never thought she would be caught dead in a strip club.

I looked back at Sharon and told her I thought the lady in back of me was a stripper and expected that she was the entertainment posted on the sign outside. I suggested we quickly finish our beers and leave before the show started at nine o'clock. It was about eight forty-five and I figured we had at least ten minutes to get out of there. I had barely finished my sentence and the stripper walked up to the stage and started her act early, with all of the men that had been congregating in the bar area starting to close in behind us.

After being trapped there for about twenty minutes of the stripper's eye-opening act, Sharon and I backed out of the bar as fast as we could. Once we were back in the car and heading back to Winona I sensed that Sharon was a little taken aback. I suggested we go back to Winona, find a pizza place for a bite to eat – and not mention our little experience to our folks. I could already hear my mother's voice in my head scolding me for taking my poor innocent little cousin to a strip joint. Not to mention that my uncle, Sharon's dad, was a military man, who later retired as a Lt. Colonel in the National Guard. I sure didn't want him to know about this little adventure of ours either.

Sharon and I went back to Winona, found a great place for pizza, and had a good laugh over our evening in search of live entertainment. We went back to her folks' house with no one any the wiser.

Thankfully, this was the first and only time I got Sharon into one of my fine little messes.

CHAPTER 10

Stepping Up in the World (1967)

A fter my accident, my family and Rick Winokur's family became very close. Once I was out of rehabilitation and living at home, Rick's family would come to our house in South Milwaukee, Wisconsin, about once a month and bring a great lunch with fixings from their favorite delicatessen in Evanston, Illinois. After the first three or four visits to South Milwaukee, the Winokurs invited my family and me to visit their home in Evanston.

We very much wanted to visit the Winokurs in their home. However, we knew there would be a problem because they lived on the second floor of a three-story apartment building that did not have an elevator. When we raised the question about how difficult it could be to get a wheelchair into their apartment, Rick said that it would not be a problem and assured us he had the situation handled. Although skeptical, we decided that the next time we got together with the Winokurs, it would be at their Evanston apartment.

Still having our doubts about getting up all those apartment stairs, the next month on the scheduled day my dad put me in the family car, loaded my push wheelchair in the trunk and he, mom, and I headed out of the driveway toward Evanston.

One Flight, Two Flights, Three Flights, Four

When we arrived at Rick's place, I got out of the car and had an unexpected surprise; the building the Winokurs lived in was called a three-flat and it didn't have any apartments on the ground floor. So even though the Winokur's apartment was considered a second-floor apartment, it was not just one level up from the ground, it was two levels up from the ground – and four flights of stairs. We would have to climb a flight of stairs from the ground level to a small landing followed by a second flight of stairs that put us on the first-floor apartment level. We would then need to go up a third flight of stairs to another small landing followed by a fourth flight of stairs to the second-floor apartment where Rick lived.

I couldn't believe all the stairs we were going to have to go up before we reached Rick's apartment. When I mentioned to Rick that maybe it would be better if we all went to a restaurant in the area for our visit he said, "No way!" He had arranged for a few of his high school buddies to come by and help lift me in the wheelchair up the four flights of stairs. Sure enough, about fifteen minutes later four of Rick's friends – who looked like linebackers from his high school football team – came in the front door of the building. We all introduced ourselves and, without hesitation, the guys said it would be no problem to lift my wheelchair with me in it up the four flights of stairs.

I wasn't as confident as they were.

At that time I weighed around two hundred and twenty pounds and my push wheelchair weighed around sixty. It was no easy task to lift nearly three hundred pounds up four flights of stairs, one step at a time. Two of Rick's friends got behind the wheelchair and two of his friends stayed in front. They backed the wheelchair up to the first step. The two people behind tilted the chair backward and lifted while the two people in front also lifted and held the wheelchair in place on the stairway. One step at a time we ascended the first flight of stairs. The first set of steps didn't seem to present much of a problem and we made it to the first landing in about five minutes.

We then backed up to the second set of stairs and started our way up using the same process of tilting and lifting. By the time we got to the first-floor apartment, all four of Rick's friends were starting to get a little winded. They rested on that first-floor landing for a few minutes and then regrouped and started going up the next flight of stairs. The third set of stairs was traversed slower than the second and the fourth set of the stairs traversed slower than the third but after forty minutes of a lot of lifting, a little grunting, and a good amount of heavy breathing, we finally made it – step by step – into Rick's apartment. By this time Rick's friends were exhausted and probably regretted that they ever volunteered for the task.

Although relieved to finally be on the second floor, my only thought was how the hell I was going to get down after our visit. It's one thing to pull the wheelchair with me in it up one stair at a time against gravity but another to control the wheelchair going down one stair at a time. I was not looking forward to going down all those stairs at the end of our visit and I'm sure Rick's friends weren't either. I was particularly concerned about the guys who volunteered to be in front of the wheelchair in case the people holding the wheelchair from the back lost control. I could see the headline: "Two people trampled to death by a runaway wheelchair."

Once we reached the second floor, Rick's friends left and we visited with the Winokurs for the entire afternoon. We had a great time as usual and when it came time to leave Rick phoned his friends and asked them to come back to help get me down the stairs. I half expected his buddies to give him a number of excuses saying they couldn't make it. But about twenty minutes later, every single one of them showed up to get me down the stairs.

Luckily, going down the stairs wasn't as bad as we all thought it would be and we got down in far less time than it took to get up. Rick and I thanked his friends for all their help. I'm sure they'll probably think twice before volunteering to do anything for Rick the next time he asks. But then again, that's what good friends do - help out when they can.

What a fine mess Rick and I got his buddies into.

After this incident I didn't ever again want to put myself in the position of having to go up and down flights of stairs. I once again realized how something I took for granted – like simply walking up a flight stairs – now had barriers that further limited where I could go in the future.

"It's Faster By Plane." Wrong! (1969)

While attending college, the one and only time I flew back to the University of Missouri in Columbia from my parents' house in South Milwaukee, Wisconsin, was during a Christmas break.

The drive from South Milwaukee to Columbia would take about seven and one-half hours one way. After dropping me off at school, my parents would have to drive an additional seven and one-half hours to get back to South Milwaukee. That's a long way to go for a day trip, and Wisconsin winters were notorious for being unpredictable in December. Road conditions could quickly become hazardous. I assured my parents that it would be much quicker for me to fly to Kansas City, meet a friend at the airport, and then drive back to Columbia with him.

The flight would be three short hours and I would have to wait for my ride in Kansas City for about two or three hours, but what the heck. I could spend the extra time reading a magazine in the airport.

My parents drove me to the Milwaukee airport, due to depart at one o'clock in the afternoon. I always needed to arrive early so that I could get loaded on the airplane prior to the rest of the passengers. Handicapped passengers are always the first on and the last off of an airplane.

Imperfect Landing

In those days – the late 1960s – most airports did not have telescopic walkways between the terminal and the airplane entrance door. Passengers would walk out onto the tarmac where all of the maintenance and cargo loading trucks would be and then climb the stairs of a portable stairway that was pushed under the airplane's entrance door just behind the pilot section.

Usually I was transferred in and out of a portable aisle chair and carried to my assigned seat in the airplane. This trip, however, was a little different. Instead of putting me in an aisle chair to carry me up the stairs, the airline brought over the vehicle they use for loading food containers onto the airplane. Operating similarly to a forklift, it had a large area in front that transported the food containers. I was asked to back my wheelchair onto the area where the food containers usually sat.

Once on the lift, two people held my wheelchair while we were lifted level with the airplane entrance doorway. Three people then physically lifted me out of my electric chair and carried me back to the passenger seating area, placing me in the seat next to the aisle. Although this was the first time I experienced this method of being loaded on an airplane, it seemed to go okay. My wheelchair was then lifted back down to the tarmac and loaded into the cargo bay.

Every time I am physically lifted from my wheelchair to an aisle chair and then lifted from the aisle chair and into the passenger seat, my clothing tends to get disheveled to the point where my shirt comes out of my pants and my pants get twisted up on one side and down on the other. I usually ask a flight attendant to help rearrange my clothing back to a normal position as much as possible. But since I was only getting on and off the plane once for this entire trip, I did not think repositioning my clothes was necessary.

I was flying Ozark Airlines with a scheduled intermediate stop in Cedar Rapids, Iowa, before continuing on to the Kansas City airport. The flight got off on time and we experienced an uneventful trip.

Until...

Cedar Rapids was experiencing a snowstorm that unexpectedly turned into a blizzard.

The pilot communicated to the passengers that the depth of the snow on the runways in Cedar Rapids was at the absolute limit allowed for landing. Because we were only a couple miles out from the airport they would make an attempt to land. A few more minutes – and 6 to 8 bounces later – we were on the runway and taxiing toward the Cedar Rapids terminal building.

Strange Sequence of Events

The pilot then announced that we would be sitting in the plane by the terminal building for a while. The snowplows had to finish plowing the Cedar Rapids roads prior to coming to the airport to help clean off the runways. He said that once the runways were clear we were second in line to take off behind a United Airlines plane.

Fifteen minutes passed.

A half an hour passed.

An hour passed.

Finally, the pilot announced that the snowplows were cleaning off the runways and we should be taking off soon.

Twenty minutes later the pilot told us that the United Airline flight ahead of us took off and we would be next. By this time I was getting a little worried about meeting my connection in the Kansas City airport for the rest of the drive to Columbia. Although the timing would be tight, since we were next in line to take off I would still be able to make it.

The pilot is ready. The passengers are ready. The runway is clear. The jet engines ...

...are frozen.

We were going nowhere. Deicer was quickly brought out and hosed onto the engines. But, about forty-five minutes later, the pilot announced that we would have to disembark the airplane and board a different one being moved out of the hangar. Transferring to a plane that could take us to our final destination was a great relief to most of the passengers.

Not to me.

The snow was still falling, high winds were gusting and swirling around the tarmac, and I had no clue how airline personnel would be able to get me off one plane and onto another.

Once everyone else was off the plane, it was decided I would be put into a narrow aisle chair and carried down the stairs of this plane, across the tarmac and up the stairs of the new plane. So that's exactly what we did.

With all of the lifting from the seat to the chair to the new seat, my pants and underwear were starting to do some debarking of their own. But once on the new plane all I wanted to do was get to Kansas City. This was before cell phones so all I could do was hope my connection would find out the new arrival time in Kansas City and wait for me. As we all settled in for the final leg of this flight, the pilot took the microphone in his hand and made one last announcement...

... we were grounded.

Weather conditions in Cedar Rapids had worsened to the point that the airport was not allowing any takeoffs or landings. We would have to disembark the second plane and go into the terminal.

This Can't Be Happening

Once again, I was lifted into an aisle chair, carried back down the stairs and into the terminal. Once in the terminal I was lifted from the aisle chair into my wheelchair. To my surprise and delight, my pants were still with me.

I sat in the Cedar Rapids terminal not knowing anyone and wondering how I was going to get from Cedar Rapids to Kansas City. As I listened to conversations around me, there was talk from the airlines about putting everybody up in hotels for the night.

This was a great idea for some people, but a disastrous idea for me.

Traveling alone, I had nobody who could help get me in and out of bed, undressed and dressed, or assist with my personal hygiene, which included changing my Texas catheter and emptying and cleaning my urine collection devices. About all I needed to top off this day was an unexpected bowel movement.

As luck would have it, a large group of disgruntled passengers refused to be put up for the night in Cedar Rapids and wanted to continue on to Kansas City by taxicabs. If I could get myself with this group, at least I would get to Kansas City even though my ride would have been long gone.

Ozark Airlines managed to hire four taxicabs and we left Cedar Rapids about two hours after getting off the last airplane. I was in the lead cab sitting next to the driver, which later turned out to be the one fortunate part of this trip.

Driving conditions were poor with low visibility. We passed many cars that were stranded in ditches and along the roadside. As we approached Des Moines, Iowa, the road conditions were so bad that the cab drivers were talking back and forth with one another about stopping the caravan to Kansas City and instead staying overnight in Des Moines. I began to wonder how much more of this great news I could take.

Since I was sitting upfront with the driver, I explained my impossible situation for spending the night in a hotel or motel without someone to assist me. For whatever reason – perhaps because he felt sorry for me – he decided to drive a few miles farther to see if the weather conditions might ease up. Conditions didn't get better, but they also didn't get worse so he kept going. Many hours later we pulled into the Kansas City airport.

It was now midmorning in Kansas City and my three-hour flight back to school had turned into a 20-plus hour plane trip from hell.

My final challenge was to get from Kansas City to the Columbia, Missouri, airport where I could be picked up by one of my friends. Ozark Airlines was well aware of all the problems we had with our flight. They quickly found me a connecting flight from Kansas City to the small airport in Columbia. Finally, I was only an hour away from putting this nightmare to an end.

I was boarded onto a turboprop airplane using the usual method of lifting me from my wheelchair, to an aisle chair, and then into a passenger seat. As I started to feel some relief, an Ozark airline representative came over, sat next to me, and asked if I wanted them to make arrangements for me to go back into the terminal.

What?!

I asked, "Why would I want to go back to the terminal when I just boarded this plane less than twenty minutes ago?" I was then informed that the snowstorm had disrupted everybody's schedules and they were still calling throughout the Kansas City area to pull together a flight crew.

I informed the airline rep that I had been on and off airplanes and in and out of taxis seven times during the last twenty hours and would be staying onboard until a crew could be found for the plane.

My Last (Humiliating) Hurrah

Three and a half hours later – yes, I said three and a half hours – a crew was assigned and we were ready to take off. I asked a flight attendant to call ahead to make sure that a friend of mine was notified and would meet me at the Columbia Airport. An hour and a half later we touched down and the plane trip from hell had finally come to an end.

Or so I thought.

There was one final humiliation to endure that put a perfectly lousy ending on this perfectly lousy experience.

Since there were only about five other passengers on the plane, it didn't take long for the plane to empty. From my window I could see that they removed my wheelchair from the cargo section and had it sitting on the tarmac. After waiting what seemed like an inordinate amount of time for people to come and lift me off the airplane, three people finally showed up – but without an aisle chair to carry me in.

No one at the small airport could find an aisle chair to use for my transport so the collective decision was to just carry me off the plane and put me in my wheelchair. I had one person under each shoulder and one person lifting me under the knees. Add to this the fact that they were turned in the wrong direction, taking me off the airplane backwards.

So here's my parting shot at the end of this adventure: I am being carried down a flight of stairs headfirst, pants and underwear creeping ever closer to my kneecaps from all the lifting done in the last twenty-six hours. My wheelchair is about twenty feet from the bottom step and that final twenty-foot walk is lined with passengers waiting to board the airplane for its continuing flight. I could hear snippets of whispers and questions being asked of no one in particular wondering if I was the victim of a heart attack, or perhaps I was dead, and why were my pants and underwear nearly off?

Fortunately, my ride back to the University was waiting for me and my three-hour-turned-twenty-six-hour flight was finally over.

Even with the best of intent, this was another fine mess I'd gotten myself into.

CHAPTER 12

The Jell-O Mixer (1971)

Wen living off campus at the University of Missouri, my two roommates, Ray and Edward, and I decided one night that we wanted
to make whipped Jell-O® for our evening dessert.

The recipe is relatively simple. Mix up a package of Jell-O and let it
sit until it was just starting to get firm. Add to it a couple of scoops of Cool
Whip™ or vanilla ice cream and use a mixer to blend it altogether.

After mixing the Jell-O and setting it aside to firm up a bit, we got
busy doing other things. When we finally remembered the Jell-O it was
already pretty hard and we wondered whether or not we would still be
able to mix in the ice cream.

American Ingenuity

The only mixer we had was a simple non-electric hand mixer, more
commonly used to beat eggs. It had a handle on top and a wheel on the
side with a crank connected to a knob. To rotate the beaters, you turn the
knob in a circular motion.

As suspected, the Jell-O was already too hard to be able to turn the
hand crank to get the beaters moving. But we were three industrious
college students and were not about to give up and start over. We were
determined to find a solution to get that mixer to mix.

I suggested that we could easily make a modification to the mixer
by cutting off the little knob, and straightening out the metal piece connected to the rotating wheel. This produced a three-inch piece of metal

that resembled a drill bit. All we needed to do now was find the electric drill and we'd be well on our way to getting that Jell-O whipped.

To some, the combined brainpower of three determined college guys might be frightening. To us, it was exhilarating and we thought our solution was ingenious. A quick hunt for the toolbox produced the electric drill we needed.

Ray attached the electric drill to the side of the hand mixer. Edward put a firm grip on the handle of the mixer and held the beaters close to the top of the Jell-O. And I – the proud innovator of this invention – watched closely in anticipation of success.

We were "all systems go" and, as Edward touched the beaters to the Jell-O, Ray squeezed the trigger on the electric drill. Just as we had planned, the drill spun the beaters at rapid pace. And in the blink of an eye we were all drenched with Jell-O and ice cream. It splattered throughout the kitchen from the floor, to the walls, light fixtures and ceiling. The one thing we realized too late was that the electric drill only had one speed: super fast.

As with all great inventors, a snafu on the first try did not dampen our determination to make this idea succeed. There was still a little Jell-O left in the bowl, and we saw it as an opportunity to perfect our technique. After a brief discussion we decided that we could achieve more control if the trigger of the drill was lightly touched to start it and then immediately released. Four or five short bursts in succession might mix the ingredients without sending it flying out of the bowl and into the far corners of the kitchen.

This new strategy proved successful and we used our invention several times in the following months to make perfectly whipped Jell-O.

Mix Masters

Quite proud of our accomplishment, we had the occasion to show off our new invention when my parents came to visit our off-campus apartment. When we described our modified hand mixer, my mother thought we were kidding. Mom was pretty conservative and learned how to cook from her mother. She wasn't too fond of changing the methods of how food was to be prepared. Despite her continued protests, we were enthusiastic about how well our technique worked and insisted that she let us show her how it was done.

Ray mixed up a box of Jell-O and we let it sit for a while. As it started to get hard, we put our apparatus together, added a couple scoops of ice cream, and Ray started up the electric drill. Proud as can be, Ray pulsed the drill as the beaters touched the Jell-O, and in mere seconds Ray, myself, the kitchen – and my mother – were covered with Jell-O and ice cream.

Needless to say, mom wasn't impressed and we were embarrassed. Why is it that something can work perfectly time after time until you want to show off your genius to others?

Not more than fifteen minutes passed before my mother sent my dad to buy us an electric hand mixer with more than one speed.

Having the new mixer certainly eliminated any future whipped Jell-O disasters, but to tell you the truth, Ray and I kind of missed using our old invention.

Looking back on that day when I witnessed my mother covered in Jell-O, I know she would never have uttered these words, but she certainly had to be thinking, *"Son, this is another fine mess you've gotten me into."*

CHAPTER 13

Slide Rule? (1972)

I really enjoyed attending the University of Missouri and it prepared me for my future career in data processing. At that time (1969 to 1973) the computer industry was in its infancy. There was no such thing as a Computer Science degree and computer courses were taught in the math department. If you wanted to get into the computer field, you needed to get a degree in math.

Back then, every science student used a slide rule to solve math problems in their math and science courses. Many people today don't even know what a slide rule is or how to use one. As a matter of fact my grandson, Eric, who is now taking physics courses in college, asked me what kind of portable calculator I used to solve physics problems when I went to college. He was somewhat amazed when I told him that there were no such things as portable or pocket calculators until after I graduated with my master's degree.

For those of you who do not know, a slide rule is a very unique and accurate calculating device. It is essentially made up of three rectangular sticks, resembling a standard ruler, held together with braces near the two ends with the middle stick being able to slide back and forth between the two outer sticks. All of the sticks have very precise marked scales on them so that when the middle stick is moved into a certain position based upon the type of math problem you want to solve, you can read the numeric answer contained under a hairline piece of plastic or glass located between the two braces. To see a picture of a slide rule, see the photographs in the Addendum at the end of this book.

Slide rules were used all the time in science classes and I always had difficulty trying to manipulate one because I could not use my fingers to move the middle sliding bar. I would have to grip the middle slide between my teeth and then pull or push it into a position where I could then wedge my finger between the two outer rectangular scales to more accurately position the slide. Using this technique to solve numerous problems was not good for my teeth and certainly would not be considered proper hygiene.

A slide rule was very inconvenient for me to use and was a big reason I learned how to program computers.

I purchased a programming manual in the Fortran IV programming language from the University bookstore and used the computer equipment in the physics building to learn how to program from examples given in the book. Majoring in physics required me to take two or three physics courses plus one or two math courses per semester. This involved solving lots of math related problems with a great number of calculations.

I found it much easier to write small computer programs to solve these problems rather than to try and work them out on a slide rule. Fortunately, the physics building had a room with a computer in it. It was one floor down from my physics building graduate office and on the other side of the building. While earning my bachelor and master degrees in physics, I shared a graduate office space in the physics building with Errol, another physics graduate student, and spent a good deal of time in that office.

As I became more proficient in programming the small computer in the physics building, I found that I really enjoyed programming and actually started thinking of it as a career path. I talked to a few professors to see if they had any research projects with which they might need computer help. One of the professors specializing in solid-state physics and my astronomy professor both had research projects that I could help out with using the computer.

One of the professors had a Navy contract and I earned a little bit of spending money working with him on it. He paid me $2 an hour for the computer work. I thought that was easy money because I really enjoyed programming and working with the computers. I programmed theoretical energy curves based on data his solid-state physics lab would generate experimentally from their lab equipment. But my main project was programming model universes for the astronomy department professor.

Finding the Right Universe

My astronomy professor was trying to show the difference between two competing theories of our universe. Each of the two theories had a mathematical model that I could program into the computer. The program would generate calculations from what was considered the start of the universe (Big Bang) at time zero and evolve the two mathematical models in time until the models reached a set of astronomical parameters that we could both directly and indirectly measure in 1970. These models would evolve a theoretical universe from time zero to a time frame measured in billions of years.

This might sound complicated but it was really only a matter of converting mathematical equations into a computer program. The program required a set of starting points each time it was run. Once the program was executed the computer would perform millions of calculations before it would finish. Once it was finished it would print out about ten numbers. These numbers would later be used as points on a graph. I would then change the initial starting points and run the program again. Each time the program was run a new model universe was generated. The program needed to be run more than forty times in order to generate enough data points to graphically plot the differences between the two competing theories.

My astronomy professor had hoped that the graphical lines generated by the data this project collected could be used to distinguish which one of the two competing theories was correct. The results were very interesting because the two theories did graphically diverge but at that time our knowledge of the universe was not sufficient to definitely identify which divergent line was correct. The divergence was just too small to make a definitive conclusion as to which of the two theoretical models was correct. The results of this modeling would need to wait until future advances in observational astronomy could provide more accurate information about the universe we live in.

Late Nights of Computing

I programmed the astronomy project on the small DEC PDP 11/40 computer located in the physics building. Since I spent most of my day at the physics building in class or in my office, the computer in that building was convenient for me to get to.

There was a much larger IBM computer in the math building, but that was a few blocks away and it was not pleasant to travel back and forth repeatedly between the two buildings in a wheelchair, especially on cold rainy days. Also, the IBM computer was used for all university computer projects and it was difficult to get enough computer time allotted for a single large research computer project. When constructing my program that had thousands of lines of computer code it was much easier to test and correct everything on the computer in the physics building.

Once my computer program was finished it would take seven to eight hours to run a single model universe on the computer and while it was running nobody else could use the machine. This would also have to be done more than forty times to complete the project. The only way I could get that much time alone on the computer was to come in to the physics building late in the evening when there was usually no one around. I could then start my program and monitor it while it was running. I was able to run one model universe for each full night I spent in the physics building.

Evening Cleanup Crew of One

During those years Edward Weishaar was my caregiver and we have been very close friends ever since. Edward and I shared an apartment off-campus about four blocks from the physics building. He would pack me a few sandwiches and a thermos of coffee, and get me into the physics building computer room at night. The doors to the computer room were very difficult for me to get in and out of by myself so once I got into the computer room I was pretty much stuck there until somebody came by to let me out.

Most of my research was done during the summer semester when there weren't a lot of people around taking classes. I would usually get into the physics building computer room around ten or eleven in the evening and then call Edward in the morning around six or seven o'clock to come and get me.

Unfortunately, there were many times when I had to call Edward much earlier in the morning because the Texas catheter that I was wear-

81

ing would leak, leaving a puddle of urine all over the physics building computer room floor. My pants, underwear, and wheelchair cushion would also get very wet and that was not healthy to sit in for long periods of time because my skin would start to break down. In the fifteen to twenty minutes it would take Edward to get there I would shut down my computer program, pack up the desk work I was doing, and be ready to leave. Needless to say that would be a wasted night with little to no research completed.

When Edward arrived at the physics building he would go straight to the graduate office I shared and get our handy dandy little mop and bucket that was kept at the back of a little alcove for just such an emergency. He would use the large utility sink in the lab close to my office to fill the bucket with some water and detergent. Edward then wheeled the bucket and mop into the elevator, took the elevator down one floor, pushed the bucket down a long hallway past the professors' offices, and then into the computer room at the other end of the physics building. He would then mop up the computer room floor to eliminate all traces of the mishap.

Edward would also bring a large towel with him from the apartment so that he could shove the towel between my wheelchair cushion and pants to prevent my leaving a trail of urine back to my office. When we got back to my office he would empty and rinse the bucket and mop in the lab and put them back into the office alcove. With this secret mission accomplished, we would then go back to our apartment so that I could get out of all my wet clothes and no one would be the wiser.

This was another fine mess I got Edward into. I always wondered if the administrative staff in the physics building ever knew they had this special janitorial service working in the dead of night.

Barnes, Ronnie C. and Prondzinski, Robert: "A Comparative Study of Brans-Dicke and General Relativistic Cosmologies in Terms of Observationally Measurable Quantities", *Astrophysics and Space Science,* Vol. 16, Number 3 (June 1972): 499-504

CHAPTER 14

Quantum Burst (1972)

Attending university classes all day long while wearing a Texas catheter had some benefits but it also had many downsides. On the plus side it was an external catheter instead of indwelling so that it was less prone to bladder infections. The downside was that it was attached with just a small amount of surgical adhesive and elastic tape. If the adhesive or tape came loose, the next time you urinated it was all over your pants, wheelchair, and floor. Every morning when I got up a new Texas catheter was put on while getting dressed and I would spring a leak about once every couple of weeks. The frequency wasn't a problem but I had a lot of embarrassing moments in public because of that Texas catheter.

I sprung a leak a few times during regular class hours and had to exit the physics building, leaving a trail of urine in the hallways. I would hurriedly drive my electric wheelchair back to my apartment, which was about four blocks from the physics building. I always wondered what people thought as they walked through those hallways after I left the building, and hoped they would think that it was water that leaked from some lab project being carried from one place to another.

Battle of the Bulge

One time I was taking a Quantum Mechanics course final exam. I looked down from my test papers and to my dismay saw a huge bulge in my crotch area.

Nasty, nasty! No, it's not what you think.

I evidently had a twist at the end of the condom that makes up part of my Texas catheter. That end of the condom has a hole in it and is attached to surgical tubing that drains into a disposal bag attached to my leg. If the condom or tubing gets twisted it blocks off the urine flow to the leg bag. The result is that the Texas catheter blows up like a water balloon when I urinate. Since my bladder at that time could hold around a liter of urine this bulge was very huge.

What the hell was I to do? I thought of only three options:

1)   Just ignore what was going on with my Texas catheter, finish the test, and leave. But there was a pretty good chance that the adhesive or elastic tape would loosen and I would flood a good portion of the back of the room around me. I didn't think that the students sitting next to me would appreciate that very much.

2)   Excuse myself from the room, go back to my office, and burst the bulge. This would create a large puddle on my office floor that would need to be dealt with later, but I could then go back and take the rest of the test.

3)   Excuse myself from the room and try and make it back to my apartment so I would not have another embarrassing moment in the physics building. I could call the Quantum Mechanics professor later and explain why I had to leave in the middle of the test.

I chose option number two – but later wished I had chosen option number three.

I left the testing room and went back to my office. Once there I burst the balloon, leaving a huge puddle on my office floor. As I went back to the testing room I was reminded of the children's story, Hansel and Gretel. The young brother and sister left a trail of breadcrumbs behind to find their way home but, instead of breadcrumbs, I was leaving a telltale trail of droplets that dripped from my urine soaked wheelchair cushion.

I went back to the testing room and, after sitting there for another half-hour finishing the test, another small puddle had accumulated under my wheelchair. Since I was sitting in back of the room, as the other students finished their tests and handed them in, they would walk past me to go out the door. I became really embarrassed when a few of them would look at the floor and then stare at me on their way out.

When I finished the test and went back to my office, Errol, the other graduate student I shared that office with, was staring at the large puddle on our office floor. I shared with him what had just happened. He was a great guy and very understanding. He knew about some of the problems

I had in this area. He got out the bucket and mop we had in our office for just that reason and cleaned up the office, the hallway, and the floor in the room where my test was taken.

This was another fine mess I got somebody into. I just hope he didn't have to explain to any of the professors why he was mopping up the testing room floor and hallway.

CHAPTER 15

The Mississippi River Houseboat (1973)

As I mentioned in Into the Twilight Zone, I have a lot of ties to the town of Winona, Minnesota. The scenery around that area is magnificent and the town is partially surrounded by beautiful bluffs, with the Mississippi River separating Minnesota from Wisconsin.

Denny, my cousin Sharon's husband, owned a marina on the Mississippi and, at one time, also owned a nice houseboat. I was fortunate enough to take a couple of trips up and down the Mississippi on that houseboat and each trip was adventurous in itself.

Trip #1: Maiden Voyage

Denny purchased the houseboat from a dealer in the La Crosse area. La Crosse is about thirty miles downriver from Winona and is located on the Wisconsin side of the Mississippi. The day Denny was scheduled to pick up the houseboat in La Crosse and drive it up the river to Winona, my family was in town for the weekend visiting Sharon's family – my Uncle Louie, Aunt Florence, and cousins Jim and Susan. Denny invited my brother and me to go along with him and Jim to pick up the houseboat.

When Denny proposed the trip, my mother was totally against me going on that houseboat. She worried that something disastrous would happen. Well, that's my mother. She was always worried about something and, since my accident, she became extremely over-protective. Mom was insistent that I not go and I, of course, was just as stubborn insisting that I would go.

My father stayed out of that argument – he knew better than to get in the middle of an argument between my mother and me. I know however that he had no trouble supporting me going if I wanted to take the chance.

My brother Bill came to the rescue and helped me win the argument. He told mom that he would be going with me and would make sure nothing happened. I kept saying to my mother, "What could go wrong with Bill there to watch out for me?" By now you'd think I would have learned not to tempt fate by saying, "What could go wrong?" but I kept saying it anyway. And Bill and I both repeatedly reminded her it was going to be a short trip. The plan was to pick the houseboat up in La Crosse around eight o'clock in the morning and be back in Winona by mid-afternoon the same day.

Although still not happy with the situation, my mother finally caved in and said, "Fine. Go." However, she made sure she had the last word and laid one of those little guilt trips on me by saying, "Nothing better happen – and if it does, remember that I told you not to go." By this time, Denny was also in a little hot water with Sharon. She also thought it was a bad idea for me to go and was mad that Denny started this whole uproar. I think he was beginning to wish that he had never have asked my brother and me to go with him and Jim to pick up the houseboat.

Sputters and Stops

The next morning we drove to La Crosse and Denny signed the papers to purchase the houseboat. We immediately went to where it was docked to get onboard, leaving the car we drove to La Crosse to be picked up later in the day. The houseboat had a railing completely surrounding the outside with a small gate for entry and exit that was not quite wide enough for my push wheelchair to get through. Bill and Jim lifted me out of the wheelchair while Denny folded it up a little bit, pushed it onto the deck of the houseboat, and opened it again. Bill and Jim then carried me on board and put me back into the wheelchair. It was a little inconvenient getting me on to the houseboat but Bill and Jim were strong and they managed without any problems.

We were on our way up river to Winona by about nine o'clock. When we left the La Crosse area, the sun was shining and it looked like a great day for a trip along the Mississippi river. But the weather soon turned bad and we got caught in a huge downpour about eighteen miles north of La Crosse, just as we passed the town of Trempealeau on the

Wisconsin side to our right – I know I should use the word, "port" or "starboard" but I don't know which word means "right" and which word means "left."

As we cleared the lock and dam located just south of Trempealeau and were traveling the main channel just north of the dam, we heard an unwelcome sound – the houseboat's inboard Volvo engines sputtered and then stopped. Denny got the engines running again but a short distance farther, they again sputtered and stopped.

There we were – in a houseboat with no power drifting in the strong Mississippi current back toward the dam with no way to stop. This could quickly become a very dangerous situation.

Jim took over piloting the boat while Denny went below to see if he could find out what was wrong with the engines, thinking there might be some water in the fuel line. There wasn't much time to try and clear out the fuel lines before we were carried back to the dam by the current.

Once again Denny managed to get the engines started but, again, they soon stopped. We were probably about a mile above the town of Trempealeau and Denny aimed toward the Wisconsin shore. With continuous spurts of the engine starting and stopping he managed to get the boat to the dock just below Sullivan's restaurant north of Trempealeau.

Marooned!

We were all relieved to be tethered to a stable dock and certainly dodged one potential disaster but we weren't out of the woods yet. Denny and Jim tried to get the houseboat engines running consistently but it was just not happening. It was now getting late into the afternoon and Denny had National Guard duty that evening so he had to leave. We were all right but it looked like we would probably have to spend the night in the houseboat docked below Sullivan's.

I couldn't believe it!

How lucky could I get? I was going to be able to spend the entire evening on a houseboat on the Mississippi. Instead of having just a short boat cruise up the river this was turning into an opportunity to sort of camp out for the night. This was fantastic!

I was ecstatic.

Denny had to call someone to get a ride so that he could change clothes and make it to his National Guard duty while Jim needed to call my uncle's house to let them know what was happening. There were no such things as cell phones when this incident happened, so Denny and Jim walked up to Sullivan's restaurant to use a phone. When they left, Bill and I talked about how cool it was going to be to spend the night on the Mississippi – we were like kids in a candy store. This was going to be a great night and we thought things couldn't be better.

When Jim came back he relayed the conversation he had with my uncle. My mother was on the verge of hysterics and telling my dad over and over again, "I told you they shouldn't go." Sharon was not a happy camper, either, and was very worried about how we would survive the night.

I couldn't wait to spend the night on the houseboat. By this time, the rain had stopped and it was turning into a beautiful and very enjoyable evening on the Mississippi. My brother and I were having a great time while apparently everybody at my uncle's house was in a panic.

The houseboat had four drop-down beds inside the cabin area. They were very narrow and not very long but more than adequate for sleeping. The cabin was down a couple of stairs from where I sat on the deck so Jim and Bill pulled open one of the drop-down beds and then picked me up out of my wheelchair and carried me from the deck down to the bed. They then brought my wheelchair down and put me in it until we were ready to go to sleep for the night. Docking just below Sullivan's restaurant was a perk with plenty of fantastic food available to us just a short distance up the embankment.

As we were eating our carryout dinners of steak and shrimp with all the trimmings from Sullivan's, we heard a loud commotion on the dock and Bill quickly went outside to see what was going on. My Uncle Louie, dad, mother, and Sharon had come to see for themselves that we were not dead. Mom looked like she had been crying for a long time – and still was – when they came on board the houseboat. I believe the first words out of her mouth were, "I told you so. I told you not to go."

After seeing that we were having a great time and in the middle of a fantastic meal my mother calmed down and asked how we were going to get off the boat. We said we weren't going to get off and would be spending the night sleeping on the drop-down beds.

Mom immediately started crying again.

My dad explained that it would probably be better for us to stay rather than trying to carry me up to the steep embankment and into a car but she wouldn't listen. Denny told my uncle that he would come back early the next morning in one of his powerboats with new gas canisters and the appropriate equipment to clean out the fuel lines. My uncle and dad were pretty cool guys and thought that was probably the best idea. Uncle Louie, who eventually retired from the National Guard as a lieutenant colonel, was used to analyzing situations quickly and coming up with a plan. He thought the plan that Denny proposed was probably the best at the time and told my mom that if the boat wasn't running by noon the next day, they would get enough people to carry me off the boat. He calmly explained that getting me off the houseboat and up the incline was not as simple as it looked.

Sullivan's dock was attached to a very rocky area built for a railroad track. Once you climbed up the narrow path along the fifteen-foot rocky slope you had to cross railroad tracks and go down the rocky slope on the other side of the railroad tracks. Once there, you still have to cross a small ten-foot wide area connected to a twenty-foot high slope that leads to the front of Sullivan's restaurant lot. From there was a pretty straight shot to get to Sullivan's restaurant parking lot but, despite being a relatively short distance, clearly the whole traverse would not be easy.

After hearing the anticipated degree of difficulty to get me off the boat that night, my mother calmed down somewhat and they left about forty-five minutes later – but not before mom declared she wanted to stay with us that night. It took a group effort, but everybody finally convinced her to go back to the house.

Boy, were we glad when they were gone so we could continue our party on board the houseboat. The beautiful evening turned into a great moonlit night and was a fantastic experience. Every once in awhile a large barge would pass by with its headlight rotating left to right from bank to bank, and as it passed the water would gently rise and fall causing the houseboat to rock back and forth in a very soothing way. Sometime during the evening a train went by on the railroad tracks just above where we were docked, which was also interesting and not to be missed.

Thank God the engines failed or I would never have had that experience. As I fell asleep that night I reflected on the range of my emotions for the day. What started out as a great experience could've easily ended in disaster but turned out better than my brother and I could ever have expected. The only real negative of the entire experience was knowing how upset my mother was throughout the ordeal.

Reluctantly Rescued

The next morning Jim got up early, went into Trempealeau and called my uncle's house to let everybody know that we had a great night and everything was okay. When he got back to the houseboat both Bill and I were up and they proceeded to get me onto the front deck of the houseboat. I thoroughly enjoyed the scenery around me, and the great morning sun.

We thought ahead enough to buy some eggs, bacon, biscuits, dough-nuts, orange juice, coffee grounds, and milk from a local grocery store the night before and Jim went down into the cabin to make breakfast in the galley.

The smell of bacon frying and coffee brewing drifted up to the front deck where my brother and I were sitting. The aroma, mixed in with the fresh air and fantastic scenery along the Mississippi, was a unique experience. I don't remember a breakfast ever tasting so good as it did out there in the open air with the houseboat gently rocking back and forth as a barge passed by.

Not too long after we finished breakfast we saw a powerboat coming our way. It was Denny – still in his National Guard uniform – bringing fresh gas for the engines. He had a couple of people with him that quickly cleared out our fuel lines and put in the fresh gas. After a short while the houseboat was running without a single sputter and we were ready to finish our journey.

Denny left in the powerboat and Jim piloted the houseboat back to Denny's marina in Winona, around ten miles upriver. It was a fantastic morning. The weather was clear and sunny and the scenery was spectacular. I couldn't believe our luck in having the houseboat engines breakdown the previous afternoon.

As expected, my mother was waiting for us at the Winona dock. She wasn't crying anymore but it didn't look like she got any sleep that night either. And you can be sure that throughout the day Bill and I heard an, "I told you so," every now and then.

Well I sure got into another mess by taking this river trip but, to tell you the truth, I didn't care. It was a magnificent experience. When we went back to Milwaukee, we both had a great story to tell our friends.

By the way, although it now has different owners than the time we camped overnight on its dock, Sullivan's restaurant is still there and still serving great food. It has a fantastic view from the dining room windows of the Mississippi and surrounding bluffs. If you ever find yourself in the La Crosse, Trempealeau, or Winona area it would be well worth your time to stop in and have dinner. I would highly recommend starting with their beer battered mushroom and onion ring baskets. They are the best I've found anywhere. You can see a photo of Sullivan's river view (and menu) at: http://www.sullivanssupperclub.com.

Trip #2: All Hands on Deck

A year after our Mississippi River adventure, I was living in Chicago and working at G.D. Searle. After relating the houseboat story to a few close friends they said they wished they, too, could take a trip on a houseboat on the Mississippi. I asked them if they were really serious and they each said, "Yes." If you know me, you know that my response was, "Okay, let's do it." They then asked me if I was serious and I assured them I was. They told me that if I could make the arrangements they would be very excited about going.

I called my cousin Sharon and asked to speak with Denny. I asked him if a couple of friends and I could use his houseboat some weekend later that summer. He told me that if I could find somebody who knew how to pilot the houseboat on the Mississippi he would have no problem with us using his houseboat.

Because of the size and strength of the Mississippi there was no way any of my friends would be able to pilot a houseboat. The river has a lot of commercial barge traffic and the pilot needs to be familiar with all the navigation rules for traveling the waterways. Denny suggested I call my cousin Jim and asked him if he would be willing to pilot the houseboat for us. Since Jim was part of the first houseboat trip I thought that was a great idea.

I called Jim and told him about my hope to bring my friends for a river trip on the houseboat and that Denny said we could use it if we had a pilot who knew the river. Jim said he was more than willing to take us 2out if we could coordinate a weekend sometime just after Labor Day. When I relayed the information to my friends they were surprised and eager to make this trip happen. We settled on a weekend when everybody could get together.

Balancing Act on Bouncing Barrels

When the weekend for our houseboat excursion arrived, my friends and I drove to my uncle's house in Winona, arriving on a Thursday night. We wanted to spend most of Friday and all of Saturday traveling up the Mississippi to camp out overnight on one of the many islands north of Winona. The friends who came with me on this journey were Edward Muldoon, Sudhir Arora, and Roman Raszeja. Jim also brought along his friend, Gary, to go with us. We all left my uncle's house early on Friday morning and went to the docks to board the houseboat.

The first order of business was to somehow get me onto the houseboat. When we arrived in Winona after the first trip we got off at the gas dock, which was a stationary dock. But the assigned space to park the houseboat in the marina was alongside a floating dock. A floating dock is kept afloat by using barrels placed underneath the wooden planks and the dock rises and falls along with the water level. This kind of dock moves up and down and rolls a little when anyone walks on it and I felt more than a little uncomfortable taking my wheelchair to the end of the dock. One of my friends pushed me there and held on tight to try to keep me fairly steady. The next trick was to actually get me on the houseboat.

As I mentioned earlier, the houseboat's perimeter was lined with a metal railing to keep people from falling off once they were on the houseboat and the gate was too narrow to get my wheelchair through. A few of my friends would have to lift me out of my wheelchair while another positioned it on the deck of the houseboat to set me back into. As my friends lifted me out of the wheelchair at the end of this rolling dock, the dock started to rock, sinking deeper into the water because of all the weight concentrated at that one point. Fortunately my friends managed to keep their balance and step onto the deck of the houseboat. However they were not looking forward to going through this routine again once we returned from our trip.

We untied from the dock around nine o'clock in the morning and our journey upriver began. The weather forecast for the weekend was clear and sunny with only a slight possibility of rain showers. As we pulled away from the marina it was bright and sunny without a cloud in the sky and the temperature was in the mid-eighties. It was a great start for our trip.

Rear Ended

A little after noon, Edward went down into the galley and fried up some hamburgers and hot dogs. There is nothing like having lunch on the deck of a houseboat while traveling on the Mississippi and watching the spectacular scenery as we slowly cruised along the river. The afternoon was warm but a brief rain shower cooled things off just a little bit. At about three o'clock in the afternoon we decided to pull in and anchor at one of the sandbars to spend the night.

There were a great number of other people in boats who were doing just what we were doing. Some of them had houseboats and some just had regular sporting boats that they would beach and then set up camp for the night. You could see a few pitched tents up and down the beach and a lot of campfires glowing. There were also a lot of people swimming at the beach area and enjoying the great afternoon and evening.

Just after we beached the houseboat, Roman decided he needed to take a big dump. We could not use the houseboat's lavatory facilities due to problems with the chemical toilet so Roman grabbed a roll of toilet paper from the lavatory and walked out onto the beach. He walked up the sandbar toward the center of the island where there was a lot of brush and scrub trees. We saw him walk onto what looked like a path and lost sight of him as he went behind the brush.

About four or five minutes went by and we heard Roman cussing and swearing from somewhere in the brush. Two minutes later he came running out of the brush area with his underwear up but his pants still halfway down to his knees. When he got to the boat we were all concerned that he might have hurt himself but found out it was a lot less serious.

Evidently, Roman found a log in the brush area that he could drop his drawers down and squat over while he was doing his "business."

One of the things he didn't realize immediately was that the brush area – especially after a rain – had thousands of mosquitoes all around. Let me set the record straight: it is no exaggeration that Minnesota mosquitoes are huge.

Roman told us that when he wiped himself and brought his hand forward the toilet paper was all bloody. The blood came from all the mosquitoes he squashed while wiping his butt. By the time Roman got his skivvies up he literally had hundreds of mosquito bites on his two cheeks. Once he got onto the boat he actually dropped his drawers and bent over to show us. His entire ass was red and pimpled with hundreds of mosquito bites. I couldn't believe that all of us were actually staring at Roman's butt.

It's a sight I hope never to see again.

Roman had a tough time sitting down and kept rubbing lotion on his cheeks to stop the itching. That is the last time that Roman ever ventured into the brush. The rest of our crew took note and performed their duty elsewhere. Where, I can only guess and imagined a couple of them hanging their butts over the side rail after it got dark.

A couple of my friends went swimming and then started a small campfire towards evening. We brought along some steaks, potatoes, and beans, which were cooked over the campfire. Although I couldn't get off the deck they constructed the fire close enough to the houseboat so I could still talk with them without having to shout. We all had a marvelous time that afternoon and evening – except for Roman who was still nursing his rear end.

It was very pleasant sleeping on the houseboat that night. My friends and I slept in the drop-down beds located inside the cabin. Jim and Gary slept in sleeping bags on the roof of the houseboat. We could hear the frogs and insects making their nightly noises while the houseboat gently swayed up and down with the waves. It was very soothing.

Around midnight when the mosquitoes disappeared, Edward and Sudhir climbed to the roof of the houseboat with their pillows and blankets and slept under the starry sky. Occasionally a big Mississippi barge would pass by and the smooth rocking motion of the houseboat would get a little more intense but it was still very pleasant. It was a great night on that houseboat. My friends said it was an experience they would never forget and I agreed with them wholeheartedly.

Locking Through

When the morning came, Edward fried bacon and eggs on the galley stove and made fresh coffee. Just as I remember from my first houseboat trip, the aromas of breakfast cooking and coffee brewing drifted up to the front deck of the houseboat and made my mouth water. It just doesn't get any better than this.

After breakfast we stayed on the sandbar for a couple of hours before traveling a little farther up the river. Under Jim's guidance, each of my friends had a chance to pilot the houseboat and we figured that we could probably travel up the river until noon before we would have to start heading back down. The return trip downriver would be much quicker because of the strong, rapid river currents.

My friends also had a new experience when we traveled through a series of locks. A lock is a chamber separating one side of the dam from the other. Since the water level is different on each side of the dam, each boat that wants to cross to the other side enters the chamber, is locked in, and the water level is either increased or decreased in the chamber to bring the boat to the same level as the side it exits. It's quite a process and on a busy weekend it's not unusual to see a line of boats waiting to go through the locks.

Saturday turned out to be another day of nothing but great experiences for everyone and by the time we got back to Winona everyone was exhausted but couldn't stop talking about the experience. When we got back to my uncle's house, it took quite a while for us to unwind. I guess at least this journey was one of the rare times when I didn't get my friends into another mess (except maybe for Roman's mosquito mishap).

Memories and Mud Bogs

My friends and I woke up the next morning, ate breakfast, and started driving back to Chicago, but not without one last little twist of events.

On our way out of Winona, Sudhir wanted to get a couple final pictures to keep as memories of this trip. So we stopped along the shoulder of the road about four miles out of town where there was a very nice view of the Mississippi looking toward the Wisconsin shore. Sudhir got out of the car, crossed the road and disappeared over the embankment. We waited there for around fifteen or twenty minutes with no sign of Sudhir.

Just as one of my friends was going to see what was taking him so long, we saw Sudhir walking on the shoulder on the opposite side of the road. He looked a little strange in the distance and as he got closer we found out why. When he went down the embankment on the other side of the road, he tried to position himself for a better picture and jumped onto what he thought was solid shoreline. Instead, it turned out to be a mud bog that had about three feet of water under it.

Sudhir was soaked in a filthy mud from his waist down to his shoes.

Sudhir is an Indian from Delhi and part of the upper society in that culture. He was always immaculately dressed and meticulous about keeping clean. For him to be covered in mud from the waist down was a disastrous experience for him. When he got back to the car there was no way we were going to let him get in and then drive back to Chicago for the next six or seven hours. He was full of mud and it stunk to high heaven.

Sudhir opened up the trunk and took clean pants, underwear, and socks out of his suitcase. It was fortunate that we always carry a gallon bottle of drinking water in the car when we travel so that at least we had some water that he could use to wash himself up a bit. We opened both of the passenger doors so that Sudhir was somewhat sheltered from passing traffic.

There we were on the shoulder of the interstate with Sudhir naked from the waist down washing himself with drinking water and putting on new clothes. He was extremely embarrassed and did not want to talk about it the rest of the way home. But his unwillingness to talk about it didn't stop the rest of us from getting a good laugh out of it. What a trip!

To this day my friends and I still reminisce about the great night we had on the island and the entire experience of traveling on the Mississippi River. Although Denny doesn't have the houseboat any more, I hope that sometime in the near future I will be able to have that experience again.

It's possible to rent a houseboat for vacations and they come complete with instructions and training to learn how to operate, pilot, and navigate the boat on the river. If you're looking for a unique family vacation that's a little out of the ordinary, I highly recommend a slow-paced getaway on a houseboat. There are all different styles of houseboats to rent. You can choose one to travel in comfort or go all out and travel in complete luxury. Being sequestered on a houseboat while traveling and stopping at various islands on the Mississippi can provide many memories of quality time with the family. It will be an experience you and your family will remember for the rest of your lives.

CHAPTER 16

Condoms for Everyone (1974)

There are times I have gotten my friends into trouble or embarrassing situations without even knowing it. That's exactly what I did to Rick Winokur's wife, Patty.

Medical Supply Needs

When I returned home for good after my accident, there was a long list of medical supplies that I needed to keep in constant supply for the rest of my life. Things like:

- Tight elastic socks to aid with blood circulation
- Sterile latex gloves
- Regular medical tape
- Disposable bed pads of various sizes
- Urine drainage bags that strap around my leg when I am in a wheelchair
- Urine drainage bags that are used when I am in bed
- Lubricant used to assist in my bowel regimen
- The materials necessary to make Texas catheters – something I need at least once a day – including:
    - Surgical tubing
    - Surgical tubing connectors
    - Special surgical skin adhesive
    - Elastic medical tape
    - Condoms

While I was at the Sister Kenny Rehabilitation Institute, we quickly discovered that the Texas catheters available in the commercial marketplace did not work well for me because they kept falling off. It is not a pleasant experience to be sitting in a wheelchair and have your Texas catheter either loosen or fall off. In addition to being publicly embarrassing, it has adverse affects on the skin when you sit in urine-soaked clothes. And then there's always the cleanup once you finally get out of the wheelchair and into bed. It became safer to construct my own Texas catheters, so my family members learned how to assemble them before I left the Sister Kenny Rehabilitation Institute.

My mother was primarily in charge of the process for making me 90 to 120 Texas catheters each quarter. She made an extra number of catheters because sometimes there might be too much glue applied or the elastic tape did not adhere properly. When that happened you had to start over until you got it right. After a few mishaps of leaking in the wheelchair it became very obvious that putting a Texas catheter on correctly was extremely important.

A "Special Reservoir End" Shortage

I was fortunate enough during my first few years at home to obtain these supplies through a foundation that helped people like me. I usually received three month's worth of supplies at a time so I literally had a small truckload of boxes that had to be picked up each quarter.

One time Rick Winokur went to pick up my quarterly supplies and found out that the foundation was out of the condoms that I needed to make my daily Texas catheters. He was also informed that their supplier would not be able to get any for quite awhile. Being a man of action, Rick immediately called his wife, Patty, and asked her to go to their local drugstore to pick up a supply of condoms so we could make our Texas catheters. Patty agreed and drove to their local drugstore.

In the early 1970's, anyone going into a drugstore to buy even one package of condoms was looked at with suspicion and a judgmental "evil eye." Condoms were an item that couples never talked about in public and anyone who bought them tried to keep the purchase inconspicuous.

Perhaps a good analogy is the plight of the teenage boy who decides to go to a drugstore to try to buy a *Playboy* magazine. First he would search for a drugstore a few suburbs away from where he lives so that nobody could recognize him. Then he might sandwich a *Playboy* between a *Time* magazine and *U.S. News & World Report* to purchase at the checkout counter, thinking he could sneak it through with as little notice as possible. If he's lucky, he walks out with the magazine and no one is the wiser. This is the way I've heard it's done, mind you. I'm not admitting that I did this myself. (That's my story and I'm sticking to it.)

Keeping this mentality of the times in mind, imagine Patty going into the drugstore and telling the pharmacist that she needed a gross of Trojan condoms with the Special Reservoir End. Well, she not only stunned the pharmacist behind the counter but everyone around her who was in hearing range. All eyes were on her.

Patty grew up in a small farming community in northwestern Iowa with many brothers and sisters and was raised Roman Catholic. The taboo of even talking about condoms was doubly horrendous if you were Catholic. Sex was a very private matter. I can imagine what all of those people staring at her were thinking: "What in the world does a little innocent looking Catholic farm girl want with 144 Trojan condoms – especially ones with the Special Reservoir End?"

I knew nothing about this until she brought the condoms to the house. She later admitted to me that she felt that everyone around her was wondering what kind of a woman she was, and she just wanted to crawl into a hole and die at that moment. To this day, she vividly remembers how embarrassed she was that day.

It's weird how some of the ancillary items a quadriplegic needs could become a source of embarrassment to others. *Obviously I unknowingly sometimes put my friends – or my friends' wives – into "another fine mess" situations.*

Recalling this incident also made me realize something else. After getting home from rehabilitation in 1965, whenever I ran out of condoms, my own sweet, shy, conservative mother would drive to the local pharmacy to get what I needed. I now wonder how she felt asking her hometown pharmacist for a couple dozen Trojan condoms with the Special Reservoir End.

CHAPTER 17

Footballs and Footfalls (1975)

About a year after I graduated from the University of Missouri, the fifth-ranked Missouri football team was going to play against twelfth-ranked University of Michigan in Ann Arbor. I had a cousin who could provide me with as many tickets as I needed. I saw this as a great opportunity to get together for a long weekend outing with some friends of mine from the Chicago area.

Ray, Roman, Sudhir and I made reservations at a hotel near the campus for Friday and Saturday night. Not wanting to spend any more money than we had to, we reserved one room with two queen-sized beds.

Basset Barks

We arrived at the hotel late on Friday night and immediately went to bed. But every few hours we were awakened by the sound of barking dogs and wondered what the heck was going on.

When we went to breakfast the next morning we discovered there was a basset hound convention and breeders show going on in the area. A lot of the breeders happened to be staying at the same hotel we were.

After breakfast we headed for the parking lot to get in the car and drive to the University football stadium for the game. When we got outside we found ourselves in a sea of canines. The parking lot was filled with basset hounds – more than two hundred of them. There's nothing like the sight, sound – and smell – of two hundred basset hounds out for their morning walk-and-squat. As I was accustomed to hearing, my friends looked in my direction and said nearly in unison, *"This is another fine mess you've gotten us into."* We didn't realize this statement would again be uttered before this weekend adventure ended.

Leg Tap

We arrived at the University stadium gate and were ushered to the area where I would be able to sit next to my friends, positioned in the aisle next to the seats. As the stadium began to fill with people, we noticed a lot of what seemed like uniformed Boy Scouts starting to sit in all the aisles. I asked one of the stadium personnel what was with all the Boy Scouts. He told me that they did not expect a large crowd so they invited Boy Scouts from around the State to attend the game.

Unbeknownst to stadium officials, the game attracted a record crowd of 104,578 people. With seats packed and Boy Scouts filling up the aisles, I quickly realized that it would be impossible to execute my usual "Plan A" which is to drive my wheelchair to a concession area where one of my friends would have to empty my leg bag when it got full. So I made a contingency plan with Ray. I told him they all needed to drink a lot and save the cups just in case I couldn't get through the crowd and we'd have to empty the urine bag right where I was. The plan was to drain my leg bag into the empty cups and keep them under the seats. When one of them got up to go to the bathroom, he could take a cup or two with him to empty.

Near the end of the second quarter, my leg bag did need to be emptied. So there I was in the middle of an aisle surrounded by Boy Scouts with my friend Ray undoing the plug at the bottom of my leg bag to drain it into the empty cups. I suddenly had a lot of attention. The Boy Scouts sitting all around me thought I was loading the cups up with beer, and started telling all of their friends about it while pointing to my leg bag. One of them even asked where he could get a beer bag like the one I had strapped to my leg.

Who was I to tell them anything different?

Beer Crap

In a total upset, Missouri lost the game with a score of 31 to 7. As we waited for the stadium to clear out before attempting to leave, we decided to go somewhere for dinner and something to drink. In talking with some local students, they clued us in on a popular local bar called Dooley's.

Dooley's was a great little bar and we thoroughly enjoyed ourselves. My friends had been drinking for a while but I refrained because I learned early on that if I drink too much beer I'm prone to getting diarrhea (the "Big D"). But as the night wore on I thought, "What the hell?" Maybe I could chance having a few glasses of beer.

Many pitchers later, the bar closed and we went back to our basset hound hotel.

Ray and Roman took one bed and Sudhir and I took the other. My friends got me undressed and covered up in bed. "Thank God," I thought to myself. I dodged the bullet on this one and I was diarrhea free. Comforted with this knowledge, I passed out and did not wake up until morning – with a huge hangover.

Although awake, I was not quite ready to get up, so I put my head under the covers to get comfortable. I immediately noticed a foul smell coming from beneath the covers. Sure enough, I had one of the worst bouts of the "Big D" I ever had in my life. My bedmate, Sudhir, also woke up wondering what the awful smell was.

As bad as it was for me, it was worse for Sudhir. He dresses impeccably and everything about him exudes the concept of being clean and spotless. When he found out I had diarrhea in the same bed he was sleeping in, he freaked out.

Ray and Roman finally woke up and we explained the situation to them. None of us quite knew what to do. The bed was a mess. The sheets were a mess. The mattress was a mess. And I was a mess with my own excrement all over my body.

It was 9:30 a.m. and check out time was 11:30 a.m. so whatever we were going to do, we had to hustle. We finally decided the best way to get this situation under control was to get me into the bathtub and use the shower nozzle to clean me off. Ray grabbed me under the armpits and Roman grabbed me under the knees, carrying me across the room to get to the bathroom. With each step they took, I left another brown puddle behind.

I've never seen so much crap in my life. It was on the carpet, on the bathroom floor and soaked into the bed mattress. They managed to get me washed off pretty well but the diarrhea wouldn't stop. We decided I would stay in the tub with the shower running and they would clean themselves off and as much of the carpet as they could. They balled up the sheets and dragged the mattress outside, putting both into a dumpster behind the hotel.

Once they cleaned the room as much as possible they hurriedly got me dressed and into the car – lining the car seat under me with as much newspaper as they could in case my bouts with the "Big D" continued. Ray went into the lobby and signed us out. Once he got in the car, we drove away as fast as we could.

Unfortunately, we had hours to drive before we'd be home and the diarrhea did not stop. We kept the windows open almost all the way convinced that, if we didn't, we would assuredly die from asphyxiation.

This was quite literally another BIG mess I'd gotten my friends into.

CHAPTER 18

Water, Water, Everywhere (1976)

When I started my first job at G.D. Searle in 1974, I moved into an apartment in the Chicago suburb of Des Plaines. At the time, the apartment complex was called the Greens of Golf Mill. It was a very nice location because I could drive my wheelchair to the large Golf Mill shopping center located only a few blocks away.

The apartment was very roomy and the floor plan was such that it was easy for me to get around. The only downside was that, like a lot of other northern suburbs in the Chicago area, the surrounding small creeks tend to flood during springtime. Greens of Golf Mill had one of these small creeks on the other side of our parking lot.

Lake View

During the spring the creek would overflow the banks but usually the parking lot was covered with only a few inches of water. Actually, if you didn't have to leave the apartment, the minor flooding was quite nice because looking through the glass patio doors it felt like living next to a small lake. However, having to leave the apartment to get to work, and get in and out of a car was always a real problem for me if the parking lot was flooded. And it was also common for the parking lot to develop numerous potholes during spring that I needed to maneuver around.

I used to ride back and forth to work with my friend Rick. This was convenient for both of us because Rick also worked at G.D. Searle at a different complex about a mile from where I worked. He also lived only a couple miles from where I lived and would pass my apartment complex to get to and from work.

When I started my first job I could not afford to purchase a handicap van. And even if I could there were few places at that time that could outfit one with the appropriate equipment. So I spent a few years running back and forth to work in a regular car. To make things easier I had two electric wheelchairs so I could keep one at work and one at home. Electric wheelchairs are not something you want to have to take apart and load into a trunk of a car each and every time you need to ride.

Rick and I had a simple daily routine. Rick would come by in the morning, meet me at my door, and I would drive my wheelchair out to where he was parked. He would open the front passenger door, remove the left armrest from my electric wheelchair, and use my sliding board to get me into the front seat of the car. He would then close the car door and push my electric wheelchair back into my apartment. The process was reversed when we got to work.

At the end of one particular day of heavy rains, we arrived at my apartment after work to find that my parking lot was flooded. Usually the parking lot nearest my apartment didn't flood because it sat on a little higher ground than the apartments further down the street. But we had constant rain for a few days in a row and the parking lot was flooded a lot more than usual. Upon our return that day we found that the street and sidewalk in front of my apartment were under water.

Rick had to wade in ankle deep water to get into my apartment and bring my wheelchair out to where it was dry enough for me to get into. The water had actually risen over the curb and sidewalk and was slowly creeping up into the grassy area in front of my patio door.

Once Rick got me into the chair and onto the sidewalk I was able to easily maneuver to the front door of the apartment because the foot pedals of my wheelchair were about three or four inches above the flooded sidewalk. Unfortunately Rick's feet were covered with some very unhealthy looking water – or I should say, unidentifiable liquid.

Rick stayed with me in the apartment for a while as we waited to see if the water would get any higher and start seeping through the patio door. After a few hours the water started to subside a little so he left and was to pick me up the next morning for work as usual.

Human Projectile

By the next morning the water had subsided enough to be contained in the parking lot, leaving the sidewalk clear. The parking lot where Rick usually parked his car was filled with other cars so he had to park a little bit further down the street.

As usual, Rick met me at my apartment door and I proceeded down the sidewalk in the wheelchair. We were across the street from where his car was parked so Rick helped me down the curb and onto the parking lot. The parking lot only had an inch or two of standing water so I could travel easily in the electric wheelchair to Rick's car, which was only about twenty feet away.

What happened next seemed to go in very slow motion for me. About ten feet from Rick's car, my right front wheel suddenly dropped down into a pothole that was hidden by the standing water in the parking lot. My wheelchair tipped over, throwing me about five feet away from it. I lay there looking up from the parking lot pavement with filthy water lapping halfway around my body. All my clothes were soaking wet.

There was no way that Rick alone could get me lifted back into the wheelchair. He was finally able to find a few people in the parking lot who could help lift me out of the street and into the wheelchair. Rick got me back into the apartment and into bed where I could get stripped down and washed up, checking carefully to make sure I didn't break any bones. Fortunately I only had a few scrapes and bruises. Needless to say, I called my office and told them I wouldn't be coming to work that day.

Getting thrown out of the wheelchair has happened to me many times throughout my life and it is never a pleasant experience. Every incident teaches me something new that I need to keep in the back of my mind for the rest of my life. This incident taught me that hidden dips, cracks, and potholes were my new enemies and, from then on, I needed to be extremely careful anytime I would have to go over a puddle in the street or across a parking lot.

My scrapes, bumps and bruises were not the only casualties in this two-day flooding period. The filthy water really did a number on Rick, giving him the worst case of athlete's foot he ever experienced in his life, and for many weeks thereafter he could hardly wear a pair of shoes.

This was another fine mess I inadvertently got my friend into.

CHAPTER 19

Chicago Blues (1979)

My friends and I all enjoy good live music and in the Chicago area you can always get your fill. Though I tend to enjoy live rock bands, I also like to attend live blues and jazz concerts.

Our favorite blues haunts were near the corner of Lincoln Avenue and Halsted. During the 1970's there were some really great blues bars in the area. The two we frequented the most were the Kingston Mines and the Wise Fools Pub.* I heard many memorable performances in each of these clubs.

At that time the clubs were not in elaborate new buildings or fancy rooms as you might find today in downtown Chicago. They were considered – I guess the word that comes to mind is – dives. They were small little bars that smelled of smoke and stale beer, and often had under-sized "stinky" bathrooms that were not well ventilated. Although they might've been rather earthy, these bars had a lot of character and were very intimate places to listen to live blues. We loved them.

One Monday afternoon in 1979, I received a call from Rick, who now worked for Bristol-Myers Squibb and lived in St. Louis, Missouri. He said he was going to be in Chicago at a manufacturing convention the following week and wondered if I had anything going on for the up-coming weekend. I told him "no" and he asked me if he and a couple of his fellow workers could stay at my place from Friday night to Sunday afternoon before they had to check in to their hotel for the convention. He thought it would be great to get together and have some fun in Chicago before their convention. I thought it was a great idea and told him to come up with his friends.

I was living in Des Plaines, a suburb north of Chicago, in a fairly large apartment so there was enough room for Rick and his friends to sleep on my living room sofa and floor. Their flight arrived on Friday night and we went to a great restaurant for dinner.

On Saturday we toured a few places around Chicago and then Rick said he would like to take his friends out for some live music – I never turn down an invitation to go out and listen to live music. He told me to pick the place because he hadn't lived in Chicago for quite a few years and didn't know of a good place to go. I asked him if he thought his friends would enjoy some good, live Chicago blues and he thought they would. So with that, I decided we would go to the Kingston Mines.

I always need to go to the clubs early when they have live entertainment otherwise the places are so packed it's hard to get through the door, especially with the wheelchair. So we arrived at the Kingston Mines about an hour and a half prior to the start of the entertainment. It gave us a chance to get better acquainted and eat a lot of the free popcorn they always had on the tables.

We picked a table positioned in the middle of the room. It was still very close to the stage but also close enough to the back of the room so we could get out later when we wanted to. After being there about forty-five minutes the place really started to fill up and, by the time the band started, it was standing room only.

Bathroom Barricade

Toward the end of the first set my urine drainage bag attached to my leg was full and it needed to be emptied. There was no way I could get out of the club to have it emptied because of all the people behind us. My only chance was to try and get into the men's bathroom but, when looking over toward it, I knew that idea would not work. A huge plumbing pipe was right in front of the bathroom door that went from the ceiling down through the floor. It would be impossible to get around.

I mentioned my dilemma to Rick and he got up and went to the bar area. After talking with the bartender, the bartender signaled one of the bouncers to come by. Rick explained the situation to the bouncer and they decided to have me use the women's bathroom. The women's bathroom was only a few feet from me and would be a straight shot to get into. The bartender then told one of the waitresses to make sure nobody took our places while we took care of business.

Rick came over and wheeled my chair into the women's bathroom after the bouncer made sure that all the women were out of it. It was pretty cramped quarters in the bathroom and we could not shut the bathroom door behind us so the bouncer and Rick's two friends guarded the door. Rick threw my leg over the toilet bowl and then opened the valve on my leg bag so that it could empty.

That was the first and last time I ever took a pee in a women's bathroom. As I looked around the bathroom I was shocked and amazed at all of the graffiti on the walls. I swear that some of the sayings and little poems were grosser than the worst ones I have ever seen in the men's bathrooms. I had always imaged women's bathrooms to be clean and tidy – so much for that illusion. I just smiled and chuckled as Rick and I reported to his two friends what the inside of the women's bathroom actually looked like.

We stayed for the second set of music and had a great time. While trying to maneuver through the crowd, one of the waitresses spilled a pitcher of beer on Rick and one of his friends. After she brought us a free pitcher of beer Rick and his friend didn't seem to mind having to sit in beer-soaked clothes for the rest of the night.

On Sunday Rick and his friends left my apartment in Des Plaines and went downtown to check in to their hotel for the convention. I don't know what Rick's friends expectations of me were before we ever met, but Rick told me afterward that his friends told him on the plane trip home that they were surprised that I was just like a normal guy. In truth, that is one of the greatest compliments I could ever receive: to be just one of the guys.

When Rick's friends got home they had many stories to tell about their Chicago trip and Rick told me they especially like to tell others around the office about having to guard the women's bathroom door. I guess you could say, *"That's another fine mess I'd gotten 'friends of my friends' into."*

---

*Since we frequented these blues bars in the 1970s, many of these "dives" have developed into some of the biggest and best entertainment spots that Chicago has to offer. The Kingston Mines moved (but not far) from its original location in 1980 and has since been voted best blues club for eight years in a row by the Chicago Music

Awards (http://www.kingstonmines.com). Wise Fools Pub was sold and renamed in the early 1990s and revamped into an upscale bar and restaurant. But in 2001 the Wise Fools Pub was resurrected and today continues to be one of Chicago's most historic music venues (http://www.myspace.com/wisefoolspub).

CHAPTER 20

Suckling Pig, Anyone? (1980)

After living and working in the Chicago area for a while, I accumulated a great group of friends. One group would meet at my house every weekend to listen to music, eat a lot of junk food, drink a lot of beer and wine, and play board games like Risk™, or another game that was just starting to become popular, Dungeons & Dragons™.

In addition to playing games we also liked to program computer games since all of us were in the computer field but worked for different companies. We each had our own personal computers as soon as the first ones became available to the general public. We got together for literally most of the weekend. People would crash on my living room floor or on my sofas for the night. And there were many evenings when the games started at eight in the evening and didn't end until five o'clock the next morning. Then we'd go out for breakfast at a nearby Denny's restaurant for chili and eggs before going back home and getting some sleep.

One of my friends in this weekend crowd had a sister who also had a group that met regularly on weekends. He thought it might be fun to get both groups together, meet at a restaurant in downtown Chicago, and get acquainted while having a good meal together. We all thought it was a great idea and we decided to make it happen.

Too Much of a Good Thing

We wanted to do a little something out of the ordinary so we first found a great Greek restaurant that, with a few days notice, would prepare a suckling pig for a party of more than ten people. This "private pig roast" included the use of a room separated from the main dining area by a curtain. Between our two groups, we had more than a dozen people who were going to attend so we decided it would be weird – and memorable – to order a suckling pig for dinner. And we wanted it to look just like the roasted pigs you see in old Hawaiian luau movies and TV commercials with somebody carrying a large platter to the table with a whole roasted pig on it – head and all.

We made early reservations so that we didn't have to contend with the regular Chicago dinner crowd. However, after arriving at the restaurant it was evident that they were already busy and we were informed that they did not yet have our area ready. The owner was very apologetic about the inconvenience and moved our entire group to the end of the bar area, providing us with free ouzo and metaxa as they were readying a private room. Except for me, this group was made up of pretty big drinkers and they all made the most of it.

By the time our private room was ready, everybody was officially "three sheets to the wind" from the free drinks at the bar. And once seated, we ordered more bottles of ouzo and metaxa for the table. After a short time, the waiter brought out our suckling pig. Just as we had imagined, the platter presented contained the whole pig, head and all. After we all stared at it for about thirty seconds, the waiter took the platter back to the kitchen area to be cut up and served with the rest of the meal.

My friend Ray sat to my left side with his girlfriend sitting to the left of him. By now Ray was pretty well intoxicated and very hard to understand because he kept slurring his words. But that did not deter him from continuing to delve into the liquor bottles being passed around the table. He seemed to be having a great time.

Drowning in Gravy

Before long the waiter returned. The suckling pig had been carved into generous portions and served to each of us on individual dinner plates. The pork slices were smothered in rich brown gravy and dinner was absolutely delicious.

As we neared the end of the meal everyone commented how fantastic this was and how we would have to do it again sometime.

Then…

I heard a thud to my left, glanced over, and realized that Ray was slumped forward in his chair with his face firmly planted in his dinner plate, still filled with pork gravy. I knew he was still alive because I could see the gravy bubbling next to his cheek as he started snoring. Everybody around the table – including the waiters – stared in astonishment.

Ray's girlfriend, along with one of my other friends, managed to pull him back into a sitting position, cleaned his face, and woke him up enough to keep his eyes open, although I wouldn't exactly describe him as being "alert" at the time. We knew we had a problem on our hands and by this time the waiters had told the owner what was going on.

The owner came back to our area and told us we all had to leave his restaurant. He ignored the protests by the rest of the group, as most of us were still not done with dinner and there was a lot of liquor and half filled bottles still scattered around the table. After negotiating a while with the owner, to our surprise, he bought everyone one last round of ouzo as the waiters packed up the remaining liquor bottles and food so we could take it all with us in a giant doggie bag. It was abundantly clear that we had to get out of there before there was any more trouble.

Parting Gifts

Two or three people managed to get Ray out of his chair and maneuver him through the restaurant and out the door with the rest of us following behind until we reached the sidewalk in front of the restaurant. As we turned to go down the sidewalk to get in our vehicles, Ray suddenly broke free from the people holding him, turned back toward the restaurant, and vomited. The entire entrance way was now filled with a pile of wet regurgitated food and drink.

As the high-class dinner crowd began to arrive at the restaurant, two of my friends quickly grabbed Ray and rushed him out of there. None of us wanted to be found in the area so we ran back to our vehicles as fast as we could before the owner could call the police.

As we high-tailed it down the street, I took one daring look behind me and saw a well-dressed couple, walking arm in arm toward the front of the restaurant – the man in a dinner jacket and the woman with a fur shawl draped over her elegant evening gown. Oblivious to what had just transpired, I always wondered if they ruined their high-priced shoes by stepping into Ray's suckling pig surprise as they entered the restaurant.

This was the only restaurant I ever got kicked out of in my entire life. And even though the food was delicious I was always afraid to go back.

At least this time it was merely another mess that I was in with my friends – not one that I created.

CHAPTER 21

Stargazing from Michigan Avenue (1981)

Although we worked at different companies in the Chicago area, most of my Chicago friends worked in the computer field. A lot of the companies where my friends worked used IBM mainframes as their main computer hardware. A few times each year, IBM invited representatives from its customer companies to the IBM Plaza in downtown Chicago for special new product demonstrations and seminars. This was always a great chance for my friends and me to get together during a weekday in downtown Chicago.

We would all meet at the IBM Plaza and attend the presentations, which usually lasted an hour or two. We then took the opportunity to spend the rest of the day having a few drinks together and dining at one of the great restaurants Chicago has to offer. We usually stayed downtown well into the evening to avoid the horrendous traffic going out of the city at the end of the workday. Staying later also gave us a chance to enjoy some of the nightlife in the city.

Sleazy Bars

One afternoon four of my friends and I met for one of IBM's product presentations. Larry, Susan, Bob, Ray and I attended the IBM presentation and then went out for dinner at one of the fine downtown restaurants. After dinner we sat for a while and enjoyed a couple of drinks. When Larry and Susan decided to go home, Bob, Ray and I thought we would stay in the city to do a little bar hopping. It was a nice warm summer evening and none of us had any immediate need to go home.

Since I don't do a lot of drinking myself because of problems with my digestive system, I would nurse a drink as we went from bar to bar and sometimes not even finish it before we left for the next one. As the night got longer, the bars got sleazier, many of them located down some of the side streets and away from the main drag.

We finally wound up at a small bar I don't know the name of and could probably never find again. But I do remember that it was down a side street with a huge slope because I needed someone to hold on to my wheelchair to keep it from rolling down the street on its own. I had taken a non-electric portable wheelchair that could easily be folded and put into a trunk of a car. Without an electric motor, my friends had to push me around wherever we went.

At times it was more convenient to use the portable wheelchair if we were going into areas that might have curbs and stairs. Being lighter, the chair could be tilted back and I could be pulled up stairs. There was also a support rod on the back of the chair. One of my friends would simply need to step on the rod to lift the chair's front wheels up onto the sidewalk and then use the handles to lift the back of the chair over the curb.

The small bar on the sloping street was darkly lit with only a couple tables but they were already occupied. Bob, Ray and I managed to find some space along the corner of the bar. Since the height of a bar is much taller than I can reach, I usually sat sideways and my friends would hand my drink down to me and put it back up when I was done taking a few sips. It was a very pleasant and comfortable bar to be in and it had one of those local friendly bar atmospheres. The bartender and a lot of the customers seemed to know one another quite well.

Ray struck up a conversation with one of the ladies sitting next to him and as a table cleared they moved to the table to continue their conversation. Bob and I were talking to another very good-looking lady who sat down next to Bob on the bar stool just vacated by Ray. She told us her name was Dawn and Bob and I introduced ourselves. She was intrigued by Bob's last name – Honesty – and mentioned it more than once that night. I soon realized that she was what some would call a professional lady of the evening. We were all having a good time and she evidently was not immediately concerned about finding her next client.

After a while I noticed Bob taking out a pen and business card and wrote her name and number down on the back. I also saw him hand her a small sheet of paper on which he scribbled something. I thought to myself that if he wanted to give her his telephone number and address more power to him.

By the time we got out of the bar it was very late and Bob and Ray were pretty well blitzed. Ray pushed my wheelchair out of the bar and up the incline of the sidewalk but I had to keep telling him to slow down in order to avoid the cracks and ruts in the sidewalk. I finally hooked my arm around the back of one of my wheelchair back support rods so that I would not fly out of the wheelchair as it bounced over some holes in the sidewalk. It seemed that Ray was oblivious to whatever I was saying but we finally got onto better terrain once we turned onto Michigan Avenue.

Visions of Road Kill

It was now about one o'clock in the morning and the streets had very little traffic, which was extremely fortunate. We had to cross Michigan Avenue to get back to the car but, instead of going to the end of the block to cross, Ray decided to take a shortcut in the middle of the block.

Crossing in the middle of the block was a very, very bad move. Without realizing we'd be going down a curb, Ray pushed my wheelchair off the sidewalk to get across Michigan Avenue. As my wheelchair lunged off of the sidewalk and down the curb my front foot pedals hit the street first and stopped me dead in my tracks. I went flying out of the wheelchair about four feet in front of it, landed on my side, and then rolled on my back. There I was in the middle of the busiest street in downtown Chicago at one o'clock in the morning staring up at the stars.

Since I really can't feel anything from the chest out I didn't know if I was hurt or had any broken bones. Bob and Ray came to see how I was and it didn't appear that I had broken anything but now they had to get me off the street and into the wheelchair before I got hit by a car. In fact, there was a taxicab coming right towards us and Bob got in front of me to motion for it to stop. The taxi did stop and the driver got out. Seeing what had happened, he helped Bob and Ray lift me back into the wheelchair. It always amazes me how people are so willing to help in pretty weird situations.

Bob pushed my wheelchair the rest of the way to the car and I was very grateful because he was steadier on his feet than Ray was at the

119

time. I got home and went to bed without any repercussions from the fall I had taken.

Temptation

The Saturday after our outing I was sitting at my desk in my family room at home when I got a strange phone call.

It was Dawn.

I couldn't believe it. Evidently the note that I saw Bob pass to her a couple nights before did not contain his name and number but mine. She had my address and wanted to come over that afternoon to spend some quality time with me in my bedroom. I have no clue what Bob told her about me but I made a mental note to myself that the next time I saw him I was going to kill him. *Clearly this was another fine mess he was determined to get me into.*

I was very polite to her and said I really wouldn't get much pleasure out of the experience. I explained that I have no feeling from the chest down and did not feel it would be worth her time to travel up to the suburbs. She was pretty persistent and indicated that there was always oral pleasure to be had. I pictured that in my mind for a second and then, again, I said thanks but no thanks. But before I hung up I thought I would return the favor to Bob.

I gave her Bob's home telephone number and address and told her he really enjoyed her company at the bar. I also told her how he mentioned to me how beautiful she was and how he was very sorry he did not take the opportunity to leave the bar with her for an hour or so. I also said that he didn't stop talking about her all the way home and that he would really appreciate it if she called him because he forgot to give her his number. Of course this was all bull but I thought that one good turn from a friend deserves another.

I then politely ended our conversation and hung up.

A couple days later I found out that Dawn did call Bob and he had a difficult time getting rid of her. Believe it or not, *he* was actually ticked off at *me!*

CHAPTER 22

Romance at the Playboy Club (1982)

After my girlfriend, Diane, and I had been seeing each other for around a year I had a discussion with two of my friends, Larry and Ray, to see if they might be interested in spending the weekend with their girlfriends at the Playboy Club in Lake Geneva, Wisconsin. They both thought it was a great idea so we made reservations and surprised the ladies a week and a half before we were set to go.

When Diane found out, she was delighted to have the opportunity to spend a romantic weekend together at Lake Geneva's legendary Playboy Club. This was the first time we would ever have a bed large enough to hold the two of us. I was living in Northbrook, Illinois, at the time and always had a hospital bed to sleep in at home. Since they're only about thirty-four inches wide it was impossible for Diane and me to lie next to one another. With no feeling from the chest down, physical sex to me doesn't mean the same thing as it would to a normal able-bodied person. However I wanted to be able to lie next to Diane so that we could share some physical closeness.

Trapped on the Sofa

Diane and I actually tried to get closer once when I used a sliding board to transfer onto a sofa I had in my family room. It was a great room with a cathedral ceiling and a large fireplace that set the mood for romance. But the romance soon evaporated because I kept losing my balance while sitting on the sofa. When we realized things weren't going as planned we decided I'd better get back into my wheelchair but it

121

turned out that Diane couldn't transfer me back into it by herself. Since nobody else was around, she had to actually lay me on my left side now and then to prevent pressure sores from developing, which was more likely to happen without my wheelchair cushion under me.

We stayed on the sofa with me being repositioned from time to time until my caregiver came back many hours later. When he came in the house and saw me on the sofa he had a strange quizzical expression on his face. I'm sure he wondered what the hell was I doing – or attempting to do – because he never ever saw me out of my wheelchair except when I was in bed. Together he and Diane finally managed to get me back into the wheelchair and I was glad my caregiver never wanted me to get into the details about how I got there in the first place.

Friday Night Fatigue

Diane and I were both looking forward to making up for the sofa debacle in my family room, and we arrived at the Playboy Club late on a Friday evening. All three couples had to work until five o'clock on that day so by the time we arrived in Lake Geneva and checked in it was probably around nine o'clock.

After getting our room assignments Diane and I moved in our luggage and went to meet the other couples for a late dinner at one of the Playboy Club's fancier restaurants. I even remember my appetizer from that night – escargot. Everyone needs to try snails at least once in their life, right? No they don't!

The snails were served in a little tin or ceramic pan that looked like a cupcake pan but the place where the cupcakes would be were only about an inch wide, with only six places for the snails. I ate them but didn't like them very much.

Although I didn't personally care for the snails, we had a great dinner with my friends and their girlfriends and then we all walked around the hotel a bit before going back to our rooms.

It had been a long day of work and travel. Diane looked at me and I looked at her and we both knew that once we got into bed we would just go to sleep. I later learned that the two other couples were so tired that they pretty much did the same as we did that Friday night.

Saturday Night Surprise

The next day we all met and had breakfast together at the Playboy Club. After breakfast each of the couples had different things they wanted to do that day but we all decided to meet up again at the Club later in the afternoon around five.

Diane and I decided to drive into Lake Geneva and spent our time shopping and sightseeing until late afternoon. It so happens that the Dungeons & Dragons™ role-playing game that my friends and I often played was founded in Lake Geneva, so we visited the shop where it all started and picked up some materials for the next time my social group got together to play.

The three couples all met back at the Playboy Club for cocktails before dinner. I had only one martini before dinner since drinking too much liquor can cause trouble with my digestive system. We all had another fine dinner at the Playboy Club. I stayed away from alcohol during the dinner but had an after dinner drink with our group in the bar when we left the dinner table.

We all exchanged stories of what we did in Lake Geneva that day and were all pretty well rested. The other two couples stayed in the bar area while Diane and I retired to our room a little early. The two of us were so looking forward to spending at least one romantic evening together before we had to leave on Sunday and go back home.

Diane got me settled into bed and then came in to snuggle beside me. We had a great king size bed with plenty of room so that I didn't feel like I would be falling out onto the floor. As we cuddled together it wasn't long before I started to get a whiff of something behind me. I immediately knew what it was and five seconds later Diane did too. This was my first romantic evening in nearly twenty years and I let loose the unholy "Big D."

What incredible timing.

Diane spent the next couple of hours cleaning up both the bed and me. *This was another fine mess Diane had to clean up for me.* We had to get new linens from the hotel housemaid and I've always wondered what she thought when she picked up the soiled ones.

Needless to say that incident pretty much ended our romantic evening for the night. We didn't mention what happened to our other friends the next morning and just said that we had a fantastic evening together. Diane and I left after breakfast and went back to Northbrook. I know that we both wondered if our future would contain many other romantic evenings like the one we just experienced.

If nothing else, living the life of a quadriplegic is always an adventure.

CHAPTER 23

A Foreign Visitor (1983)

Diane and I both worked at Baxter Healthcare. She was in the computer department and during the early 1970's and 1980's often traveled to Baxter's facilities in Europe, especially Brussels, Belgium. In the early 1980's while visiting the European facility, she became acquainted with an employee in Brussels by the name of Jean-Paul. Diane asked Jean-Paul to recommend a nice French restaurant in the city and offered to take him to lunch there during their lunch break – her treat. Jean-Paul did know of a great French restaurant so they went.

Diane later told me that she had a great lunch but was very surprised when the bill arrived. Lunch had just cost her more than $200 U.S. dollars. That's the last time Diane ever asked Jean-Paul to recommend a restaurant and felt that Jean-Paul had taken advantage of her. Although their offices in Brussels were in the same office complex, Diane never worked with Jean-Paul on any projects so when she came back to the States she thought she would never hear from Jean-Paul again.

She was wrong.

The next fall Jean-Paul was sent by his department to the United States to work on a special project at Baxter's corporate office complex in Deerfield, Illinois. Jean-Paul did not know anyone at Baxter's U.S. offices and had never been to United States. The only person he remembered was Diane. He called Diane to let her know he was coming into town and thought they would be able get together for lunch. Diane still had a bad taste in her mouth from the last time she went out to lunch with Jean-Paul but once he arrived, she invited him to join the two of us for lunch one afternoon in Baxter's cafeteria.

Jean-Paul was very short and thin in stature and spoke very little English. He also had some difficulty understanding English so we spoke very slowly and sometimes repeated what we were saying until he indicated that he understood by shaking his head. Despite the language barrier, after awhile we were able to communicate fairly well together. Jean-Paul or I would periodically have to repeat a phrase or two to get across what we were trying to say but with patience on both our parts we seemed to communicate just fine.

Jean-Paul and I hit it off right from the start. Diane was, of course, far less enthusiastic about wanting to renew her acquaintance with Jean-Paul but said if I wanted to hang around with him while he was in town then so be it. She would make other plans for the week.

I took it upon myself to show Jean-Paul a good time. Since this was his first time in the United States I was determined to take him to places he would not be able to go to in Europe. I also thought he might enjoy trying foods he probably couldn't get in Brussels. Jean-Paul would finish his project at the end of the week on Friday and was scheduled on a flight to return to Belgium the following Monday. This gave my friends and me Saturday and Sunday to show him a little taste of America.

As chance had it, he was in town during the Wisconsin State Fair in West Allis, Wisconsin. West Allis is a suburb of Milwaukee and only about an hour and fifteen minutes drive from my house in Northbrook, Illinois. Each year my friends and I try to attend the fair at least one out of the ten days it runs. We always have a great time and if you've never been to the Wisconsin State Fair, I highly recommend it.

The Fair has food of every kind imaginable plus beer tents with live bands all over the fairgrounds. Of course there are also buildings full of agricultural exhibits and farm animals but my friends and I usually focus in on the beer, food, and live entertainment. I thought this would be a perfect opportunity to show Jean-Paul something a little different.

Food and Frenzy at the Fair

I talked to my friends and they agreed it would be a great idea to have Jean-Paul come along with us to the Fair. They were all eager to show him a good time. When I asked Jean-Paul he said that he had nothing planned for Saturday and would be happy to go with us to the

Wisconsin State fair. At that time I had a large handicapped van that could comfortably seat five people in addition to myself. Around seven o'clock in the morning my friends Bob, Bruce, Susan, Ray, and Jean-Paul met at my house and we all headed to the Wisconsin State Fairgrounds, arriving there by eight o'clock.

My friends and I wanted to make sure that Jean-Paul tasted food from all of our favorite food stands and we had many of them that we patronized each and every year. Wisconsin is the Dairy State and the Fair is well known for its cream puffs. They are huge, extremely rich, and delicious. They make them throughout the day but it is best to get the cream puffs in the morning because the lines later in the day can stretch all the way around the building.

Besides the cream puffs, we always make a point of stopping at Millie's Italian sausage booth at least twice during the day. We also make Millie's our final stop just before we leave the fairgrounds to buy plenty of Italian sausages with peppers to take home to eat over the next couple days.

The New Berlin sweet corn roast area is also a must stop with its sweet corn on the cob freshly roasted in the husk over charcoal fires. As the husks are peeled back you dunk the entire ear of corn into a large bucket of melted pure Wisconsin butter. Add some salt and the taste is pure heaven. The Wisconsin State fair is usually held the first or second week in August each year at the peak of sweet corn season. We go to the New Berlin booth at least three times during our visit and sometimes more.

And then there is Rupena's charcoal roasted barbecued chicken, suckling pig, and lamb dinner. You could get all three items on a sampler plate – boy, are they tasty.

Over the course of an eight- or ten-hour visit to the Fair, one could consume an awful lot of food and wash it down with many fine Milwaukee hometown beers. That year was no different and we made sure that Jean-Paul had a taste of every one of the aforementioned delights.

Not being able to drink much without adverse affects on my digestive system it was particularly disheartening to go to the Wisconsin State Fair with my friends and abstain from drinking beer with them. They all realized the problems I could get into when I drank alcohol and then had a bout of the "Big D". Yet, it always seemed wrong to me to spend an entire day at the fair listening to live music with my intoxicated friends and me being sober.

But after years of trial and error (mostly error) to find alcoholic drinks I could somewhat tolerate I did find a solution that worked most of the time – although it is still always a crapshoot (no pun intended… okay, the pun *is* intended) as to when drinking has negative effects and when it doesn't. I seem to be able to tolerate Carlo Rossi's Paisano, an inexpensive red table wine that I can usually pick up in gallon-sized jugs.

When I go to the Wisconsin State Fair I usually take a bottle of Paisano with me as well as an old army surplus canteen to keep it in when I move around the fairgrounds. That way when my friends are slugging down their beers, I am slugging down my Paisano. As I understand it, Paisano means "friend" so what wine would be more fitting than this to enjoy with my friends?

We all started eating and drinking as soon as we arrived at the fair. Since most of the live bands didn't start until noon we roamed around the fairgrounds all morning stopping every twenty minutes or so for more food and beer or an occasional trip to the horse, cattle, swine, pigeon, and rabbit exhibits. I usually went only to the pigeon and rabbit exhibits because I didn't care for the smell in the other barns.

Around noon we were all sitting and talking in one of the beer tents listening to a band warm up. The live entertainment was about to start. I turned around to ask Jean-Paul a question but he wasn't there. I asked my friends where Jean-Paul was but they didn't know either. We all realized that none of us had seen him for some time.

Where was Jean-Paul?

Jean-Paul was nowhere in sight and there were literally tens of thousands of people visiting the fair by now. It would be very difficult to find one small Frenchman amid the elbow-to-elbow crowds packed on this very large fairground.

My friends and I decided that the best plan of action was for each of us to go in a different direction to look for him. We would then meet back at the beer tent we were currently at around one o'clock.

One o'clock came and everybody met at the tent but nobody had found Jean-Paul. Jean-Paul's English was not very good and he certainly wasn't familiar with either the Milwaukee or Chicago area. Someone suggested going to the lost a found booth where parents and kids reunite after their names are announced over a loudspeaker. But it seemed kind of silly for us to go to the lost and found booth. What were we going to tell them? If we told them that we wanted to find a short little European guy named Jean-Paul who didn't speak or understand much English and has never been in the United States before last week what do you think they would say?

Well, this was another fine mess I got into – I lost a little European.

Most of my friends decided to have a couple more beers at the beer tent while trying to figure out what to do next. While everyone was discussing our next move, I asked Ray to take me back to the van so I could empty my leg bag and fill my canteen with more Paisano. As we put down the wheelchair ramp in the van there was Jean-Paul lying in a fetal position on the floor, snoring away. He was sleeping off the morning drunk and when we got him up he was surprised to find out we were all looking for him.

When we got back to the beer tent where the rest of my friends were enjoying more beer they were surprised and relieved we had found Jean-Paul and we continued our ritual of eating, drinking and listening to live music.

We decided to leave the fair around five in the afternoon. By that time not one of us could stuff another corn dog or ice cream sandwich down our throats. My friend Bob stopped drinking just after we found Jean-Paul and became our designated driver for the trip home. Within minutes of being on the road everybody but the driver was asleep and snoring. By the time we got back to Northbrook a little over an hour later everyone had pretty much sobered up.

A Night for Blues and Building Lights

Since it was only a little after six o'clock Ray suggested that we take Jean-Paul to a couple of the blues clubs in Chicago. I asked Jean-Paul if he had ever been to a blues club before and he said 'no' but that he would like to go. So with that, Ray, Bob, Bruce, Susan, Jean-Paul and I got back in the van and headed to the intersection of Lincoln Avenue and Halsted.

We decided to go to the Wise Fools Pub. By the time we got there the place was starting to fill up but we managed to find a very small table, pulled a bunch of chairs around it, and ordered some drinks while we waited for the music to start. Most blues clubs around this area are pretty dark inside and smell of smoke and stale beer. At times you also get a good whiff from the bathroom as people go in and out. At the time that was the mark of a real Chicago blues club and Wise Fools was no exception.*

The band started and Jean-Paul seemed to really enjoy the first set. Between sets most of the people at our table went to their appropriate bathrooms for relief. As a second set started everyone had returned to the table except Jean-Paul. Ray went to check the bathroom and the rest of the club but he came back to the table and said that Jean-Paul was nowhere in sight.

We lost the little critter for the second time that day.

This time at least we were in Chicago, and if we couldn't find him he could hopefully find his way home. Ray and Bob went outside the club to search for him. Ray finally found him about four or five blocks away walking with a drunken smile on his face and staring up at all the building lights. It was now around midnight so Ray escorted Jean-Paul back to the van while Bob came back to Wise Fools to get the rest of us. It had been a long and tiring day and everybody was ready to go home and get some rest.

But that was not to be.

The Night the Music Died

Although it was sunny all day at the Wisconsin State Fair, it had been raining in the Chicago area for the last three days. When it rains a lot, many of the suburbs experience some flooding. Northbrook was no exception but I didn't worry about my house because it was somewhat elevated from the lower areas. The southwest corner of the block flooded quite regularly as the street sewers would fill up and the water would then overrun the road and creep up a good portion of my neighbor's lawn.

When we got back to my house and turned into the driveway we could see that the street in front of my neighbor's house, as well as his lawn, were pretty much underwater. My yard and driveway were fine so we went inside and made up the living room sofa into a bed so Jean-Paul could sleep it off for the night. My friends left and went home except for Ray who was living with me at the time while he was between apartments. Ray had been living in my finished basement for about two months and because my caregiver was away for the weekend he put me to bed that night.

I did not yet have an overhead lift to help get me in and out of bed and used my sliding board, which was straddled between the edge of my wheelchair and the edge of the bed so I could slide from one to the other.

Both Ray and I were still a bit intoxicated and I did not quite get my wheelchair close enough to the bed. As I slid onto the board it came out from under me and I wound up on the floor between my wheelchair and the bed. Because I have no feeling from the chest down I thought everything was fine and I just needed to be picked up off the floor. Ray is a strong guy and he managed to lift and maneuver me into bed.

Finally the day was over and we could all get some sleep.

Just moments after Ray left the room and went downstairs I heard him swearing at the top of his lungs and he came back up the stairs from the basement. This was immediately followed by a loud pounding noise in the kitchen. Ray came back into my bedroom and informed me that the whole basement was flooded.

Evidently the flooded sewers in the area had backed up into my basement drain. All of his belongings were underwater including his huge record collection that he started when he was just a kid. Ray had over 700 record albums in his collection and it was worth quite a bit of money. But Ray didn't really care about the money. Each album reminded him of a specific time and place in his life and it was really the only hobby he ever had.

Ray loved his music. His albums were now all underwater and I had never seen Ray as mad as he was right then. I don't know what he did the rest of the night but I must have finally fallen asleep because when I woke up it was early the next morning.

We called my parents early on Sunday morning and told them that my basement was flooded. They lived in South Milwaukee, Wisconsin, which was about an hour's drive from my house in Northbrook, Illinois. They immediately got into their car and drove over.

Sometime during the night, the floodwaters subsided and the water in the basement disappeared back down the basement drain, but the damage had already been done. While I was still in bed we called all of my friends to see if they could come over and help clean up the basement. Everyone said they would get there as soon as they could so I thought I'd better get up and into my wheelchair before they arrived.

My mother started getting me dressed and when she started putting on my socks my left ankle flopped to the side in a very awkward position. She could hear the bones crunching on one another when she moved my foot. To my dismay, I did not escape injury-free after the fall I had taken the night before so, as my friends started to arrive, I had to be taken to the hospital emergency room.

Sure enough, after the emergency room staff took a couple of x-rays I was told I had broken both my fibia and tibia. I returned home with a cast over my entire foot that went all the way up to my mid thigh. This was not a good way to travel around in a wheelchair but there was nothing I could do about it. I would have to make the best of it until the cast was removed about six weeks later.

When I entered my family room I could see that all my friends including Jean-Paul were on my patio trying to clean Ray's belongings that were brought up from the basement. Ray's record albums were spread out all over the patio in an effort to dry off the album covers. My dad had rented a Shop Vac from the hardware store and was vacuuming up the basement floor while my mother followed him around with a broom washing the floor with bleach.

When I went into the kitchen I noticed a big one-foot circular hole in the wall. It suddenly dawned on me that the sound I heard the night before was Ray putting his fist through the kitchen wall when he came up from the basement after discovering the flooding.

My household insurance would not cover the loss of Ray's belongings. I was told that without a specific flood insurance policy it was considered an Act of God and exempt from coverage. I helped Ray replace as many of his items as I could but there were a lot of record albums that were out of print and irreplaceable. Ray's record collection meant everything to him. Something he had spent a lifetime collecting was destroyed in one single evening. Although Ray has been dead for many years now, I still feel sorry for what happened to all of his things that night.

This was one fine mess I'd gotten Ray into that I truly wish had never happened.

Au Revoir

By Sunday evening the basement was somewhat back to normal and my friends and Jean-Paul left. Jean-Paul thanked all of us for showing him a great time and said that he would never forget the time we spent together. He had never before experienced the variety of wonderful foods he ate at the Wisconsin State Fair and he enjoyed the live music he heard both at the fair and at the Wise Fools blues club in Chicago.

Jean-Paul expressed that he was also glad he could help out with the cleanup that took place all day Sunday at my house. What a way to spend his last day in America. I am sure that when he left on Monday he would take with him experiences of America he would never forget just like we would never forget our experiences that weekend with Jean-Paul.

---

*Wise Fools Pub was sold and renamed in the early 1990s and revamped into an upscale bar and restaurant. But in 2001 the Wise Fools Pub was resurrected and today continues to be one of Chicago's most historic music venues (http://www.myspace.com/wisefoolspub).

CHAPTER 24

Puerto Rico Here I Come! (1986)

When I was working as manager of the data processing department at Baxter Healthcare in its Fenwal division, I had to travel to one of the manufacturing plants in Puerto Rico. The company planned to install some new computers in the plant and upgrade the manufacturing software. Since I was ultimately responsible for making sure that we selected the right equipment and software, it was important for me to see their operations firsthand.

Pre-flight Arrangements

Travel for me, especially at that time in the 1980s, required a lot of logistics planning prior to making reservations. I knew that once I arrived in Puerto Rico I would need a handicap van to get from San Juan to the other side of the island where the Maricao manufacturing plant was located. Back then there was little focus on making handicap vans available for rental in the United States much less in Puerto Rico.

After spending quite a bit of time without success in finding any available handicap transportation on the island, my superiors used their leverage and contacted the Puerto Rican Governor's office to try and arrange for a handicap van. After some discussion it was determined that we were able to rent one from a school that was located near Mayaguez, where I would be staying at a nearby hotel.

The plan was to arrive in San Juan on Saturday and stay the night at a hotel there. Arrangements were made for the handicap van to pick me up from the San Juan hotel on Sunday morning and drive me to a hotel in

Mayaguez. Then each morning for the next four days the handicap van driver would pick me up in Mayaguez, drive me to the Maricao manufacturing plant that was twenty miles inland from Mayaguez, and return me to the hotel at the end of the day. Once my business was finished, the handicap van driver would drive me back to San Juan where I would get my flight home.

The company made arrangements with the school, granting me priority to be driven to and from the manufacturing plant. In fact, they actually changed the class time for students in order to accommodate my schedule. In gratitude for the willingness to alter their schedules, the company later gave a large donation to the school.

With my island transportation secured, I could make final flight arrangements for the trip. Because I needed a traveling companion to get me dressed and undressed and help me with my daily hygiene the company paid for one of my friends, Ray, to accompany me and help take care of my daily needs. We were surprised and appreciative when the company upgraded us to first-class seats.

All Aboard...

The day we were scheduled to fly to San Juan Ray and I arrived at Chicago O'Hare Airport early. Since I am the first one on and the last one off of any flight, we wanted to make sure that we had plenty of time to get on the airplane before the regular passengers. As usual, I would have to be lifted into a portable aisle chair and then carried and placed into my assigned seat, which was normally a three-man job.

Because of a union agreement at the time, Chicago O'Hare Airport required a skycap person to do the lifting, so one was summoned and one – just one – arrived. He was about 65 years old and might have weighed all of 120 pounds.

Well, I am 6'2" and weighed about 250 pounds at the time. And that's dead weight. That means any lifting is done without help from me. How was this skinny, aging, fragile-looking guy going to lift me (twice) without help?

The skycap's superior gave him strict instructions that he was required to do the transfer alone. So we entered into a discussion that quickly escalated into an argument, lasting nearly twenty minutes before the skycap finally realized and admitted that there was no way he could lift me into the aisle chair without help. Since I was the first passenger to board the airplane, airline personnel were pushing us to get a move on. The other passengers were ready to board and if we didn't get me into the plane soon, we would delay the flight's departure.

One of the pilots came back to help. He and Ray lifted me into the aisle chair and got me seated aboard the plane. I'd like to tell you that the skycap issue only happened this one time, but I had similar experiences more than three or four times when flying out of O'Hare Airport.

Hot Wiring My Wheels

Our flight to San Juan was without further incident – a nice change of pace from most of my plane rides. After a long flight, I looked forward to settling in to our hotel room for the night.

We were on a flight scheduled to continue on to another destination so passengers who were getting off in San Juan disembarked the plane. Ray and I waited for our turn to get off. Usually while the passengers are disembarking, airline personnel are taking my electric wheelchair out of the cargo hold and bringing it up to the telescopic walkway attached to the front door of the airplane.

As Ray and I sat there for what seemed like a longer time than usual one of the airline cargo handlers came rushing out of the airplane's kitchen area toward me with a very angry look on her face. She was screaming at me, accusing me of almost killing somebody in her cargo crew. I had no idea what she was talking about and tried to get more information from her but she just kept on screaming the same thing over and over.

The woman, still in a panic, extended her clenched fist and opened it, palm side facing up. She had been clutching a great number of fuses and wires that she promptly handed over to Ray. As we looked at each other wondering what the hell was going on, she pointed out the passenger window. Leaning forward a little, I was able to look over Ray's seat and out the window. There on the tarmac was my electric wheelchair – or I should say the remnants of my electric wheelchair – with various pieces strewn every which way.

This time, it was my turn to panic.

What the hell happened and what was I going to do without a wheelchair?

The screaming woman finally composed herself enough to explain. Rather than take my wheelchair through the terminal, to the gate, and down the telescopic walkway, several members of the crew tried to physically lift my 275-pound electric wheelchair and carry it up the utility stairs from the tarmac to place onto the landing at the door of the airplane. Two-thirds of the way up, one of the people helping to carry the wheelchair up the stairs slipped and went tumbling down the stairs with my electric wheelchair close behind.

Since this was a connecting flight to one of the other Caribbean islands, there were passengers still on board awaiting departure. A fast decision had to be made about how to get me off of the airplane so the flight could continue on schedule.

Airline personnel lifted me into an aisle chair and took me up the telescopic walkway and into the San Juan airport terminal. One of the terminal employees found an old push wheelchair for me to be placed in while they collected the bits and pieces of my electric wheelchair from the tarmac.

It was getting to be very late in the evening and the area of the terminal we were sitting in was closing down. But Ray and I were allowed to stay there until my wheelchair parts were gathered and brought up.

After about an hour, we found ourselves staring at the pieces that used to be my electric wheelchair. The foot pedals were both bent out of shape as well as both wheelchair armrests. But the most severe damage was to the electronic controls that powered the chair.

The people in charge of the terminal sent up the only maintenance engineer they had on duty that night. He was a nice elderly Puerto Rican man that could not speak any English. One of the bilingual airline people explained to him what happened and then had to leave. But it soon became evident that the engineer understood the gravity of the situation as he proceeded to work on my wheelchair.

Ray and I watched as the engineer began to reassemble the various parts, and were a bit taken aback when he started cutting and stripping wires with his pocketknife and teeth.

After about an hour of tinkering and testing he had the wheelchair assembled into one usable piece.

The engineer was able to hot wire the controls well enough so that at least the power was on and the motor was running. To turn the power on we needed to twist two wires together. And to turn the power off, we needed to untwist them. But thanks to this man's know-how and willingness to help, we were finally going to be able to leave the airport with a working wheelchair so I could complete my manufacturing plant trip.

Ray and I managed to find a couple of airline personnel still in the terminal to help transfer me from the manual wheelchair into my now working electric wheelchair. We left the terminal in search of a taxicab that could drive us a few miles west of the airport to the Hilton Hotel where I could finally lay down and get some much-needed rest.

The Taxi and St. Chris

Ray and I made our way outside of the terminal and stood near the taxi stand with no taxis in site. After about fifteen minutes or so we were relieved to spot an approaching taxi. As it got closer, I began to shake my head in wonderment and looked at Ray to see if he noticed the same thing I did.

The front of the taxi had a hood ornament about a foot and a half tall. It resembled one of those figureheads you might see on an old-time sailing ship. It was sculpted like a mermaid with an arched back showing bare breasts on her torso with long flowing hair on each side of her head. Well you certainly don't see that in Chicago too often – as a matter of fact, I've never seen that in Chicago. This was going to prove to be an interesting ride.

When riding in a taxi I usually get into the front passenger side and sit with the driver, using my sliding board to get in and out of the vehicle. As our San Juan taxicab driver got out and opened the passenger door for me, a second surprise awaited. All along the top edge of the front window and the top edge of the back window were little red and white dingle balls hanging and bobbing in the wind.

In addition to the fuzzy dingle balls, the entire length of the dashboard was covered with St. Christopher medals – probably a dozen or more – that had little flags protruding from both sides of each medal. If I didn't realize it before, I certainly realized it now; we were no longer on the United States mainland.

As I proceeded to transfer into the front seat using the sliding board I leaned over a bit too far and hit my forehead on one of the St. Christopher medals. It didn't fall off the dashboard so I didn't think much of it and I finished the process of getting into the taxi while Ray loaded my wheelchair into the trunk. Off we went.

When we arrived at the Hilton the doorman came out and opened the passenger door while Ray and the taxicab driver went to the rear to get the wheelchair out of the trunk. As the doorman looked in to greet me he became very flustered. Blood was dripping down my forehead and across the entire side of my cheek and he thought I was seriously injured. Evidently when I leaned into the cab and hit the St. Christopher medal with my forehead, it gave me a small gash that bled quite a bit – unbeknownst to me.

The doorman finally calmed down enough to go inside and bring me a wet towel to wipe the blood off my face. I then transferred into my wheelchair, checked into the hotel, and Ray and I finally got to sleep around one o'clock in the morning.

It was a long day of travel and turmoil, and we had to be up and ready to leave by nine o'clock when my handicap van was scheduled to arrive and take us to Mayaguez.

San Juan to Mayaguez

Around seven o'clock in the morning Ray got me up, dressed, and into my wheelchair. We went downstairs to have a small breakfast so that we would be finished well in advance of the 9 a.m. arrival of my handicap van.

About quarter to nine we went outside to wait for the van in the Hilton's arrival driveway. Nine o'clock came and went. Ten o'clock came and went. Since this was before cell phones, all I could do was hope that the person was on his way because I really had no way to get in touch with him.

Around eleven o'clock we saw a big blue van entering the driveway. Even though it was so late, I hoped this wasn't the handicap van we were going to use. It was a normal height van and I need a high top van. I conveyed to the people at work that I needed a handicap van with a high top so I assumed that detail was transmitted to and understood by the people we were going to rent the van from here in Puerto Rico. (Yes, I know what they say about assumptions…)

As the blue van pulled up and the driver waved to me I knew we were in trouble again. Not only was it a regular size van, but there were seats throughout with no place for me to park my wheelchair inside. However, the one thing it did have was a ramp so if we could manage to get out some of the seats there was at least the possibility that I could get into it.

Everyone Ray and I met in Puerto Rico was extremely helpful and willing to bend over backwards to make things right and this new challenge proved to be no different. In talking with the hotel personnel about the situation, they were kind enough to bring up a couple of their engineers to look over the situation. The engineers went back into the hotel and soon came out with a bunch of tools to unbolt the seats and take them out of the van. They offered to store the seats in the hotel basement until I came back to the Hilton on my return trip in a few days.

As I started to drive my wheelchair up the van ramp I realized I was going to have a major problem actually getting into the van. When I reached the top of the ramp my entire neck and head were looking over the van roof. Somehow – and with great difficulty – Ray and the driver managed to bend my body sideways and then forward enough to get me under the doorway and into the van.

There I was, sitting in the van with my body bent forward so far in my wheelchair that my head was almost completely between my legs. The only thing in my line of sight was my own crotch. I knew that the road winding around the perimeter of the island leading to our destination in Mayaguez was smooth, so all I could do was hope that this would be a quick trip.

After about twenty minutes on the road my head was really getting sore because as we drove the roads got worse and the crown of my head was continually rubbing against the roof of the van. Not only was the roof not covered with cloth but it was made out of a press board type material that had tiny quarter-inch holes every inch or so. As my head rubbed across the ceiling my hair got caught in these holes and was pulled out by the roots. I began to wonder if I would be partially bald by the time we arrived at our destination.

As we continued our journey Ray mentioned that he was surprised he could not see the Caribbean waters surrounding the island. The driver then informed us that he was taking a much more picturesque route over the Puerto Rican highlands and rainforest area instead of the coastal route because all you could see was water.

Excuse me? We're taking the scenic route?

While I appreciate his enthusiasm to show us the beauty of the island, did our driver not remember that I was wadded up in an uncomfortable ball behind him and all I could see was my own crotch?

As we wound around the mountain curves I could feel the van swaying from side to side violently. At one point Ray leaned back from where he was sitting and whispered to me that he needed a drink – he also proceeded to inform me that *this was another fine mess I had gotten him into.* Personally, I thought he had it pretty easy. I was the one who was staring at my crotch for hours on end while my hair was plucked out follicle by follicle.

After about another two hours' travel on this scenic route, we arrived at our destination. By the time the van finally stopped my head was numb and I could hardly breathe from being bent over for that length of time. We pulled into the hotel parking lot and Ray and the driver managed to push my head far enough under the doorframe so I could go down the ramp. My only thought at that moment was that I was going to have to go through getting in and out of this van for the next five days. Trying to stay positive we thanked the driver and wished him a good evening.

We checked into the hotel and Ray immediately threw me in bed so that I could stretch out and relax a bit before getting up later to have dinner. I never thought that lying down would feel so good. Ray mentioned that a good chunk of my hair was missing on the top of my scalp but, at that point, I didn't really care. After the ride we just survived, all I thought was, "That's just one of the little things!"

After resting for three or four hours, Ray and I went to the dining area and had a great dinner, topped off with excellent fresh tropical fruit for dessert. The hotel had a casino so we played craps for a couple of hours. I had to be ready to leave for the manufacturing plant by seven thirty the next morning so I finally went to bed around nine o'clock.

Ray got me up and dressed around six o'clock so that I could have breakfast before having to get in the van. My driver arrived promptly at seven thirty. Before getting in the van the driver said that he had hoped once I arrived at the manufacturing plant he could leave immediately because he had the school children to pick up. I told him that it should not be a problem because I was having somebody at the plant meet me in the parking lot upon our arrival.

I then asked the driver about the school children. He told me that the children he picked up were handicapped but that none used a wheelchair to get around. He also said that their ages were between seven and twelve. It finally dawned on me that I should've asked more questions of the people in Chicago who secured this handicapped van for me. Of course it would not have to have a high top. These kids were probably no more than four feet tall. Hindsight sure is enlightening.

You may be wondering why I didn't just rent a car and get in and out of it using my sliding board. That method is very strenuous on everybody. Having to take apart and reassemble a 275-pound electric wheelchair is not only time consuming, it requires strong people to be able to lift it into the trunk and then take it out again. I also wanted to avoid having my wheelchair disassembled and assembled by someone who didn't know how to do it. In the past when I depended on strangers to assemble and disassemble my wheelchair my controls shorted out because the wrong wires were plugged together. Also, since I am susceptible to quickly developing pressure sores, it is not good for me to sit without a wheelchair cushion, especially for any length of time.

I resigned myself to the fact that I only had to survive four days of van rides back and forth to the plant. That's only eight trips of about a half-hour each. And for Friday's final trip in that van from Mayaguez back to San Juan I would make sure we traveled via the coastal route, anticipating a much smoother ride than going across the scenic Puerto Rican mountains.

Ray and my driver managed to get my body bent over enough to once again get into the van. We arrived at the manufacturing plant within half an hour, and were met by my counterpart in the computer department who was waiting for me in the parking lot. His name was Luis and he and the driver proceeded to unbend me and get me out of the van.

Picnic in the Parking Lot

I told Luis that I would like to go to the cafeteria to get something to drink and get a little bit more organized before going with him to the computer area. We had refreshments at the cafeteria and then proceeded to have our morning meetings, which went well. I mentioned to Luis that I would like to have a working lunch with him and a couple of his employees. He said that would be fine.

When getting out of the van that morning I noticed a helicopter pad in one area of the parking lot and a couple of picnic tables in another area. I suggested that we have lunch at the picnic tables. He gave me an odd look but proceeded to tell his employees in Spanish what I had suggested. They all stared at me.

Coming from Chicago where temperatures were below zero to Puerto Rico where it was in the eighties I thought it would be a great treat to get out of the air-conditioned building and have lunch in the great outdoors. Arrangements were made and we met for our working lunch outside. After about an hour I realized that the people attending were wiping the sweat off their brows. Although the temperature was only in the eighties, the humidity was probably also in the eighties because the plant was located in the tropical rainforest area of the island.

As we headed back to the building I noticed that there was what seemed like a heated discussion in Spanish between Luis and his employees. There was a lot of hand gesticulation, and the voice levels and body language coming from Luis' employees indicated to me that they clearly were not happy campers.

It would be many months later when Luis visited Chicago before I found out what the ruckus was all about. Evidently I asked to do something that no one else ever did at the plant – eat outside on the picnic tables. The tables were there only as a place for people to sit while waiting for the helicopters to land on the heliport. Luis and his employees – but mainly his employees – thought I was just another bizarre corporate type visiting the island.

There's Something Fishy Going On

When I returned to the hotel in Mayaguez that Monday afternoon, I got out of the van and nearly gagged from the stench that was sucked through my nostrils. It smelled like dead rotting fish all around me. The odor was so bad that it was impossible to take in a full breath. To this day I have never smelled anything so bad in my life.

When I got into the hotel I asked a person at the registration desk what that overwhelming dead fish stench was. I was told that there was a tuna packing plant located a few miles downwind of the hotel. Staying in the hotel room alleviated the problem because the air conditioner was always on. However, neither Ray nor I would venture out for walks in the area when the wind came up from the packing plant.

I would never have guessed that I would look forward to getting in that van and riding up to the plant every day, but the smell of the tuna cannery changed my mind.

The business trip was very successful and after a while I actually got used to being bent in and out of that van. By the end of the week it became a relatively simple routine. My business concluded Thursday afternoon and we were ready to head back to San Juan on Friday. However, this time we took the long way around the island on a nice smooth highway along the coast. We even stopped at a couple of picturesque points where I could get out and relax for a half-hour or so.

When we arrived back at the Hilton the maintenance people put the passenger seats back into the school van. As I write this, I now wonder where the schoolchildren sat without any seats in the van for four days.

Ray and I stayed overnight at the Hilton on Friday, taking time to do a little gambling at the casino and enjoying a great dinner. We went to bed around midnight knowing we did not have to get to the airport until five on Saturday afternoon. On Saturday Ray and I had a chance to relax and sip a few piña coladas at the beach. Around three o'clock we loaded our belongings into a more traditional taxi that was dingle-ball free and arrived at the airport in plenty of time to catch our six o'clock flight back to Chicago.

The plane trip home was thankfully very uneventful and I reflected back on everything that happened on the island. In some ways I was amazed that I managed to survive the trip. Life is always an adventure to be consumed with gusto. Or so I always try and tell myself.

CHAPTER 25

Office Cactus Incident (1986)

I have had many wheelchairs in my life. One unavoidable fact is that at some point in time they all need maintenance. Finding a good medical supplier with a repair shop for wheelchairs is much like finding a car repair shop. There are good ones and bad ones and when you find a good one you always stick with them.

It is also helpful to know of a good welder. Many times the back supports on a wheelchair will crack or break and need to be welded. This usually does not present a problem because you can see the crack starting and take care of It before it gets too bad. It is always good to have a good – or at least working – backup wheelchair when your main one has to be repaired.

Backward Summersault

One morning when I was working in the Fenwal division of Baxter Healthcare I noticed that one of the main supports in the back of my wheelchair was cracked about halfway through. I knew this would quickly become a problem so I decided to enlist the help of one of my employees to drive me home so I could switch to another wheelchair.

As I got out from behind my desk both of the back supports on my wheelchair cracked completely off. In less than two seconds I flew backward in my chair, making an awkward and ungraceful somersault-like move that dumped me in a heap on the floor.

I yelled out to one my employees located just outside my office door to come in to help. Carol and Marly rushed in with surprised looks on their faces to see me sprawled out on the floor. I was flat on my back with my feet propped on top of the three-foot tall cactus plant that fell over when I did. After asking them to close my office door so that I wouldn't attract any more attention than I had to, I told them what happened and what we would probably need to do next.

There was no way I could sit in my wheelchair because the entire back was off. I could not be lifted into another chair because I have no balance sitting in a chair without side rests, nor could I sit in a chair without a cushion. I would have to stay on the floor until we could get my spare wheelchair from home back to the office.

I didn't seem to be hurt but was not in a very comfortable position. I asked Marty to take my house and van keys and go back to my house to get my spare wheelchair. In the meantime, Carol straightened out my body on the floor and put my wheelchair cushion under my head so I was more comfortable until Marty returned. She then started to clean up the floor where the cactus turned over and discovered that she could not get the cactus out from under my feet. Dozens of three-inch cactus spines were lodged in my shoes and ankles. After spending the next ten minutes pulling the cactus out from under my body she began pulling all the cactus spines out of me. The spines had gone clear through my leather shoes, stuck into the back of my ankles and partially up my calves. I had puncture wounds in my legs for a week.

By this time, people were knocking on my office door wondering what was going on. Carol explained and told them that everything would be fine when Marty came back with my extra wheelchair. Luckily I lived only about fifteen minutes from work and Marty was back with the spare wheelchair about forty-five minutes later.

However, getting my spare wheelchair was more eventful than Marty ever expected.

Marty unlocked the door to get into the house and immediately went to my bedroom, making quite a bit of noise as he pulled my spare wheelchair out of the closet. I had already been at work for an hour or so, but Diane happened to be in the bathroom getting ready for work herself.

Diane was not expecting anyone. My bedroom closet shares the same wall as the bathroom Diane was in so when she heard noise coming from my bedroom, she had no idea what was happening. Thinking there was an intruder in the house, Diane started to panic. She locked the bathroom door but didn't have a phone to call the police.

Marty was also startled when he heard noises coming from the adjoining wall. He did not expect anyone to be in the house, either. He finally realized my wife was still home and eventually convinced a panicking Diane that he had just come from my office at my request. He explained to her why he was there and that I had given him the keys to the house.

Diane was still shaken up, but at least she believed Marty's story and he headed back to the office with my spare wheelchair.

When Marty returned with my wheelchair he placed it in the hallway outside of my office. With me lying on the floor, my office was too small to get both wheelchairs inside. Carol found four strong bodies to help lift me off my office floor and into my spare wheelchair. After about a half-hour with half the people from the entire office floor congregating around me and asking questions about what happened, we got back to a normal office day.

Ka-Boom!

I remember one other time that I had half of the office personnel congregating around me. In a previous job I occupied one of several cubicles in a large room. One day one of my wheelchair tires blew out and, in such a confined space, it made a horrendous noise that sounded like an explosion. You would think that people would run away from a sound like that but, instead, they started running straight to my cubicle.

Both of these incidents make me wonder what dinner conversation is like for my office mates when they get home. "Guess what happened at work today, honey?"

Chances are that the spouse never guesses correctly.

CHAPTER 26

Northern Exposure (1992)

When my brother and I were growing up, Dad used to take the family for vacations in northern Wisconsin and Minnesota. It was always great to get away from the city for a few weeks and spend the time in the north woods doing a lot of swimming and fishing. One year my dad had a chance to purchase some land on the Wheeler (sometimes called Townsend) flowage near Townsend, Wisconsin. Townsend is located in the Nicolet National Forest a little over an hour north and west of Green Bay, Wisconsin. The town at that time consisted of a very small post office, pizza parlor, combined grocery and hardware store, filling station, and two taverns.

My dad purchased one lot with a hundred-foot frontage on the flowage for only $500. My uncle bought the lot next to us and the lot on the other side of us went to my mom's friend from work. Our lot was a little less than an acre. These lots were totally wooded and wild with ferns and brush. The first few years we spent the weekends clearing the land until the front part nearest the lakeshore had some grass. We put in a well with a pump for water and planted many pine trees. Around 1960 we had a small trailer home moved from Milwaukee and placed on our property. From that point on we called it our cottage up north.

The cottage had two bedrooms, a bathroom, and a combined kitchen and small living room area. One of the bedrooms had a bed that was only about five feet long. The hallway going to the back bedrooms was so narrow that we would practically have to turn sideways to walk through. It was a very (very) small home, but it didn't matter to us. It was a great place to go because the fishing and hiking in the woods were exceptional. It was even fun to be up there during the winters. Ice fishing on the flowage was a great experience and never to be forgotten.

I vividly remember standing on frozen snow that blanketed the flowage, staring up at the sky in the middle of the night, undisturbed by city lights. The Milky Way on a crisp clear winter's evening was incredibly beautiful. Once in awhile we could also see the Aurora Borealis (Northern lights) shimmering in fantastic colors against a backdrop of stars. These experiences at our "cottage up north" fueled my interest in astronomy from a very young age. The cottage was located only a few hours drive from our home in South Milwaukee, Wisconsin. We would travel up north almost every weekend, and also spend a few weeks there during the summers as we were growing up and throughout high school.

After my accident I would periodically go to the cottage with my friends or family and continued to do this throughout my years of living in the Chicago area. In fact, for many years my mother, Aunt Phyllis, and friend, Edward Weishaar, took an annual one to two-week trip "up north."

Bees, Bugs, and Bullheads

I always loved to go up north with my mother and aunt because my mom would make all my favorite foods – and I had a lot of favorites. My van was usually packed to the roof with ice chests containing meats, soups, and other dishes she had prepared for the trip. One year the four of us went up to the cottage in my handicap van and it turned out to be a bit more eventful than any of us expected.

Leaving from South Milwaukee, Edward loaded up my van with suitcases, my medical supplies, and the (nearly literal) tons of food my mother and aunt prepared. With the four of us – and my wheelchair – there was little room left in the van to maneuver around. My Aunt Phyllis sat next to me in the back of the van in a fold out lawn chair because she refused to sit on my van's rear bench seat. In her defense, not many people liked to sit in that seat.

When I bought the van we took out the bolts that fastened it to the floor so that the seat could be removed if we were hauling a lot of stuff. Anyone sitting on that bench seat would have the added treat of bouncing up and down in tandem with the seat as we rode over bumps and railroad tracks. One of my friends likened it to a carnival ride. Since my Aunt Phyllis had traveled in my van's backseat once before and almost hit her head on the ceiling during one of those bounces, she decided to take her chances with a lawn chair this time around.

The lawn chair proved to be a disappointing alternative to the bench seat. As the van turned or swerved from side to side, the lawn chair's legs would lift off the ground depending on the direction we were turning. Each lift tilted Aunt Phyllis back and forth, forcing her to engage in an unwelcome three-hour balancing act.

We stopped for a picnic lunch at a wayside rest just north of Green Bay, with a side benefit of giving my aunt a break from the armrest-clutching ride in her lawn chair. The further north we traveled the more primitive the rest stops were, so there were no fancy buildings with in-door plumbing to use. This wayside rest was located at the edge of very deep woods and only had two small rustic outhouses set a short way from the picnic tables.

As we all contended with the usual swarms of mosquitoes and deer flies, Aunt Phyllis was stung in the arm by a yellow jacket while she was eating her sandwich. If you've never heard of a yellow jacket, it is one of the most aggressive members of the wasp family with an extremely ven-omous sting. Attracted to sugar, yellow jackets are notorious for crawling inside an open soda pop can and stinging the unsuspecting person who eventually takes a sip from the can. I have been stung by yellow jackets more than once and it is not a pleasant experience. Clearly this was not my aunt's lucky day – who knew she would find herself looking forward to getting back into that bump-jumping lawn chair?

We managed to arrive at the cottage in late afternoon without fur-ther mishap and proceeded to do the usual prep work to make it livable for the week. An electric box in back of the home housed four fuses that turned on the electricity in and around the cottage. The refrigerator fuse was always connected but the remaining three fuses needed to be connected to power the outside lights and lights inside the cottage. The propane gas tanks needed to be turned on and the pilot lights for the kitchen stove needed to be started. The coverings were removed from the pontoon boat that was tied to the pier. Finally, it was time to unload the car – a time-consuming feat because of all the stuff we brought with us. As the car was unloaded my mother and aunt packed its contents away in the appropriate areas of the cottage.

After the car was unloaded and everything was put in its proper place we washed up a little bit and headed out for dinner at one of the local restaurants. As much as I looked forward to delving into all the favorite foods my mother would be making, even I was willing to give my mother a break from cooking for that first night. After a day of travel, opening the cottage, and a fine meal, we went to bed. I slept in the living room on the fold out sofa bed while my mother and aunt shared the back bedroom, and Edward slept in the tiny bedroom scrunched up on the five-foot long bed.

The next morning when we woke up, Edward got me dressed and into the wheelchair and we went outside to enjoy the clear summer morning while my mother and aunt made breakfast in the kitchen. There's nothing like the smell of bacon and eggs wafting out from the cottage into the clear northern fresh air. As I write this, saliva is accumulating in my mouth just thinking about those mornings. We ate breakfast outside at the picnic table, a mere twenty feet from the lakeshore.

Following breakfast my mother ordered Edward and me to stay out of the cottage because her next task on that first day was to clean the entire inside of it.

My mother and aunt were notorious for making sure everything was in its right place at all times and completely spotless. I pitied the poor speck of dust that dared to land on the furniture. My mother's highly trained eye would hone in and pounce on that poor dust speck like a hawk diving on a mouse. That microscopic flake would never have a chance.

I'll admit the place probably did need some cleaning. A few of my friends and I were up there a few times prior to this trip with my mother. We always tried leaving the place in pretty good shape so that I could avoid the inevitable lecture from my mom when she finally came. But no matter how tidy my friends and I thought we were leaving the place, she could always find something that didn't meet her standards.

While Edward and I were sitting on the pier enjoying the morning sun we could hear my mom and aunt inside going through their cleaning frenzy. After about a half-hour the door swung wide open and my mother shouted for Edward to come inside and to bring the bug spray that was stored in our little maintenance shed. My mother was flustered, anxious, and pleading for him to take immediate action.

As we approached the cottage, mom was frantic, yelling about having moved the sofa bed away from the wall in order to vacuum the carpet, and discovered an infestation of bugs. My aunt and mother said there were hundreds of big black bugs all over the carpet and we needed to get some bug spray to kill them immediately. My mother was certain that the entire place was now infested with these bugs.

Edward went inside to check out what was going on and before long came back out looking perplexed. He said it appeared that all the bugs were dead. As he opened his hand to show me a few of the big black bugs he picked up off the floor, they didn't really look like bugs at all.

I finally realized what these disgusting bug-like carcasses were.

When my friends Ray, Bob, Bruce, and I spent time at the cottage we usually had a full day outside or on the pontoon boat, drinking a few cases of beer throughout the day. By the time we were ready to settle inside to watch TV for the evening, one of them would run into town to get a couple of "garbage" pizzas with everything on it from the Golden Eagle restaurant. The Golden Eagle made some of the best pizzas I have ever eaten. For a small little restaurant in northern Wisconsin they sure know how to make a damn good pizza.

Ray wasn't fond of the black olives that were included on the garbage pizza so, without the rest of us knowing, he used to pick the olives off his slices and toss them behind the sofa. After several visits – and several pizzas – the discarded olives piled up into the "disgusting bugs" that my mother uncovered behind the sofa.

I braced myself for the long lecture I knew was coming my way. I took my lumps and promised it would never happen again (at least I hoped it wouldn't). My mother vowed that when she got home and saw Ray she was going to give him a piece of her mind. I didn't envy Ray's next meeting with my mom.

Once the black olive bug scare was over, things around the cottage settled down. My mother and aunt had the place cleaned to their satisfaction by mid-afternoon. We had lunch outside at the picnic table and then went fishing in the small pontoon boat I had docked there.

After we came back from fishing Edward went into town and picked up a nice large Golden Eagle pizza with the works, but this time no one threw the black olives in back of the sofa.

We enjoyed a number of activities throughout the week. A lot of our meals were eaten outside at the picnic table unless it rained. We would barbecue most evenings and when we didn't we would head out to one of the local restaurants for dinner. Many of our afternoons were spent fishing or driving around Nicolet National Forest sightseeing. We even took a drive to Copper Harbor in upper Michigan. It's a beautiful drive that takes up most of the day. In the evenings when we stayed at the cottage we would fish for yellow belly bullheads. They are a very good tasting fish when filleted and pan-fried.

Fishing for bullheads is best done after it gets dark. We usually put out two or three cane poles on the pier using a glob of worms as bait. A heavy rock or bucket filled with water is then placed on the end of the cane pole that sits on the pier so if a fish takes the bait, it won't drag the cane pole in the water. This hands-off style of fishing let us sit inside and every once in awhile shine a flashlight through the window to check if the cane pole bobbers were still floating or underwater. If they are underwater, it's likely you've caught a bullhead and you run out to the pier to pull it in, take it off the hook, and put it into what is called a "live box" overnight. It's not unusual to catch about six to ten nice bullheads in the three to four hours immediately after it gets dark. In the morning you take the bullheads out of the live box and fillet them for dinner.

One evening while fishing for bullheads Edward shined a flashlight out the window to check the bobbers as usual. He saw that one of the bobbers was under the water and ran out to the pier to pull in the fish. When he lifted the pole the line stayed in the water and seemed to be stretched under the pier near the shore. As he pulled harder and harder the cane pole started to jerk wildly and he yelled for someone to come out with another flashlight so they could see what was happening.

My aunt grabbed a flashlight and ran outside to join Edward at the end of the pier. When she shined the flashlight toward the shoreline they saw that a muskrat was all tangled up in the fishing line. It must have gotten tangled in the line when it was swimming into its burrow under the pier.

Forty-five minutes later they finally had the muskrat untangled without hurting it or being bitten by it. Edward decided to give up bullhead fishing for the rest of that vacation. There was no way we wanted to take a chance at getting that muskrat tangled in a fishing line after dark.

Shear Pin Panic

Two days before we were scheduled to go home we boarded the pontoon boat to go fishing on the flowage. My mother and aunt always sat in the backseat while Edward piloted the boat from the seat behind the control panel. I sat in the front area of the pontoon boat with very little room to move around.

The three or four hours just before dark are good for fishing during the summer months. Usually during the day the fish are not biting but as the evening approaches they seem to be more active. After a pleasant late afternoon of fishing for bluegills we had about a dozen good size fish to take back with us. It was getting close to dark so Edward fired up the boat's engine and we started heading back to the pier. All of a sudden the outboard motor on the pontoon boat hit an underwater stump.

Hitting a stump is not unusual and happens every so often when boating on a lake flowage. A lake flowage is usually created by cutting down a lot of trees in a valley that has a river running through it. The river is then damned up downstream and the water rises in the valley to create a lake. Flowages are great for fishing because of the many areas fish can hide in for protection, but they are very bad for boating because outboard motors periodically hit the tree stumps that are just below the water level.

To help prevent damage to the motor, a good rule to follow is to keep your outboard motor release lever in a released position rather than in a locked down position. By having it in a released position when it hits a stump, the outboard motor will lift up a little bit as it traverses the stump. It is difficult to identify the areas where a stump might be under the surface because the water level changes from time to time. You can travel the exact same path over and over again without hitting a stump and the next time you go over that same path, you hit one.

When our pontoon boat's outboard motor hit one of these underwater stumps, it broke the shear pin in the propeller drive shaft assembly. Shear pins are designed and manufactured to break if an outboard motor hits an object so that the outboard motor does not get damaged. Boaters commonly carry spare propeller shear pins for just such an incident.

The pins can be replaced easily by tilting the outboard motor up and out of the water and taking off the cotter pin on the cap that holds the propeller to the drive shaft. When the cotter pin is taken out, the cap comes off so the propeller can be removed. You can then push the broken part of the shear pin out, replace the propeller, put in a new shear pin, place the propeller cap back on, put back the cotter pin, and you're ready to take off again. It's no big deal. So Edward reached into the tackle box where we kept all our spare shear pins.

To Edward's surprise – and ours – there were no shear pins in the tackle box. We brought the wrong box with us.

When my mother heard that there were no replacement shear pins in our tackle box she went into a panic. My mother worried about everything. In fact, I often wondered if she'd be happy if there was nothing for her to worry about. She was a very short, thin lady who was the best mother anyone could have, but she was a worrywart, probably from the day she was born. With darkness not far away, she was very worried about how we would get back to the cottage.

We could not use the motor and, with just a small canoe paddle in the pontoon boat, it was impossible to try rowing any distance. We were about three hundred yards from the nearest shoreline and the lake water was still and smooth as glass. With absolutely no wind, there was no way we could hope to drift ashore.

In an attempt to calm my mother down I told her that we would just sit for a while and see if another boat might go by that we could flag down to help tow us back to our pier. She bought this for a little while but, after about ten minutes with no other boats in sight and the evening getting darker, she started to panic even more and took matters into her own hands. So she stood up in the middle of the boat and in her feeble little voice started yelling over and over again, "Help! Help!"

Her voice was quivering so much when she talked that I don't think her calls for help could possibly carry more than ten feet beyond the boat. The rest of us tried to calm her down and assured her that we would eventually get back to the cottage. To our relief we finally saw another boat on the lake about fifteen minutes later. Edward stood up and waved his arms while we all yelled to get its attention. The boat came over and towed us back to our pier.

By the time we reached the pier, got off the boat, and were safe and sound inside the cottage, my mother was a basket case. I felt really bad because I knew this was the way she reacts in stressful situations and that would never change. *This was another fine mess I'd gotten mom into.* Out of all the people I have managed to get into unusual and weird situations, she is the one person I never wanted anything to happen to.

The remaining days of our vacation went without a hitch. Before we left my mother and aunt again cleaned the cottage from top to bottom so that it would be in great shape for the next time we went up there. After the three-hour ride to the cottage, my aunt did not look forward to using the lawn chair on the trip home and said she would prefer the back seat.

We covered the boat, turned off the electric and gas, loaded the van and were off – my aunt bouncing on the rear bench seat all the way back home to South Milwaukee.

CHAPTER 27

Reeb Traf (1993)

The Deal of a Lifetime

During the mid-1990s, my friend, Mark Perkins, invited me to go with him to a boat show in downtown Chicago. I had never gone to a boat show before so I thought it would be an interesting trip. Mark was interested in talking with some of the marina owners who were in attendance about storing his current boat on the Chain O' Lakes, also known as the Fox Lake chain, which was about an hour from my house in Northbrook, Illinois.

While he was talking with one of the marina owners, I noticed that they had some really nice pontoon boats on display. I started talking with one of the salespeople about how impractical a pontoon boat is for a person in a wheelchair. I owned a small pontoon boat that was kept at the cottage I had in northern Wisconsin. I knew from experience that they had narrow entrance gates and lacked enough space between the passenger seat and pilot station area, preventing the ability to sit toward the back of the boat.

The salesperson I was talking with represented the pontoon boat manufacturer and told me he could customize the pontoon boat so that I could easily get on and off by installing wider gates for entry and exit. He said he could also modify the backend area to allow more room in the center of the boat by the driver's station so that I could fit between the seats. This sounded great to me.

I asked about price for all this customization and found it relative-ly reasonable. He put together a price quote for a brand-new 28-foot pontoon boat with a 120 horsepower outboard engine. The owner of the marina that represented the salesperson's line of boats offered me a great package deal which included the price of the new pontoon boat along with a free docking berth at his marina facility for that summer. Of course, the deal only lasted for the duration of the boat show so that if I was going to actually purchase a pontoon boat I had to do it that day or I would not get the great boat show pricing. I knew this was a lot of sales hype and decided to just keep the offer in the back of my mind.

As the afternoon went on I got all excited about the prospects of having a boat that I could actually use on the Fox Lake chain. Mark and I discussed the offer they made me and he thought it was a great deal. Mark was also very enthusiastic about the possibility of having a pontoon boat on the Fox chain. He had a growing family and did a lot of boating and fishing in the area so for him the pontoon boat represented a great way to take the entire family along.

After a short discussion, we decided we would purchase the boat as equal partners. We signed a deal at the boat show but the agreement stated we had the option to cancel within two weeks.

Despite what seemed to be all the right reasons to buy the boat, all I could think of after signing the deal was what the hell I was going to say to my wife when I got home. "Gee, honey, I went to this boat show with a friend and guess what? We now own a 28-foot pontoon boat!" Clearly I had some serious talking to do when I got home. But I figured that if she was vehemently opposed the idea, I could always cancel the agreement within two weeks. Mark had the same problem. He, too, was going to have to convince his wife of what a great deal this was.

As we continued to look around the boat show my excitement about being a boat owner grew. I noticed an area where people were lined up to buy large custom-made decals to put on their boats. As I contemplated how ridiculous it was for people to put cutesy names on their boats, Mark asked me what we were going to name ours. After a few more minutes of listening to people request names that refer to their dogs, cats, wives, lovers, and monetary status, I, with my more bizarre sense of humor, decided that whatever we named our boat it should have some hidden meaning. I confided to Mark what I was thinking and, although he thought it was a little weird, he said to go for it.

I got into the line and when it was my turn to talk with the vendor about my custom decals I told him that I wanted something in a very elegant script with a nice nautical symbol between the two words I was proposing. He showed me a variety of script fonts and I found one that I thought was perfect. It had lots of curly loops and was somewhat slanted to the right. We then looked at various symbols and I picked out a nice looking nautical steering wheel that you might typically see on the sails of a yacht.

The vendor showed me the final mockup and I had him generate two decals – one for each side of the pontoon boat – that measured about three feet long and eight inches high. Each decal had two four-letter words generated in a very fancy and elegant script. The illustration of the nautical steering wheel I picked out was placed between the two words. The first word to the left of the illustration was "Reeb" and the second word to the right of the illustration was "Traf". I figured these two words would have people wondering what the name of my boat was all about. In fact, a couple people who were lined up to get their boat name decals asked me what language the phrase was written in and suggested it was some sort of cutesy French phrase. I nodded and chuckled to myself, confident that I'd picked the right name for the pontoon boat.

Mark and I left the boat show and went home with the receipt for a new pontoon boat in our pockets. We now had to figure out what to say to our wives.

We agreed to blame the purchase on each other. We could each say we were helping out a friend and emphasize that it was really a great deal to only have to pay half of the purchase price. And wouldn't it be a great family picnic boat to go boating with on the Fox Lake chain?

Another argument was that we didn't even have to worry about spending money on a trailer to haul it around because we cut a great deal with the marina owner to store it there. We decided not to mention that this marina deal was only for the first year.

Of course we could always tell our wives that we had two weeks to cancel the order if there was no meeting of the minds, but that was the last thing we wanted to do.

Whatever tack we took, we agreed it would be good to mention the significant savings passed on to us by buying the boat during the show. On their own, the price of the pontoon boat and marina fees would be outrageous. How could we not purchase this boat when there was a discount of over thirty-three percent? These arguments sounded completely

159

plausible while riding home in the car but we both wondered if they would be received well by our wives.

Not surprisingly, we got home, each talked to our wives, and had similar experiences – namely, the proverbial shit hit the fan.

After what seemed like hours of heated discussion, my wife – reluctantly – agreed to the purchase. In my discussion with Mark later, his experience was nearly identical. But I certainly learned to never – ever – surprise her with that sort of purchase again.

The boat show was in February and, as promised, the custom pontoon boat was ready by the start of the boating season in May. The year we purchased the boat, the company I worked for had what they called summer hours. This meant that if you work an extra hour on Monday through Thursday, on Friday you could get off at noon. This was a great way to get away for an early start of the weekend. Not every company in the area did this, so Friday afternoons were usually far less crowded around the parks and lakes. This made it perfect for boating on the Fox Lake chain on Friday afternoons.

We owned that pontoon boat for over four years and had many great times and experiences with it. It was a real party boat that could easily hold ten people. It even had a small charcoal grill in the front of the boat if we wanted to barbecue in the middle of the lake. Mark and I both used the boat with our friends and family and it was well worth the purchase price. It provided me with a new sense of freedom and allowed me to greatly expand my recreational activities.

By the way, if you haven't already figured out the hidden meaning of our boat's name, spell each word backward.

Running Aground in Grass Lake

It was always better to go boating on the Fox Lake chain during a weekday because the weekends were so crowded with boats and drunken boat operators that it became more dangerous than fun. Edward and I decided to spend a great summer afternoon on the Fox Lake chain. You could travel out of the Fox Lake chain north and then follow the Fox River a few miles into Wisconsin. You could also travel on the nine large lakes in the chain or go downriver about twenty miles until you reached the dam in the town of Algonquin.

One afternoon, Edward and I were coming back down from the Fox River in Wisconsin into Grass Lake, which is a very shallow lake with lots of marsh area and cattails jutting out around the perimeter of the shoreline.

It was a calm, quiet day with few boaters out at that time. I decided I wanted to find out if I was able to pilot the pontoon boat by myself. Edward thought this was a bad idea, but I persisted and said, "What could possibly go wrong while you're right there next to me the entire time?" He gave in.

In order to maneuver my electric wheelchair into the pilot's position located behind the pilot station and directly in front of the steering wheel, Edward unscrewed and removed the existing pilot seat. The pilot station has a speedometer to let you know how fast the boat is going. With a high horsepower motor we could hit a maximum speed of about 27 miles per hour, but as I took over in the pilot area Edward set the initial speed at about three miles per hour.

I positioned my electric wheelchair so that the toes of my shoes touched the back of the pilot station. The steering wheel was directly in front of me and the throttle that controls the speed was to my right. The throttle is just a single lever. When pushed forward the boat's speed would increase. When pulled back, the boat's speed would decrease. Simple enough. However, since I can't use my fingers to grab and hold on to anything, I needed to use my wrists and lower arms to control the steering and throttle.

I had my left hand resting on the spoke of the steering wheel and my right hand positioned with my wrist over the throttle. Edward aimed the boat straight down the channel going into Grass Lake. With the speed set at three miles per hour I had no problem controlling the boat and felt confident that this was a piece of cake. I planned to drive this boat many more times in the future.

Because I have very little balance when sitting in a wheelchair on the water, I use a seat belt to keep my upper body positioned upright. Although I could noticeably feel that my balance was a little off from the unfamiliar extension I was putting on my arms, I was still fairly comfortable. As we got out of the channel and into Grass Lake I thought I would speed the boat up just a bit.

I must have pushed the throttle too hard because the boat lurched forward and my wheelchair jerked backward. (My electric wheelchair doesn't have any brakes. The chair depends on friction to keep the wheelchair stationary.) I lost my balance and, as my upper body fell forward in the wheelchair, my left hand turned the steering wheel sharply to the right while my other arm pushed the throttle to full speed.

As the boat surged forward, the wheelchair tipped over backwards and my back hit the deck. The boat was now going about 26 miles per hour and heading directly for the marsh and cattails. Edward, who had been standing next to me to ensure nothing bad would happen, was also sprawled out on the pontoon boat floor. We could feel the impact of hitting the marsh at full speed and it seemed like forever before the pontoon boat finally stopped.

When the boat did stop, the motor was still grinding away at full speed. Edward managed to get off the floor and turn the engine off. He then saw that I was lying on my back on the floor still strapped into my wheelchair. After struggling quite a bit, he managed to get my wheelchair upright with me at least halfway in it so that we could maneuver my body back around to regain some of my balance.

You know how people say things seem to go in slow motion when in the midst of a crisis? I can tell you for a fact that it is true!

It must have been less than a minute from the time I first hit the throttle to the time Edward lifted me up from the floor, but to us it seemed like an eternity. We took a few moments to catch our breath and calm down a bit. Only then did we wonder how the pontoon boat had faired.

We couldn't believe what we were seeing.

The boat had managed to jump up and onto the more solid part of the marsh, stopping about thirty feet from the water in the channel. The pontoons were actually on top of dry land in the marsh. The outboard motor was completely exposed and up in the air. We were about one hundred and fifty yards from shore, and there was no way that I would be able to get off the pontoon boat and get to shore, with or without my electric wheelchair.

Eventually some boaters came by and pointed to our boat sitting atop the middle of the marsh. We yelled to them and explained that we needed help. They were more than willing to help and called in to one of the largest marinas on the Fox Lake chain to see if they could get a high-powered boat out here to drag the pontoon boat out of the marsh.

As the boat from the marina approached us we could see the two people on board pointing in our direction and laughing hysterically. To them it probably looked pretty funny to see a 28-foot pontoon boat completely exposed in the middle of the marsh. To us, however, it was a little more serious and before long it was also a little more serious to them.

After explaining how we managed to get ourselves hung up on the marsh they threw over some towing ropes. We attached them to the pontoons so they could drag us back into the water. They arrived in a huge double inboard cigar boat that had a tremendous amount of horsepower so we thought once the pontoons were tied to the towing rope it would be simple for them to pull us off and out of the marsh.

An hour later they were still struggling to get our pontoon boat to budge. It took all the horsepower they had, we had barely moved, and they were talking about giving up. That would have been an untenable situation for me. They began trying to figure out a way to get me out of the pontoon boat, with or without my electric wheelchair, without the risk of plunging me into the water.

Realizing it would be almost impossible to get me off the pontoon boat, they came up with a new plan and suggested that we tie the tow rope to the far left part of the pontoon boat as it faced them. They would then try to swivel that end of the boat toward them. We would then retie the towing rope to the right side of the pontoon boat as it faced them and they would swivel that end of the boat toward them. Using this technique over and over again they managed to pull the pontoon boat toward them foot by foot. It was a very slow process but at least it worked.

After at least two dozen times of tying and retying the pontoon boat in different places they managed to get us back in the lake waters. We gladly paid them for their services and thanked them profusely. You can't imagine what a relief it was to get the pontoon boat started and make our way back to our marina.

Running aground in Grass Lake was a very harrowing experience and even I had to admit, *"What a fine mess I had gotten us into."*

From that moment forward, I left the boat driving to other people.

CHAPTER 28

Surprise, Surprise (1996)

One day Mark and I took our 28-foot pontoon boat out on the Fox Lake chain. The Fox Lake chain has nine nice-sized lakes as well as the Fox River system that flows into and out of the chain. We spent a good portion of the late morning just cruising around the various lakes in the pontoon boat, stopped for lunch, and then did quite a bit of fishing. It was a great day to be out.

Around mid-afternoon, Mark's wife, Sharon, started calling Mark on his cell phone. Each time she called he would look at his watch and I would think we were about to get ready to go because he had to leave. But each time he'd hang up the phone and we just kept on fishing. It was about three-thirty in the afternoon when he finally suggested we head back to my house. My house was about an hour away and Mark had to travel another thirty to forty minutes to his place. I suggested that if he wasn't constrained by time, we might stop for dinner somewhere along the way but he said he needed to get back home.

We took the boat back to the marina where we had a dock rented for the summer and then stowed all the fishing gear in my handicap van and started home. By now it was about four in the afternoon.

Tow Trucks and Wheelchairs

We were on Interstate 294 heading back to my house when my van abruptly stopped and we coasted to the shoulder of the road. The gas gauge still indicated we had three quarters of a tank of gas. Mark, being somewhat familiar with car engines, got out to see if there was anything

164

he could find wrong with the engine. He looked things over but after a while determined that there was nothing he could do. We called the auto service and waited for more than an hour before the tow truck arrived. By that time Mark's wife had called another three or four times to find out what was going on.

The tow truck driver said there was nothing he could do to start the van. We were told the van would have to be towed back to my house. Sounds like a fairly easy solution, right?

Wrong.

There are laws disallowing a vehicle to be towed with a person in it. Here I was on Interstate 294 in the middle of the country in my electric wheelchair and in my van that can't be towed with me in it. Yet there was no way for me to be transferred into the cab of the tow truck. If you'd ever tried finding a handicap van in a pinch, it just doesn't happen. You can't just call a rental center.

After explaining the situation to the tow truck driver, he got me in touch with his manager. His manager had a real problem with allowing me to stay in my vehicle if it was going to be towed. After discussing it with a few other people on his end the manager finally, but reluctantly, agreed to allow me to stay in my vehicle while it was being towed. Problem solved, right?

Wrong again.

The tow truck that was on the scene could not tow my vehicle. This particular tow truck used a winch to lift the front of my van to tow it. That meant that I would be lifted with it, positioning me at a dangerous angle while in the van as it was being towed. A different tow truck had to be dispatched that had a large flatbed on the back. Using a flatbed would allow my vehicle – and me – to travel without the front end being lifted up in the air.

We waited well over another hour for the second tow truck to arrive before Mark and I were towed back to my driveway. I was very surprised that no highway patrol cars stopped us to see what was going on, but I thought perhaps the tow company contacted them about our unusual situation and assured them that everything was fine.

The tow truck driver was concerned with me sitting in the vehicle on his flatbed so he drove very slowly. Mark later told me that Sharon continued to call him while we were being towed to find out what was happening.

165

Had all gone right, we would have been at my house by four thirty that afternoon. But thanks to our series of unfortunate events along the Interstate, we didn't arrive home until after seven-thirty in the evening. With my van unloaded onto the driveway, all I wanted to do was get into the house and go to bed. It had been a long, long tiring day and I was looking forward to calling it a night.

Better Late Than Never

I entered my house through the garage doorway and immediately saw my mother, brother, and two aunts sitting on the sofa. My first thought was, "Oh my God something has happened in the family." But as I ventured further into the room I heard:

"Surprise!"

As I looked around, the whole house was filled with people – at least twenty-five and probably many more – leaving me speechless with no other thought in my head except, "I don't need this right now."

My stepdaughter, Sandy, had arranged a surprise fiftieth birthday party and arranged for everyone to be there by four o'clock so they'd be there by the time I got home. My wife knew I hated surprise parties. I even hate to attend surprise parties for others. But Sandy is the best stepdaughter one could ever hope to have and she thrives on doing stuff like this. I'm sure she spent countless days making arrangements and plans to pull off this surprise. With the unexpected van diversion Mark and I had, I guess it was more than just me who was surprised that day.

By the time Mark and I arrived – three hours late – a quarter of the people invited had arrived, eaten, and left. Can you blame them? To tell you the truth, I was exhausted and could hardly keep my eyes open. By that time I was in no mood to party but a lot of old friends were there who I had not seen in a while so, as far as I was concerned, the party turned out to be a great success.

Mark finally filled me in on all the phone calls he was receiving from Sharon. She was calling to make sure that Mark would get me back to my house by a little after four thirty.

Mark said he was already running late by the time we left the marina and was expecting to catch hell from Sharon because we would be twenty minutes to a half-hour late to begin with. He pushed the speed limit to try to make up some time on our way home when the van broke down. He told me that as far as he was concerned having to be towed got him off the hook with his wife. Once she found out my van broke down her calls to him were to find out an estimated time we might arrive so she could tell the guests. I could easily imagine both Sandy and Sharon panicking while we sat in the middle of the Interstate.

I don't know whether that was another fine mess that I got Mark into or if it was a fine mess that Sandy got me into. I think I'll call it a tie.

CHAPTER 29

Space Shuttle Police (2002)

Edward and I would frequently take a vacation trip to Marco Island in Florida. At one time we did this for four out of five years. We usually arrived somewhere around the last weekend in February or the first weekend in March and stayed one or two weeks.

The beaches of Marco Island are extraordinarily beautiful and, coming from Chicago's harsh winter, it is a real treat to sit around the beach and enjoy the sun and eighty-degree temperatures. We used to stay at the Marco Island Marriott, which has a fantastic beach area. Later we switched to the Radisson Hotel only a few blocks south of the Marco Island Marriott because the handicap rooms there were much bigger with a screened in balcony, living room, and kitchen area. The staff at the Radisson Hotel was very accommodating and would help me out whenever they could. They continually asked me what they could do to make my stay more enjoyable.

In mid-February the city would use its heavy equipment to loosen up all the sand on the stretches of beach on Marco Island. They did this to provide better nesting conditions for the turtles that would migrate there in May. This was great for the turtles, but not for me. I used to enjoy going down to the beach and finding a nice spot at some secluded part on the beach and read the books I saved up for the trip. It was extremely enjoyable sitting on the beach in the nice warm weather listening to the ocean waves breaking on the beach while reading a book. Unfortunately when the sand was loose my wheelchair would constantly get stuck. I would have to depend on passersby to help me get out of the ditches my wheelchair dug into the sand every time I tried to move.

I told a couple of the hotel staff people the problems I had with trying to maneuver around the beach. The people at the Radisson went out and purchased – at no expense to me – ten 4' x 8' sheets of plywood and laid them out adjacent to the area at the end of the footbridge that went from the hotel to the beach. Each year when I would go back to the Radisson they would bring up the plywood from storage and set aside this area for me to maneuver my wheelchair so that I could read my books and enjoy the beach area. They went way beyond what they needed to do to make my visit more enjoyable.

Taking a Chance on a Long Shot

During our 2002 stay at the Marco Island Radisson, we found out that there was going to be a space shuttle launch at the Kennedy Space Center in Cape Canaveral during the end of the week. The space shuttle Columbia was scheduled to take off just before dawn on Friday, March 1, at 6:22 a.m. The shuttle mission, STS-109, was to perform maintenance on the Hubble Space Telescope.

Neither Edward nor I had ever seen a live space shuttle launch and we decided to try to get passes for this one. Edward had a second cousin who worked at Cape Canaveral, so he called her to ask if she could possibly get us passes. She said she could, and told us she would send them to us at the hotel by overnight mail. We were thrilled.

Cape Canaveral is about 260 miles from Marco Island and about a five-hour drive. The launch was scheduled for dawn, so we decided to leave around eleven o'clock the prior evening to give ourselves plenty of time to get there. It would also allow us enough time to find and select a good site to park and view the launch.

Every shuttle launch is subject to the weather conditions and because of the cold weather that year there was only a sixty percent chance that the shuttle would launch. Edward and I knew that it was a long drive and that it might be for nothing but it was probably the only chance we would ever have to see a shuttle launch so we decided to go anyway.

By this time in my life I had to be careful about how long I sat in my wheelchair. I had continual and recurring problems with pressure sores and was trying to limit my sitting in a wheelchair to twice a day for a maximum of four hours each time. We needed to come up with a plan to

169

make sure that, while we traveled to the Kennedy Space Center, I would not put undue pressure on my butt.

I was fortunate to have with me both my reclining wheelchair and my old Ford handicap van. With the reclining wheelchair, I could push a button and the wheelchair would lean back so my feet and head were horizontal, just like I was lying in bed. This relieved the pressure areas but I was limited to lying within the narrow width of the wheelchair. We decided that we would recline my wheelchair all the way back in the van so that I would be perfectly flat. Edward would then line my sides with pillows, tuck one under my head, cover me with a blanket, and strap me in with safety belts so the wheelchair could not move while driving. With a five-hour drive there and another five-hour drive back, the longer I could lie prone while traveling, the longer I could sit upright in my wheelchair to watch the shuttle launch.

We left Marco Island a little before eleven o'clock in the evening for the Kennedy Space Center. Since late evenings and early mornings were very cold that time of year, we took extra jackets along with us and I wore a hooded sweatshirt tied tightly to keep my head warm.

"Houston – We Have a Problem"

Edward doesn't like traveling on the interstates because he feels the drive is too boring and he likes to see some of the sights along the smaller roads. He decided to take what he thought would be shortcuts on some of the state highways. We would be traveling in darkness so the sightseeing would be at a minimum, but Edward still liked to travel through the small towns and look at their storefronts. We would also get to the Kennedy Space Center in a more direct route. Edward thought we would run into very little traffic traveling the smaller state highways at that time of night and early morning hours.

After driving a couple hours, Edward and I heard a siren and saw flashes of many red, white, and blue revolving lights coming from behind us. Edward slowed down because we didn't know if it was an ambulance, fire truck, or police car. It turned out to be two police cars. When we slowed down we thought they would be passing us by on the way to some emergency but that wasn't the case. As one police car pulled up to get even with us the policeman motioned for Edward to pull over.

Edward drove the van to the shoulder of the road and stopped. The first police car pulled in front of our vehicle and the second police car moved in behind us. An officer got out of the police car in front of us, walked back to our van and stood by the driver's side window. I could barely see the officer as he approached Edward but it looked like he had one hand on his holster and held a flashlight in the other hand that was fixated on Edward through the window. Neither Edward nor I knew what was going on as Edward rolled down his window.

The officer told Edward that he was speeding. We had just passed through a small town about five miles back and I figured we got caught in one of the local speed traps. With out-of-state Illinois license plates on my van, I figured we were probably prime candidates and thought, "Okay, so Edward will get a ticket and we can be on our way again."

The officer writing out the ticket questioned Edward about why he was driving a van with Illinois license plates but his driver's license was from Missouri. The strange set of circumstances made the ticketing officer very suspicious. By this time the second officer who was in the police car that pulled up behind the van shined his flashlight through the back window of the van. He saw me, flat out and strapped down in the back of the vehicle, and said something to the other officer.

In less than three seconds, both officers had their guns drawn and the policeman closest to Edward ordered him to get out of the vehicle with his hands raised. We had no clue what was going on and Edward complied – it's not a good idea to argue with a policeman who has his gun drawn and pointed at you. The officer told Edward to put his hands on top of the van and spread his legs. Again Edward complied as he was searched for weapons.

I thought, "What the hell is going on?"

The officer nearest Edward asked him why he had someone tied up in the back of the van and Edward tried to explain that I was his friend and we were going to the Kennedy Space Center to see the shuttle launch. You could tell that the officer didn't believe what Edward was saying. Can you blame him?

There I was lying on my back surrounded by pillows, covered in a blanket with just my nose and eyes sticking out of the hood of my sweatshirt. I imagine the worst part was that there were three safety straps wrapped around my body near my ankles, abdomen, and chest, render-

171

ing me completely immobile. I probably looked like a patient from a psych ward with something stuffed in my mouth.

I could hear the officer behind the van talking with somebody on what I could only surmise was his radio unit. Up until this time I had stayed pretty quiet because I wasn't sure what was going on and it all happened very quickly. The driver's door was still open from when Edward got out of the van so I yelled out that I was all right and tried explaining why I was strapped in the back of the van, but I don't know if the officer could hear me or not. I think the officer behind us finally saw parts of the wheelchair as he continued to shine his flashlight through the back window and yelled something to the officer watching Ed.

The sound of sirens from a distance suddenly got closer and a third police car was now on the scene. The officer behind us had called for backup. When the third officer got out of his car, he went to the open driver's door and shined his flashlight toward me. I quickly explained what was going on and why I was lying all covered up with straps around me and that we were vacationing at the Radisson Hotel in Marco Island. It finally became evident to them that we were no threat. They seemed to relax a little and the tone of their voices was a little less demanding and a little more conversational. One of the officers had the dispatcher call the hotel to verify that we were guests there and when the dispatcher relayed confirmation that we were, they realized that we were just vacationers and let us go.

What another fine mess we just got out of.

The officers were extremely apologetic for the inconvenience but said that they could not take any chances when they saw that I was strapped in the back of the van. One of the officers told us that quite a few drug runners pass through the area and that they are very suspicious of vans traveling through in the early morning hours with out-of-state license plates. We told them we understood and just wanted to get back on the road because we were now starting to run late. Two of the officers got back into their cars and left. But after all the hassles we just went through, the third officer stayed long enough to finish writing out Edward's speeding ticket. I couldn't believe it. I guess those little townships need the money to help pay for their diligent police force.

As the last police car left, Edward began complaining about receiving a speeding ticket. This was the first traffic ticket he ever got in his life and he insisted he was not going as fast as the officer said he was. I was dumbfounded – after all we just went through, including a near miss of being hauled off to jail, Edward was complaining about a stupid speeding ticket.

Liftoff: Up Close and Personal

I was pretty shaken after the whole experience and wondered if we should turn around and go back to the hotel. Edward thought that as long as we were as far as we were we might as well just continue on. Our little confrontation with the police wasted a lot of time but we would have just enough time to hopefully get to the Kennedy Space Center before the shuttle launch.

We were glad to have allowed a couple hours of extra travel time before the launch. By the time we arrived at the Kennedy Space Center, crowds of people had already parked at the best spots to see the launch. When we finally found a decent spot to park the van there were about twenty minutes to spare before the launch. Edward and I got out of the van and I remember it being so cold that he had to get me the extra jacket I brought to put on.

The launch was truly an amazing sight. Floodlights surrounded the launch pad and they lit up the huge rocket and space shuttle against the black sky. The shuttle launched on time as dawn approached. It was a spectacular sight and sound as we heard the roar from the rockets as they lifted off the launch pad. Although the launch pad was pretty far from where we were parked, the launch was still spectacular and certainly very different to watch live rather than on television. It only took a couple minutes before all we could see was the contrail as the shuttle disappeared in the distance. Within ten minutes after the launch everybody got back into their cars and headed out of the Cape.

We had traveled all night and our harrowing experience with the police lasted longer than the ten minutes of watching the shuttle launch. We headed back to Marco Island, another five hours of driving.

Was it worth it? It was to us. I don't know how many Americans have ever seen a shuttle launch in person but at least Edward and I had, and it was well worth our time – and unexpected delay – to get there.

CHAPTER 30

New Orleans and the Preacher (2007)

I visited New Orleans the year prior to the devastation caused by Hurricane Katrina. Edward and I had a great time on our first trip and we decided to go back in the spring of 2007. On our previous trip we really enjoyed the food, the Southern hospitality, and the weather. I had heard that the French Quarter was pretty much back to the way it was before the hurricane, and I was eager to see how things were a year after Katrina.

Edward and I decided we'd like to first go to Gulfport, Mississippi, and then on to New Orleans, but when I tried to make reservations for the weekend in New Orleans, everything was booked. We had to change our travel plans to go to New Orleans first and then to Gulfport, so I booked reservations in the New Orleans downtown area for Thursday evening.

We arrived in New Orleans on a Thursday at noon and checked in to our hotel, which was adjacent to the New Orleans Riverwalk. I then found out why I could not book a hotel for that weekend. From Friday at noon until Sunday evening, New Orleans was staging its French Quarter Music Festival. Hundreds of bands would perform on a dozen or more stages located all along the Riverwalk and throughout the French Quarter. This was a very pleasant surprise for us because we weren't scheduled to leave until late Friday afternoon and would be able to attend a few of the outdoor concerts before we had to go.

Edward and I spent most of Thursday afternoon traveling the Riverwalk and French Quarter. Everything in that area is so close that I could easily travel nearly anywhere in my electric wheelchair. The biggest difference I noticed post-Katrina was that I could not take the trolley from one end of the Riverwalk to the other. I was told that the handicap accessible trolley was destroyed in the flood so they only had a very old trolley servicing that route. In talking with some of the French Quarter store owners, I found out that their businesses were finally starting to pick up but it was still only about sixty percent of what it was prior to Katrina. Other than not being able to use the trolley, it was still the great city of New Orleans that I remember and came to love the first time I was there.

Early Friday morning, Edward and I had breakfast and when he went back to our room to pack, I started to travel down the Riverwalk in my wheelchair to see what was going on and to enjoy the warm spring weather. Edward was going to meet me a couple of hours later in front of the New Orleans aquarium building after he checked out of the hotel and had the van all packed to travel.

New Orleans is a great town to get around in a wheelchair. You can travel for miles around the Riverwalk and French Quarter with very few – and minor – problems. The cobblestone streets that make the French Quarter charming are difficult for a wheelchair to travel, and quite a few of the old buildings in the French Quarter are a little difficult for my chair and me to enter using the main door. But other than these minor difficulties, I thoroughly enjoyed touring the city on my own.

A Riverwalk Encounter

I stopped to look at the river in front of the aquarium building, tilted my wheelchair back quite a bit to enjoy the morning sun, and fell asleep. When I woke up, I saw somebody walking toward me in a business suit. I expected him to walk past me but he stopped and asked if he could talk with me, and if I would mind if he asked me some personal questions. This has happened to me quite a bit in the past and the most typical questions are about why I am in a wheelchair. I don't mind answering these questions. I hope that the people asking them are better informed after they talk with me. I told the man that he was welcome to ask as many questions as he wished. He introduced himself and, for this story, I will refer to him as Jim.

Jim started the conversation by telling me why he wanted to talk with me. He told me he saw me there about forty minutes earlier and wanted to stop by and talk but that it looked at the time like I was sleeping. He explained that he was there for a convention and while attending one of the seminars with a few of his employees a strange feeling came over him. He broke out with sweats and was forced to leave the seminar for relief. His anxiety and uncomfortable feeling only got better when he traveled toward the Riverwalk and it completely went away when he saw me sleeping in my wheelchair. He said he was tempted to come over and wake me up but thought better of it. Since he felt better he went back to attend the rest of the seminar.

When Jim got back to the seminar he again broke out in sweats and had the same strange feelings as before. He said something told him he had to find me and talk with me. Again he left his seminar and walked to the Riverwalk where his feelings turned from uncomfortable to – as he described it – euphoric – upon seeing me again. This time I was awake and he said he knew he had to talk with me. Jim said that besides being a doctor he was also a preacher in a small town in the middle of Louisiana's Cajun country.

Jim told me his own story, saying that he used to be an alcoholic. One morning after the longest drinking binge in his life, he prayed to God for help. He said that at the time he was not a religious man but sometime during that evening God spoke to him and turned his life around. He never had a drink thereafter and has since devoted his life to his professional practice and preaching. Jim had been sober and preaching for the last ten years with a small church and congregation in his hometown. He said that when he saw me he felt that God was guiding him through his next step in life.

Jim asked me why I was in a wheelchair and I told him that I severed the nerves of my spinal column many years ago, leaving me paralyzed. He asked me if I believed in God and the Bible. I told him that I was raised Roman Catholic but that I was not practicing as one and had my own beliefs that I was very comfortable with.

I shared with him that I had my degrees in physics concentrating on astronomy and studied what I could about the physical universe, but I found it hard for anybody to outright reject some sort of power governing everything. The expanse of the universe is so large, beautiful, and intricate that I feel there has to be something behind it all. I believe that there has to be a plan to the universe and because we lived in that universe we were part of that plan.

I once heard that in this period of our human evolution we are really only using around ten percent of our brain. I always wondered what that other ninety percent was capable of. Humans can only understand a very small portion of the laws that govern the universe and I expect that in the next hundred years a lot of what we understand today will be proven wrong. Scientists today are trying to study what it means to be sentient and what consciousness and thinking are all about. They will probably discover that it is similarly governed by Heisenberg's uncertainty principle, where observing or studying it actually changes what it really is.

I don't know how Jim interpreted what I was saying but he did ask if he could lay his hands on me and pray. I said, "Yes." There are so many things in this world that can't be explained that I don't disregard the unknown possibilities through the actions of another. Jim warned me that if he started speaking in tongues I shouldn't be afraid. I assured him that I wouldn't and to go ahead with whatever he had planned.

Jim laid his hands on my shoulder and prayed over me for approximately fifteen minutes. I never did hear him speak in tongues but when he was done he felt very relieved and I felt somehow lighter. No, I didn't get up and walk or anything, but why I felt lighter I can't explain. It may have been nothing more than the beautiful sunny day that I was enjoying, but I don't laugh at or ridicule people for trying to help me. I realize they only want to help and do it the best way they know how. I thanked Jim and he left shortly after that.

I don't know if what Jim did with me helped him get to the next step he spoke of, but I hope it did. I don't ever criticize people for their religious beliefs. People's religions and beliefs might differ but if they use those beliefs for the betterment of humanity and feel comfortable because of what they believe, the more power to them.

Edward arrived about ten minutes after Jim left. By this time it was close to eleven o'clock so we walked to where some of the band stands were set up. When we got there we found out that besides live music all the famous restaurants in the French Quarter had set up food tents around the bandstands. The music started at noon and it was like one gigantic outdoor party.

We spent the afternoon traveling from bandstand to bandstand and eating a large variety of New Orleans style cooking. It was a great day and when five o'clock came I was sorry to have to leave to continue our journey. I told Edward that we should go back there the following year but plan ahead so we were sure to be there for the entire French Quarter Music Festival. I couldn't wait until the next time we could get back to New Orleans.

Lunch in Kentucky

One other time, someone asked to pray over me. During a trip to Florida from Chicago Edward and I stopped for lunch at a restaurant in a small town in Kentucky. The waitress who served us was an elderly lady and she smiled at me when we ordered lunch. When Edward went to the bathroom before the food arrived our waitress came back to my table and asked me if she could pray over me. I said she could and she spent the next three minutes praying over me. She was not ashamed nor was I.

Other people in the restaurant did not seem to pay much attention to me getting prayed over. That really amazed me. In the Midwestern cities where I grew up and now live, people are not that open about professing their beliefs.

For me, being prayed over in these two instances were strange events, but I feel they were two worthwhile encounters as well. I guess when you're in a wheelchair there are always people wanting to help in whatever way they can.

Part 3: Medical Mayhem

The following section includes additional anecdotes. But these specific stories all have a medical connection and recount some of the harrowing experiences I have had because of health conditions and during hospital stays. While none of them are particularly humorous, I include them because they are a very real part of the life I live as a quadriplegic.

Whether you have a physical disability or are able-bodied, the point I want to stress by telling these stories is that we all must be aware of both our physical vulnerabilities and the medications being administered to us by well-meaning physicians, nurses, and medical professionals.

CHAPTER 31

A Chilling Vacation (1984)

Diane and I often took vacations at Disney World. It's a great place for getting around in a wheelchair with a tremendous transportation system to get between the various areas of the park. If Diane wants to do one thing I can always go off on my own and do another. Diane usually liked to go to the Magic Kingdom while I preferred Epcot Center.

Between the ferries, monorail, and handicap buses I found that the best place for me to stay was at the Polynesian Village. The last time I went it was located adjacent to a main transportation center for the park. I often enjoyed sitting out on the Polynesian Village's dock and reading a book while Diane went off touring the park.

The best time of year that we found to go to Disney World was the week right after Thanksgiving. We nearly had free rein of the park without crowds, and making restaurant reservations was no problem at all.

One year my friend, Edward Weishaar, went with us. The prior three years the weather had been beautiful. This time, however, it was cold and rained more than usual. We still had a great time despite the weather.

With about two days left to our seven-day vacation I started to have problems. Being out in the cold and wet weather for a few days probably lowered my immune system resistance and I broke out with a urinary tract infection. I did not have any medication with me to fight the infection and thought that as soon as I got home a day and a half later I would get a prescription from my doctor to start some antibiotics.

Blood Red

The day before we were scheduled on our flight back to Chicago, the infection worsened and I began to run a fever and get the chills. I told myself that all I needed to do was stay in relatively good shape just one more night and through to the next afternoon. That didn't seem so long and I felt sure that I could tough it out until I got back to Chicago.

As the evening wore on my chills got worse and my urine turned to a bloody red – a clear indication that my urinary tract infection might have turned septic. When a urinary tract infection enters the bloodstream it is very serious. This has happened to me in the past and I knew I was now beyond being able to get rid of the infection with oral antibiotics.

Another symptom of a serious infection is the feeling that I'm urinating all the time because the walls of my bladder get so raw. Although I cannot feel my bladder I do get chills up my spine and can tell I have to urinate. The walls of my bladder contract by themselves constantly. When the bladder contracts I break out in sweats and the feeling I get is so uncomfortable I can't really begin to describe it. I imagine the feeling is similar to that of a normal person who experiences a burning sensation while urinating. For that person the burning sensation stops when they stop urinating. For me, when my urinary tract infections are so bad that my bladder walls are raw enough to bleed, the burning sensation is constant until I can start getting rid of the infection.

I stayed in bed the entire day before we left for Chicago and drank very little water because if I drink water the uncomfortable feeling of constantly urinating gets tremendously worse. Not drinking water when you are feeling sick and have a temperature will dehydrate you and actually makes you feel worse, but I only had to survive until I got back to Chicago the next day.

When we left the Polynesian Village the next morning to catch our flight to Chicago my temperature was 102.4 and I had the chills so bad that my teeth were chattering. I had the choice of trying to find a hospital in the area or try and survive another four or five hours until I could get to the hospital in Chicago. I decided to stick it out and go back home to familiar territory.

That was nearly a deadly mistake.

The sensation of urinating constantly was so bad that I had my wife get some salt packages from one of the restaurant areas at the airport. I swallowed down four packages of salt and drank just a little water to wash it down with. My thought was that if I could retain enough salt it would stop me from having the very uncomfortable feeling I had of constant urination. During that time, I wore a Texas catheter attached to a urinary drainage bag strapped to my leg while I was in the wheelchair, so it would also keep my urinary leg bag from getting full during the flight where it would be difficult to empty.

That was my second big mistake that day.

As soon as we were in the air I knew I should have gone to a hospital in Orlando. I was feeling so bad and shivering so much that the flight attendant had to bring a couple of blankets for me to be wrapped up in.

Deadly Cold

Once we landed in Chicago instead of going home we drove directly to the hospital where I immediately entered the emergency room.

A urine sample was taken immediately to send to the labs and then I was given aspirin to help bring down my temperature, which by then had gone up to around 103. I was very dehydrated from taking all that salt but people in the emergency room didn't want to do anything until they had results back from the labs.

When the lab results came back they showed that my infection had gone septic and someone in the emergency room called to request a room for me. Once a urinary tract infection enters the bloodstream, the only treatment is heavy-duty antibiotics that must be administered through an IV. I was transferred to a hospital room around an hour and a half later.

Once up in the hospital room I was bombarded with questions for more than a half hour about my medical history. It was very difficult for me to answer any questions because I was shaking so badly. They covered me with quite a few blankets and even though I had a very high temperature, I felt like I was freezing. They finally got an IV solution started to help alleviate my dehydration. About a half-hour later they also started an antibiotic IV.

As things settled down and the nurses left the room I tried to get some rest but could not stop shaking. My teeth chattered uncontrollably and there was no way I could stop it. About an hour after the nurses left the room they came back to check my vitals – my blood pressure, temperature, and pulse. Not more than two minutes after the nurse left I heard over the hospital's loudspeaker "Code 'something'" like they usually say if a patient is in dire trouble. I don't know what color was used with the word 'code' but when I heard my room number called out and saw seven people in medical garb rushing into my room, I knew that I was the one in trouble.

My temperature had spiked to around 106 degrees.

Before I knew what was going on people were turning me over and putting stuff under me. All I remember is that all of a sudden I started feeling very cold all over my skin. Evidently they wrapped me up and put me in some sort of a contraption that was like a body ice pack. For the next few hours someone kept a constant vigil while my body temperature slowly decreased.

This was one more time in my life I was very close to being dead.

With the constant intake of high-powered IV antibiotics it took about a week to get back to normal, but I knew I had to do something to reduce the risk of urinary tract infections. They were occurring more frequently and becoming septic more often.

Rehabilitation Institute of Chicago (RIC)

I went to the RIC in downtown Chicago for an evaluation. It was determined that I could no longer use the Texas catheter for keeping my bladder clear. Because the Texas catheter is an external catheter, I always had to kind of tap my bladder area with my closed wrist while I tried pushing out the urine that was trapped in my bladder. Although I have no true feeling, I can tell when my bladder gets full because I have chills that seem to go up and down my spine. When I get that feeling I push hard and can usually empty my bladder into the urinary drainage bag through my Texas catheter.

At the RIC I found out that by doing this for years my bladder stretched to the point where I would retain more than a liter of urine. When I pushed I would get most of the urine out but I was always retaining a few

183

hundred cc's that never got flushed out. This caused my continued bladder infections so I had to find another way of emptying my bladder. From that point on, I used an indwelling catheter call the Foley to make sure the bladder was empty. Using a Foley catheter decreased the number of urinary tract infections I had that would become septic.

Unfortunately there is no silver bullet. Having a catheter inserted in my bladder at all times still kept me susceptible to infections but if I could catch them earlier I wouldn't have to worry about them becoming septic. I learned that when I changed my catheter to a new sterile Foley catheter I could use a diagnostic test strip to test the first urine draining into the new urine collection device. I would then be able to tell whether a urinary tract infection was starting or not and, if so, could take a regimen of oral antibiotics to cure it within days.

Shoulda, Woulda, Coulda

This last episode really brought home the fact that I can't ignore or postpone treatment of a urinary tract infection of any kind. I should have gone to a hospital in Orlando as soon as I noticed my urine had turned bloody. Instead I didn't want to put myself into an unfamiliar hospital environment a long way from home. That was either stubborn or stupid. Probably both.

This was another fine mess I got myself into – and it was almost my last.

CHAPTER 32

Smoke and Lasers (2001)

One of the problems I have had for the last twenty years is the accumulation of stones in my kidneys. Every year I have a CAT scan done so that my urologist can determine if any of the stones are close to blocking my urethra, which can be extremely dangerous. If they are, they perform a surgical procedure call lithotripsy.

The first time I had this done they used what is called extracorporeal shock wave lithotripsy (ESWL). They performed this procedure by lowering me into a large tank filled with water. The urologist would then sit behind a huge machine that was aimed at the stones inside my kidneys. This machine would break up the kidney stones using high-energy sound waves. At the time this was a great medical breakthrough because previously they would have to be surgically removed and you would spend quite a bit of time in the hospital to recover. With this machine you could have the procedure done as an outpatient.

When the machine was triggered my stomach muscles would tighten up so quickly and so hard that it would take the wind out of me. After receiving a couple hundred of these shots I was exhausted. Afterward I was moved to a hospital room and watched for a few hours as the blood and powdered gravel from the stones passed through the bladder, catheter and into a drainage bag attached to the side of my bed. After a few hours the urine would clear up and I could go home. I had this type of procedure done three or four times.

In later years a new technique called laser lithotripsy was perfected for zapping kidney stones. I had this procedure done about a half a dozen times and liked it a lot better than the previous method. A small laser was affixed to a camera that was attached to a thin cable. The cable was inserted through the penis, bladder, urethra, and up and into the kidneys. The laser can be moved alongside the kidney stone and then zap it into a fine powder. The urologist can pinpoint the exact location of the laser by watching a television monitor attached through the camera cable.

I usually only needed a local anesthetic during these procedures. Since I really have no feeling in my lower body, pain was not an issue. I was given just enough local anesthetic that caused me to drift in and out of understanding what was going on around me. Before I started to drift in and out I often saw on the monitor the laser being inserted near the stones.

During my last lithotripsy I drifted back into consciousness to the sound of one of the surgical nurses talking frantically to the doctor. She was telling him that smoke was coming out of the laser machine sitting on the side of the table. The urologist told her to turn the machine off, wait a minute, and then turn the machine back on again. She did as he asked and the doctor continued to zap my kidney stones. I was now becoming more conscious and alert. About a minute later the operating room nurse started yelling that the machine was smoking again – and it was smoking a lot.

This time I heard the anesthesiologist from behind me say we had to wrap up and get out of there because a part of the room where the laser machine was located was starting to fill with smoke. They quickly shut the machine off and the urologist finished what he was doing as quickly as possible. As they rushed me into the recovery room I wondered if they ever finished zapping the kidney stones that I was in there to get rid of. After about an hour in the recovery room they took me to a hospital room where, unbeknownst to me at that time, I was to spend the night.

As with the high-energy sound waves technique, the lithotripsy is usually an outpatient procedure and I can leave as soon as my urine starts clearing up. When my urologist came to my hospital room I asked how the procedure went. He said it went just fine and that I wouldn't need to be back for another checkup for a year. He didn't say one word about a smoking laser machine.

I told him I wanted to leave that day but he insisted he wanted to be cautious and keep me there overnight just for observation. After a brief argument about why I couldn't go home, I agreed to stay the night. This small concession quickly turned out to be a big mistake. Isn't it interesting how a simple decision on the spur of the moment can change the path your life from that point on?

From Bad to Worse

Edward Weishaar brought me to the hospital early that morning for the procedure and was waiting for me when I was transferred into the hospital room. When I realized that I would be staying overnight I told Edward to go home for the night and pick me up the next morning. He stayed for about another hour and gave me a lot of water to drink to help clear out and flush my kidneys and bladder.

Not long after Edward left a nurse's aide came in to my room and I asked her how much urine was in my drainage bag and if the urine was starting to get clear. She looked at the bag hanging on the side of the bed and told me there wasn't anything in it.

I immediately knew I had a problem.

Edward had given me at least two quarts of water that I drank before he left. That water had to be somewhere and it wasn't going into my drainage bag. I experienced this once before when I had a lithotripsy procedure.

Normally after a procedure of this kind the urine is very bloody because of all the tubes that they used getting to the kidney stones. There is always the chance for a blood clot to get stuck in the catheter and shut off the flow of urine to the drainage bag. When this happened to me once before, I simply needed to have my catheter changed so that the urine could start flowing again.

I told the nurse's assistant to get me the nurse right away so I could explain the situation to her. The nurse's assistant said she would let the nurse know.

After the nurse's assistant left I started to sweat profusely and got a pounding headache. These were signs that I was having an autonomic dysreflexia episode.

When my bladder gets so full that it can't hold any more liquid and has expanded to the point of no longer being able to expand, a reflex kicks in and my blood pressure shoots up to more than 200/130. If I can't find a means to correct the problem I could have a stroke and be dead within a matter of minutes.

The minutes kept ticking off with no nurse in sight. And rarely is it possible for me to operate the call button located on the side of a hospital bed or on the TV remote. While lying in bed there is no way I can push – or even see -- the call buttons and this time was no exception. I knew I was experiencing an autonomic dysreflexia episode, had little time to get treatment before serious damage occurred, and I had no means to call the nurse. I started yelling out the door for someone to come in.

Nobody came.

After what seemed like a very long time I finally got the attention of the nurse's aide and asked her where the nurse was she was supposed to get me. She said that my nurse was at lunch and that she was going to tell her about my situation as soon as she returned from lunch – in about a half-hour.

There was no way I could wait another half hour.

I told the nurse's aide that I was having a very bad autonomic dysreflexia episode and that I needed professional medical attention immediately. She calmly asked me how I knew that I was having a problem and, even though my head was pounding, I managed to tell her why. She acted like I didn't know what I was talking about, but I finally persuaded her to take my blood pressure. She took my blood pressure and, sure enough, it was over two hundred. She hurried out to get one of the nurses.

A nurse came in about five minutes later. By now my skull felt like it was going to burst out of my head. I could hardly talk and it took everything I had to communicate through the pain but when I finally managed to explain that my bladder was blocked, the idiot nurse asked me how I knew. I said if she didn't believe me then she should feel my abdomen. She did and said it was very hard and distended, but she wanted to go out to the nursing station to get some kind of handheld device that would verify I had a problem.

I then told the nurse that she had to put in a new catheter quickly or I could have a stroke right in front of her and could even be dead within a few minutes. I knew she thought I was exaggerating and told me she could not put in a new catheter without talking to my doctor. As she turned to leave to contact my doctor I told her that I was holding her personally responsible if anything happened to me.

She left without saying a word and I had no idea if she would be coming back.

I was on the verge of passing out from the pain of the headache and could barely talk when I saw her come back into the room with what looked like a turkey basting syringe. She pushed in the plunger, connected it to my current catheter, and pulled the plunger back. A huge blood clot came out.

Immediately after the blood clot was extracted my urine started flowing again and more than a liter and a half of urine emptied into my drainage bag within the next two minutes. My sweats and headache subsided within the next five minutes.

I felt I had escaped death one more time.

I reported the entire scenario – and seeming lack of concern or urgency by the nurse for a very serious situation – to the head of nursing before I left the hospital the next day. She apologized, saying she would talk to the people involved, and assured me that if I ever had to stay at that hospital again a situation like this would not occur. Too many close calls similar to this one have made me cynical over the years and I thought to myself, "Yeah, right." I find it ironic that my closest brushes with death occur when I'm in a hospital environment.

Hospital care is going to be the death of me yet.

CHAPTER 33

Gone Sailing (2003)

One of the hobbies I enjoyed for years was playing with remote-controlled model electric boats. I think I started this hobby around 1985 and kept up with it until around 2001 when I switched from electric boats to sailboats. With electric boats you have to keep a lot of rechargeable batteries on hand because they only lasted about ten minutes before the batteries are drained. Although I probably had collected about a dozen different electric boats over those years I usually only took two at a time to run at a lake or pond, along with about a dozen batteries that I fully charged the night before.

My electric boats were a lot of fun but because of the short duration of battery time it could get quite cumbersome to constantly switch batteries in and out of the boats. After fifteen years of switching out batteries, my interests turned to remote-control sailboats. Four AA batteries in the actual sailboat and six AA batteries in the remote control box were all that was needed. The batteries in the sailboat would last for about twelve to twenty hours of sailing time and the batteries in the remote control box would last for six months to a year.

Renegade Runaways

Remote controlled boats were great fun but had a couple downsides. When an electric boat experienced an internal mechanical problem it would go out of control and either stop or travel in circles until the battery ran out – usually a great distance from shore. Another problem that occurred in both the electric boats and sailboats was when they would travel out of range for the boat's receiver to pick up the signal from the remote control transmitter.

There was not much you could do but watch your boats escape farther and farther in the distance with no way to get them to turn back. However, for the lake where I live, I did purchase a small dingy that was lightweight and could be pushed into the water easily. Whenever I had a runaway boat one of my friends would get into the dinghy, row over to the uncontrolled boat, haul it into the dinghy, and then row back to shore.

Retrieving runaway remote controlled craft was usually only a small mess I got my friends into except the time when my grandson, Eric, used the dinghy to retrieve one of my runaway sailboats. As he attempted to bring the sailboat into the dinghy, the dinghy tipped over and he was dunked into the middle of the lake. Eric wasn't too happy when he got back to shore soaking wet. Although his cell phone was still in his pocket, it never worked again.

Without access to a rowboat, you were out of luck if one of your boats ran amok. You would have to wait until the boat drifted back into shore or con some friend to swim or wade in the water to retrieve it. If you were lucky and running remote controlled boats in a big enough lake, another boater might retrieve it for you. Since the occurrence of runaway boats was much greater with the remote-controlled electric boats than sailboats, I'm guessing my friends were very happy when I became interested in radio controlled model sailboats and got rid of my electric boats.

Hooked on Sailboat Races

I first became interested in remote-control sailboats during my trips down to Marco Island, Florida, which is very close to Naples. One year when I was there with Edward, he found an article in the paper that talked about the Naples model sailing club that would race their sailboats at some of the local ponds on Wednesdays and Saturdays.

Edward and I attended one of the scheduled races on the Wednesday we were there and I was hooked. From that point on every time we went down to Marco Island we would go and watch the sailboat races at least twice during our visit. I was becoming a regular spectator and started talking to some of the people who were running the remote-control sail-boats. I soon found out that some of them were in a model sailing club in Chicago and went down to Naples each year to spend the winter.

When I learned that there was a sailing club in Chicago, I immediately got on the club's web site when I got home and found the local number for their treasurer, whose name was Tom. I called Tom one day and, as serendipity would have it, he lived in the same town that I lived in and was only five or ten minutes away. I told him I had spoken with a few of his club members down in Naples and he knew who they were immediately. He said that there were quite a few members in the Chicago club and that they have sailing races every Sunday during the summer at a place called Axehead Lake, near the I-294 interstate and Touhy Exit around O'Hare Airport.

I asked Tom if we could get together sometime and if he would mind teaching me how to sail a remote-controlled sailboat. I told him that I lived on a lake just a couple miles from his house. Tom said he would be happy to show me how to sail these boats and I immediately purchased one.

Before long Tom would regularly come over with his sailboat and I would take mine and we would spend afternoons down at the lake in front of my house sailing our boats and having picnic lunches in the park area by the beach. It was always a great time and I was becoming a fanatic about sailing these model sailboats. I loved it so much that I ended up giving away all of my remote-controlled electric boats to my friends who had kids who would really enjoy them. From then on I was strictly a remote-controlled sailboat fan.

Through our shared interest in this hobby, Tom and I have become the greatest of friends ever since. Whether we're sailing, playing with my model trains, or just hanging out and trying different restaurants in the area we always have a great time together.

I Sail Away

Many times some of my other friends and I would get together and spend hours down at the lake and take turns sailing my boats. One of Diane's very close friends, Dave, who later became a good friend of mine as well, saw one of my friends and me coming back from the lake with the sailboat in tow. We had purchased a red Radio Flyer™ wagon to transport the sailboats because the sailboats are very tall and cumbersome to carry around by hand. If you put the keel on the ground the top of the sail would be between five and six feet above the ground depending upon which sailboat we would use. I had two of them and would usually take out only one per sailing session.

After seeing the boats, Dave said he would like to try sailing with me some afternoon. I was always looking for a sailing partner and because Dave was between jobs at the time, we scheduled a time to get together during the early afternoon the following week. On our scheduled day, my wife was at a doctor's appointment. When Dave rang the doorbell, I was all set to go and went out into the driveway. Dave opened the garage door and rolled out the wagon with the sailboat strapped on top with bungee cords.

To get down to the lake I drive my wheelchair down the cul-de-sac in front of my house to where the housing development sidewalk starts and then travel past the tennis courts to the blacktop pathway that leads down to the lake. It's only a block or two to the start of the pathway and a very easy ride in the electric wheelchair. However there is a steep incline from the top of the path down to lake level and I have to be very careful traversing in an electric wheelchair, so when Dave and I got to the top of the pathway that led down to the lake, I hooked one of my arms over the back of the electric wheelchair in order to get better balance while going down the incline.

It just so happened that day that I was using my old spare electric wheelchair because the other one was in the shop for some repairs. This particular wheelchair had the old-style belt drive mechanism rather than the newer style direct gear drives common in today's electric wheelchairs.

As I started down the path my wheelchair picked up speed and I realized I was going too fast to control it. I pulled back on the control lever to slow the wheelchair down, but it did not slow down. I knew right then I was in deep trouble and that the outcome could only be bad. The wheelchair gained momentum as it traveled down the hill and went faster and faster. There was absolutely nothing I could do. The wheelchair was completely out of my control and I just had to let whatever happened happen. The wheelchair drive belts must have been loose. Just like the fan belts in a car, if the drive belts get too loose, there is no tension between the belt and the pulleys. The pulley attached to the motor keeps spinning, but the belt doesn't move.

As my wheelchair sped down the path, it veered to the right. The right front wheel went off the blacktop path and the right side of the wheelchair hit the dense bushes along the shoulder of the pathway. The wheelchair then bounced off the bushes and toppled over, sending me sailing into the air and I landed about ten feet further down the blacktop path at the bottom of the hill.

This was not the type of sailing I intended to do on that day.

When I hit the pavement, I landed on my right side, and smashed my head on the blacktop. The electric wheelchair continued tumbling down the path after me, and when it ran into my legs it tipped over on top of me.

I knew I was hurt but I didn't know how badly. My head was pounding and I felt excruciating pain in my shoulder. I was still conscious and saw a wild-eyed Dave running to see if I was all right. I told him I was not feeling in that great of shape. He didn't have a cell phone with him so I told him to go to some of the neighboring houses to see if he could get to a telephone to dial 911. As he left, I tried fighting back the dizziness I was experiencing, and I believe that the pain in my shoulder was the only thing keeping me from losing consciousness. This was one of the worst falls out of my wheelchair I ever had.

Dave came back about five minutes later with one of my neighbors. He told me that he called 911 and that the paramedics were on their way. When the paramedics arrived I went through a routine I was all too familiar with. As I lay there in great pain and tried to stay conscious, I had to play "Twenty Questions" about what happened. You'd think it would seem pretty obvious to them with the wheelchair toppled over next to me and me sprawled out in the middle of the pathway near the bottom of the steep hill.

After Dave and I told our stories, the paramedics said they would have to call for another ambulance because they did not have enough people to get me on a stretcher and lift me up themselves. Another ten minutes went by before I heard the sirens from the other ambulance in the distance. After about fifteen minutes more I was lifted into the back of one of the ambulances. The paramedic that was attending me in back of the ambulance asked me which one of two trauma centers I would like to go to. I said, "The closest one."

While I was being taken to a trauma center, Dave went back to my house and tried getting in touch with my wife. By that time she was probably on her way home from her doctor's appointment. Dave did not have her cell phone number, so he waited until she got home to tell her I had been taken to the hospital.

This is America! No Insurance, No Exam

When I arrived at the hospital, I was immediately taken into the emergency room where I again answered the same twenty questions. By now my head was a little clearer, but the pain in my shoulder was much more intense. I asked for some kind of medication to help ease the pain but was told that I could not have any because I did not have my insurance card with me. I would have to wait until my wife brought it from home.

Since I had never been to this hospital before, none of my medical records were available. Diane called the hospital to find out what was happening and told them she was on her way. However, they failed to mention to her that I was not being treated because they did not have my insurance information.

I couldn't believe it. I had to endure an additional half-hour of pain and they wouldn't even take me into x-ray without having my insurance card in their hot little hands. What the hell kind of medical system do we have here in America? I guess because I was conscious and could communicate they felt they could wait.

When Diane arrived and straightened out the insurance information, I finally had x-rays taken. The x-rays showed that my skull was okay but I had fractured my right shoulder. It was not a complete break so their brilliant solution was to give me some painkillers and put a sling around my neck to rest my right arm in.

I said I could not move my arm; it was completely paralyzed from the shoulder down. I was told not to worry because my arm was probably swollen and, when the swelling went down, my movement would come back. I thought to myself, "Yeah, right!"

Although I can't feel anything from the chest down, my shoulder was another story. The pain was almost unbearable every time my shoulder moved the slightest little bit. Diane brought my wheelchair with her to the hospital in case I could be released. The hospital released me but, with my right arm in a sling, I could not control the electric wheelchair myself because the control box is on the right side of the chair.

Four people lifted me off the gurney and sat me in the wheelchair, and Dave released the brakes so he could push the chair to my waiting van, but it wouldn't budge. It was bent out of shape from the fall and the only way the wheelchair would move was by engaging the belts and using the wheelchair's electric controls. So there I was going down the hallway with my wife guiding the wheelchair from behind and Dave pushing the control stick to steer the wheelchair. The drive belts still slipped, but the wheelchair was able to move on level ground.

Diane and Dave managed to get me into my handicap van and drive me home. Dave kept on saying he was sorry about what happened, but there was no way he could have done anything to stop the runaway wheelchair. It was just one of those unfortunate things that happens to me from time to time. I really felt sorry for Dave because he felt so guilty about it and there was nothing I could say or do to assuage his guilt.

I guess this was just another fine mess I got a friend into.

Six Weeks of Uncertainty

I left the hospital with orders to go about my normal routine but to refrain from using my right arm. Were these people morons, or what? They clearly were oblivious to me being a quadriplegic who needs to use an electric wheelchair to get around. Without use of my right arm, my "routine" was dramatically altered.

When I got home I could not even get into bed the way I normally do. We had to call a couple friends to lift me into bed without putting much strain on my right arm and shoulder. The pain from being lifted into bed that day was an experience I did not want to repeat for quite awhile. And there was no way I could use my overhead body lift to get in or out of my wheelchair, much less control it with an arm I could not move.

This was a no-win situation. I would have to stay confined in bed until my shoulder healed.

The doctor said it could take six weeks or more for my shoulder to heal, which was an awfully long time for me to spend in bed without ever getting up. After the first night in bed I was unable to move my right shoulder or arm at all. It felt like my entire right side was paralyzed. I called my physician and told him of my concerns. He assured me that the inability to move my arm was probably due to the swelling and that I would get some movement back as soon as the swelling went down.

After my first couple of weeks in bed, the swelling subsided and my arm and shoulder were back to their normal size. Unfortunately I still could not move either one no matter how much I concentrated. I had the same response in my shoulder and arm that I had for forty-four years in trying to move my legs.

I started to panic. I called the doctor and told him that the swelling was gone but I still could not move my arm or shoulder. As anticipated, I heard a familiar response: be patient. There is no reason the movement should not come back. Once again I thought to myself, "Yeah, right!"

After four weeks of lying in bed, my right side still felt paralyzed. This lack of improvement put me in the deepest depression I had since my original accident. If my right arm was going to be permanently paralyzed, my future looked pretty bleak. At least with the limited movement I had in my arms after I broke my neck I was able to live a relatively normal life. But without being able to move my right arm, I felt I would be bedridden for the rest of my life. That was something I could not tolerate, so I called the doctor again. Again I was told to be patient and that my shoulder would eventually get back to normal. He said to come to see him after the sixth week. It was getting harder and harder to believe him but I agreed to wait two more weeks at which time he could examine the shoulder and arm for himself.

Rescued By a Train

My friend, Bob Honesty, had a great deal to do with lifting me out of that depression and came to visit every couple of days. One day he mentioned that when I got up and around again, he and one of his friends would build a nice small model train layout for me in my office. He told me that while I was still in bed I should start thinking about what the layout should look like and what kind of equipment and scenery I would want.

Bob had been into models trains since he was a kid and always had huge train layouts in the basement of his home. My brother and I also had train layouts when we were kids but lost interest in them as we got older. Right after my accident, I had a small layout on a worktable in my bedroom at my parent's house in South Milwaukee, Wisconsin. I enjoyed operating it, but found that I could not control much of the equipment without the use of my fingers so I eventually lost interest.

Bob explained to me that model trains have come a long way and that it was possible to get something called DCC equipment. DCC stands for Digital Command Control. Trains and switches now contained small computers and DCC allows the train operator to use a simple turn knob or keypad to control trains and switches. It sounded great to me. I talked with Diane about it and she agreed to our purchasing the equipment and having Bob and his friend build a small unobtrusive layout in my office area. I spent the next few weeks on the Internet looking at equipment and planning my train layout. It really raised my spirits and kept my mind focused on other things besides my shoulder and arm. I now had something to look forward to.

Back on Track

When it was time to go for my six-week doctor's exam I was helped out of bed by a few of my friends. My shoulder did not hurt any more, but I still had no use of my shoulder or arm. I was pushed into the doctor's office in one of the portable push wheelchairs I keep for emergency purposes.

I shared my concerns with the doctor about not ever being able to use my arm again. He said there was no reason that I should not get the full movement back that I had before the shoulder injury. He told me to continue to be patient and that it would just take time.

He was right.

Slowly but surely the movement in my arm and shoulder started to come back. I would exercise my wrist, arm and shoulder every day and occasionally went for muscle massages on my shoulder. It took four or five months before the use of my right side was back to where it was before I fractured my shoulder.

If there's one thing I learned to appreciate from this experience, it's to not take things for granted. I lived as a quadriplegic for all those years but after this incident I realized that things could always be worse. You can't know how grateful I was to be back to my old self. And now I had a new hobby. Trains!

It's now many years after my "sailing" incident and I think my wife regrets the day she agreed I could start this new hobby – train layouts have taken over three rooms in our house and our entire patio.

CHAPTER 34

Rocky Mountain Low (2006)

My Train Obsession

One hobby that I began after I retired was setting up and running model trains. My brother and I had model trains when we were kids but until I built my own house, I really never had any room to construct a model railroad layout.

I enjoy all aspects of having trains as a hobby, including visiting train museums and conventions around the country, reading the history of trains, riding on old-style trains, and designing, building, and operating model train layouts. Because I really can't use my hands to build any-thing by myself I'm glad that my friends are also into the hobby so they can construct my layouts.

Bob Honesty had model trains all his life and actually re-ignited my interest in the hobby. He convinced my wife and me (although it didn't take much to convince me) that we only needed a small corner of my office to put an N gauge (sometimes referred to as N scale) train layout. Since N gauge trains, track, scenery, and buildings are very small, it doesn't take much room to set up a good layout. You can set up a pretty big layout on a 4'x 8' piece of plywood.

Well, if you've ever been a serious train hobbyist, you know that there's no such thing as "enough room" to build the layout you want, and no matter how much time you put into your layout it is truly never done. Train layouts have now taken over my entire office, my stereo room, the dining room upstairs, part of the living room upstairs, and my entire 18'x 43' patio where I have a large garden scale layout (G gauge or scale). I also have train display cases in most of the hallways in the house. I guess you could say I sometimes get a little bit carried away with things.

My wife regrets the day she ever let Bob convince us to start this little train hobby. But every time she complains to me about trains, I tell her not to blame me – it's Bob Honesty she should be chastising. Bob might tell you differently, but it is truly all his fault. My wife tells me all the time that he's lucky to be alive after getting me into this hobby and one of these days she might actually do something about it. I hope I'm not around when she does.

Fueling my obsession about model trains isn't the first fine mess that Bob has ever gotten me into but it's probably the most expensive. Oh, wait. I take that back. He recently got me into a more expensive project that I will share with you later in this chapter. Bob and I have been friends for over thirty years and you'd think I would have learned by now not to get involved with some of his harebrained schemes but somehow it keeps happening.

A Trip of a Lifetime

Once I retired, I really looked forward to doing some traveling, but hospital stays and major surgeries plagued my early retirement years. In 2006, I was in the best health I had been in for quite awhile. Bob Honesty, Edward Weishaar, and I planned a great seventeen-day trip. Our plan was to first go to Colorado, take in a few steam train rides around the state, and then head to Arizona to see the Grand Canyon. The three of us had talked about taking this trip for many years and we finally had the chance to do it.

When you're a model train fanatic all aspects of trains are interesting. The main reason Bob, Edward, and I planned this trip was to ride as many old steam trains in the mountains as we could, and visit the Colorado Railroad Museum in Golden. We planned the details out over the course of eight months and made reservations for some great train excursions at:

Royal Gorge Train Excursion in Canon City, Colorado

Cumbers & Toltec Railroad Excursion in Antonito, Colorado

Durango & Silverton Railroad Excursion in Durango, Colorado

As much as I look forward to traveling, I have always been limited in how many sights I can actually see along the way when traveling in my handicapped van. My wheelchair sits so high that if I am sitting up straight my eye level is even with the inside border of the extra high top of the van. From that vantage point all I can see through the front window is the road, two car lengths in front of the van. From the side windows, my viewpoint reaches only as far as the shoulder of the road.

Because of numerous surgeries I have had on my butt to repair pressure sores, I can now only sit straight up in the wheelchair for a few minutes at a time. The electric wheelchair I currently use is a tilt back wheelchair. When I push a button, the whole top part of the wheelchair tilts backward so that I can relieve the pressure on my butt. I usually tilt the wheelchair back about every five minutes for a minute or two. It probably sounds like a real pain in the ass (literally) – and it is – but after awhile I got used to it and it is definitely better than spending weeks in the hospital and months in bed trying to heal pressure sores.

When I am in my van I usually stay in the tilted back position ninety percent of the time. This allows me to pretty much to keep the pressure off my butt while traveling long distances. However, when I am in this position in the van, the only thing I can really see is the carpeted van ceiling. This can be very boring and annoying when the other people in the van are pointing out the windows and talking about the great sites they are seeing. After all the planning we did for our three-week trip, I didn't want to miss any part of it.

Putting the "Sight" Back Into Sightseeing

Determined not to miss a single moment of our trip, I searched for and found an ingenious way to see the sights while staring at the ceiling when traveling in the van.

I came across a web site that sold miniature TV cameras that racecar drivers put on their vehicles. The cameras attach to the outside of the van using suction cups that are supposed to hold securely even at speeds of more than a hundred miles an hour. Since we would probably not drive any faster than seventy miles per hour, I thought these would work. We attached them to the van, took it for a test drive, and the suction cups held tight. We were on our way to a solution.

The other component I needed was a TV monitor to connect to the camera, so I had a TV monitor installed in the ceiling of my van. It was installed just a couple of feet from where my head is positioned when my wheelchair is in a fully tilted position. The camera-with-monitor solution worked great and I was finally going to be able to enjoy the scenery when we drove throughout Colorado.

Although the view I see on the TV monitor is not quite the same as looking out the window it is a lot better than looking at the carpeted ceiling. If the sun is directly in front of the camera it washes out the picture to the point of not being able to see anything. So periodically I have to change the position of the cameras depending on the sun's position and the direction we are traveling. I had two cameras, one usually facing out the front of the van and the other one facing out the side. The TV monitor has a remote I use to move back and forth between the two views.

I also purchased a new 4' x 6' trailer to haul an extra wheelchair and medical supplies for the seventeen days we would be gone. Because of the modifications that were done to make my van handicap accessible, I had to have a custom-made trailer hitch installed on my van to pull the trailer. We spent a lot of time preparing for this trip and by the time we were ready to leave, the trailer was so full that we could hardly shut the door.

Going Up?

Bob, Ed, and I were finally ready to start our trip. On June 11, 2006 at exactly 8:12:46 a.m., we started the van engine and pulled out of my driveway and headed for Colorado and a great adventure. We were finally on our way for what we anticipated would be a very memorable trip.

And memorable, it was – in a very different way than originally planned.

We allowed three days to get to Colorado and since there wasn't much to see as we traveled through Illinois, Iowa, and Nebraska, we figured that our trip would really start when we finally reached Colorado with its majestic mountains. Our first train excursion was scheduled to take place on the fourth day of the trip and we eagerly anticipated the rail journey that went through the Royal Gorge, which departed from Canon

City, Colorado. But before we ever made it to Canon City, I started to have problems.

What kind of problems? The kind of problems I have from an overly inflated air cushion.

With my background in physics, I knew that as we went up in elevation the air inside the cushion would expand with the change in atmospheric pressure. The challenge for this trip would be in determining how much air to let out of the cushion based on the increasing elevations we would be traveling through during our trip. A cushion that is too hard is just as bad as one that is too soft. In both instances I can get pressure sores very quickly.

We knew it would be very hit and miss trying to adjust the air levels in the cushion as the elevation changed. As part of our trip preparations I actually did an elevation survey for the first few towns we would be traveling to in order to get a feel for what the elevation differences would be. I knew that once we got to Antonito, Colorado, we would have probably passed through the highest elevations we would encounter while traveling in the van. Here are some of the elevations I detailed:

839 feet	Chicago, Illinois
958 feet	Des Moines, Iowa
2800 feet	North Platte, Nebraska
5332 feet	Canon City, Colorado
7888 feet	Antonito, Colorado

On our first day out from Chicago to Des Moines, Iowa, there really was not much of a difference in elevation and I had no problems whatsoever. The second day of the trip we went from Des Moines, Iowa, to North Platte, Nebraska. When we arrived in North Platte, I noticed that my air cushion was a lot harder than normal. After checking my butt that evening when I went to bed, it was noticeably pinker than normal. This could have resulted from the combination of the heat, which was setting all records that summer of well over 90 degrees, and the cushion, which was harder than normal. Before I got in the wheelchair the next morning we let out a little bit of air from my cushion in anticipation of traveling into higher elevations that day.

The third day we traveled from North Platte, Nebraska to Canon City, Colorado, where we had tickets for the Royal Gorge train excursion the following morning. When I went to bed that night, my air cushion was as hard as a rock and my butt was extremely red and swollen. I couldn't believe how much the change in elevation from North Platte to Canon City expanded the air cushion.

Edward went to the back of the trailer to get the box that contained my spare air cushion. When he grabbed the box, he found that it was all ripped apart – the air cushion had expanded so much that it exploded the package it was packed in. I thought, "This is not good – not good at all." I hoped that by the next morning the redness on my backside would subside and the swelling would go down. I knew however that my chances of quickly recovering were not great. A pressure sore can develop within an hour and we had traveled over ten hours that day with me sitting on a pretty hard cushion.

Pressure sores are caused by a lack of blood flowing through live healthy tissue. They usually start from the bone area you sit on, killing all of the live tissue above it. By the time you actually see swelling and redness on the surface of your skin, the damage underneath has already been done. My only hope was that this was superficial because, even though I sat up quite a bit whenever we stopped for gas, lunch, and dinner, I was in a fully tilted position for most of the drive.

All Aboard

The next morning we checked my butt and noticed that the swelling and redness had subsided somewhat. We let a lot of air out of the wheelchair cushion so that it was about the same firmness as when we left home.

After breakfast we went on the Royal Gorge train excursion, which lasted a few hours. It was fantastic. I sat in an open-air gondola train car during the excursion as we traveled through the bottom of the gorge with the river rapids below and the sheer cliffs to the side and above. It was another day of record-setting temperatures, well into the mid and upper nineties, but it wasn't as noticeable as the train sped through the gorge. I remembered that many friends said not to worry about the heat; it's a dry heat. Yeah, right! Heat is heat and boy, was it hot!

The Royal Gorge excursion was a great and beautiful trip. I would highly recommend it to anybody traveling in the area. It's not too far from Denver and the gorge, roaring river rapids, and sheer cliffs are magnificent and memorable. I would love to take that train excursion again.

We left the Royal Gorge station in Canon City early in the afternoon and continued on to Antonito, Colorado, where we were scheduled to go on the Cumbers & Toltec Railroad Excursion the next morning. It was only about a four-hour drive and the scenery was spectacular all the way. As we wound our way through the mountains I realized we were reaching higher elevations. I was very concerned about what shape my butt would be in by the time we reached Antonito.

So Close and Yet So Far

We arrived in Antonito late afternoon and immediately went to our hotel. The hotel was actually within walking distance to the train station for the Cumbers & Toltec Railroad Excursion the next morning. After we pulled into the parking lot we heard the steam train's whistle in the distance, and ten or fifteen minutes later we saw the train pull into the station from that day's excursion.

All three of us were extremely excited about taking that same train tomorrow for an eight-hour sightseeing trip. It was the longest train excursion we had planned and was considered the highlight of our entire trip. Months before I had ordered a couple of railroad DVDs that were taken of this entire excursion with footage from different vantage points along the rail line. We watched them a few times in the months before our trip and they showed such spectacular scenery along the route that we couldn't wait to actually see it live.

After we unloaded the suitcases from the trailer, I decided I should go to bed. I immediately wondered what my butt situation would be like. When Edward turned me over and checked my backside, all I heard was, "Oh my God!"

My heart sank. I got a very bad feeling in the pit of my stomach and knew what was coming next.

I asked him how bad it was. He told me that where the swelling had been on both cheeks yesterday there were now two holes, each about the size of a nickel, that went all the way down to my bones.

I can't even begin to describe the range of emotions I went through in the next thirty seconds. I had gone through this the year before when a new cushion I was using became defective. I knew that I would have to have major surgery almost immediately. And I also knew that I would be in a hospital for at least four to six weeks and then another three or four months at home recovering.

Bob came over to take a look and confirmed that the situation was as bad as Edward had said it was. It looked like the trip we were planning on for so long was over before it really got started. I felt so bad for Bob and Edward, and guilty about what just happened.

So there I was, four days from home with an ass I should not be sitting on. What was I to do next?

After the emotional level settled down, the three of us discussed what to do next. The first thing was to let Diane know what was happening. Bob had a digital camera with a flash attachment and he took a couple pictures of my butt. We e-mailed them to Diane through the computer Bob brought with him. Once she saw the photos, she knew it was not good news and that I would need major surgery.

It was too late to do anything that night, but we did look up the telephone numbers of a few of the hospitals between Antonito and Denver. The next morning I called a few of them and explained the situation. I was told that I would first have to set up a doctor's appointment and they would determine what to do from there. I was also told it would take a few days to get an appointment.

This was nuts!

After calling the emergency rooms of a couple of the hospitals I was told that there was little they could do to treat these pressure sores except to keep them clean and bandaged until I could be evaluated for surgery. I can certainly keep them clean on my own so Bob, Edward, and I decided that we would go back to Illinois as quickly as we could.

We packed up the trailer and left Antonito just before noon. As we passed the train station, we saw the steam coming from the stack of the locomotive as it prepared to depart on the excursion we were supposed to be on. To have all our plans completely dashed because of my medical condition was a very depressing moment for all of us. We were so close and yet so far.

During the trip back home I stayed in the fully tilted position and we did not get out of the van for lunch or breaks. We stopped only for gas and to stay in a hotel each night. Whenever we arrived at a hotel, I immediately got into bed and lay on my side. Bob and Edward would go to dinner and bring me back something to eat, which I had to eat while I lay on my side. The next morning they would go to breakfast, get me dressed and into the van, and we spent another full day traveling. With both Edward and Bob driving we managed to get back home in three days.

Planes, Trains, and Motor Homes

While we were traveling home, Diane spoke with my plastic surgeon and sent him the pictures that Bob had taken of my butt. By the time we got home, Diane had already arranged for me to enter the hospital within a week and surgery was scheduled for the day after I was admitted, once blood tests were done and the lab results came back.

Surgery was actually in two parts. The day after I was admitted to the hospital I went into surgery to have the damaged area cleaned out and all the damaged tissue removed. At that time they also took a bone biopsy to make sure I didn't have a bone infection. Two days later I had major surgery that entailed moving muscle from both of my inner thighs into the area where I sit. They packed these muscles and other tissue into the buttocks area and then placed what is called "skin flap" over the entire cheeks.

As I expected, I was in the hospital and a related rehabilitation clinic for more than six weeks before I could go home. I then spent another eight weeks in bed with a vacuum pump on my butt in order to close the wounds entirely. I never want to go through an operation like this again – but I still wanted to travel as much as possible. I needed to find a better – and lower risk – solution.

I didn't want to sit around the house and go nowhere the rest of my life but I also didn't want to be caught more than a day's ride from my home in case something would happen. How was I ever going to travel to different parts of the country?

Traveling by airplane was completely out of the question, not only because of all the problems I had earlier in life but also because now it is almost impossible to get through the airports.

I checked Amtrak routes, thinking I could take the train to a specific destination and then rent a handicap van to travel around to different places in the area. It is easier to rent a handicap van than it used to be and they are available in just about any city within the United States. Although this Amtrak solution seemed doable, accommodations in an Amtrak train car are very limited, with barely enough room to turn around. Traveling for a few days at a time could be rather difficult. I started brainstorming with my friends and it was at this point that Bob Honesty got me into trouble again.

Bob suggested I make a few calls to find out if I could rent a motor home that was handicap equipped. This sounded reasonable and I spent some time searching the Web to find out where I could rent a motor home like that. To my dismay, the only places I could rent a handicap motor home were in England, Australia, and New Zealand. Not the United States. But I didn't give up on this idea.

After not being able to locate a handicap equipped motor home that I could rent, I started calling a few motor home manufacturers to see if they actually made a handicap-accessible model and how much it would cost.

When I contacted Winnebago Industries, I found out that the company has an entire department devoted to making motor homes accessible for people with disabilities. I guess with the baby boomer generation getting older but far more interested in travel than generations before, there is much more of a market for this sort of thing. After talking with the representative from Winnebago Industries I soon realized that this approach was not only feasible, it was possible.

Yes, buying a custom motor home would cost a lot of money (thank you, Bob Honesty, for once again depleting my finances). But one of the reasons my wife and I worked all these years was to be able retire and enjoy life. Diane and I talked things over and we decided we could afford to make this investment – so we ordered one.

The modifications I needed made to their standard model were actually very minimal. A wheelchair lift was installed next to the door so I had access in and out of the motor home. The back bedroom was modified to include a body lift, also called a patient lift, on a track system installed in the ceiling that would maneuver over a hospital bed. I could then move my wheelchair under the body lift, attach a sling under my legs and back, be lifted up in the air, moved over above the hospital bed using the track on the ceiling, and then lowered into the bed. With this set up, if I ever have a problem while traveling I could at least stay in the hospital bed in back of the motor home.

At the time of this writing, the motor home has been delivered and we already took it out for a quick five-day "test trip" without venturing too far from home. It worked out great. The people at Winnebago Industries did a fantastic job. The trip exceeded all my expectations. Because of the large windows, I was able to see the beautiful scenery as we traveled up the Wisconsin side of the Mississippi River and then across the state through Rhinelander, Wisconsin, and then down through Devils Lake to the south.

After all these years, I finally found a decent way to travel around the country. We already have a twenty-day trip planned to go to Florida and Louisiana in a couple weeks, and we're already talking about trying to get to Alaska in the next year or so.

I guess I should thank Bob for getting me motivated enough to research this solution. It will allow me to do the traveling I want to do while minimizing the potential for having major medical issues during the trip. Since Bob and Edward are probably going to be the two people I travel with most of the time, only time will tell how many new adventure stories I'll have to tell.

Which one of us gets the others into our next fine mess still remains to be seen.

CHAPTER 35

Two Femurs are Better than One (2007)

In September of 2007 Edward and I traveled to Forrest City, Iowa, where Winnebago motor homes are manufactured. Winnebago was custom making a motor home to fit my handicap needs with the following modifications:

- Install a wheelchair lift so I could enter and exit the motor home.
- Install a body lift in the back bedroom so that I could be lifted out of my wheelchair and into bed and vice versa. The ceiling would be reinforced so the body lift, and ceiling track it rides in, would support my weight.
- Install wheelchair tie downs so that my wheelchair would be securely fastened when riding in the front area of the motor home.

I had purchased the motor home from Winnebago Industries a few weeks before and Edward and I went there to get a fitting for the positioning of the wheelchair tie downs. The fitting went well and we left the Winnebago Industries' plant early in the afternoon. We had planned to stay in town overnight before continuing our trip to see a couple of friends of mine in St. Cloud, Minnesota. However, the weather in Iowa turned stormy. Since we were finished at the plant earlier than we expected, we decided to cancel our local hotel reservations and continue traveling north toward St. Cloud where the weather was still clear.

We decided to stop at a hotel about a half-hour from St. Cloud, figuring that we would stay overnight and have breakfast before going to St. Cloud the next morning. We checked in, went to the room, and as I was getting into bed I heard a loud crack that sounded like a gunshot. As soon as I heard that sound I knew I had broken a bone somewhere in my body but with no feeling from the chest down, I couldn't tell where. Edward finished getting me into bed and removed my trousers. My left leg looked like I had two kneecaps; one about a foot above the other.

I had definitely broken a bone.

Edward immediately went to the front desk and asked the person there to call for an ambulance. When the ambulance arrived I was taken to the local hospital and, after taking a few x-rays, they confirmed that I had broken my left femur in half.

The small local hospital was unable to admit me and I was to be transferred to a larger hospital nearby. I was told I would probably have surgery shortly after arriving at the other hospital so I was not allowed to eat or drink anything. I had not had anything to eat and very little to drink since that morning and it was now seven in the evening so I was dehydrated. They tried starting an IV but struggled to find a decent vein in either my hands or arms. On the first try they blew a vein. On the second try they blew a vein. On the third, fourth, and fifth tries they blew a vein. When they finally got one in my arm they had already tried six different locations. I guess to "blow a vein" is medical speak for, "It didn't work when I stuck the needle there so we're going to stick a needle somewhere else."

Bigger Hospital, Bigger Problems

After an hour's wait, the ambulance came and transferred me to the larger hospital. Once there I had to tell the story about what happened for about the sixth time in the last couple of hours before being taken to that hospital's x-ray department for another batch to be taken. Sure enough, it was still broken and in the exact spot the previous x-ray showed. Were they expecting to see something different?

The hospital staff wanted to get a better IV started in my arm but had the same problem as the first hospital did because of my dehydration. This time it only took five tries before they managed to get a small IV needle started in my arm and hung a one-liter IV solution from my gurney.

I was told a surgeon was being called and I would possibly have surgery as soon as he got to the hospital so I should not eat or drink anything. When they finally got in contact with the surgeon he said he would schedule the surgery for normal morning hours so I was still not to eat or drink anything. I was finally admitted and got to my room around three in the morning with the same one-liter IV solution hanging next to my bed until I awoke around daylight.

When the morning nursing shift came in one of the nurses told me that my surgery was postponed until early afternoon. Once again, I was not to eat or drink anything. I looked up at the IV solution hanging next to my bed and noticed that only about a quarter of the bag was empty. I knew the bag was unchanged from the night before and mentioned this to the nurse. Evidently the wrong drip rate was set because she looked at the IV drip gauge and then increased the rate of flow.

My dehydration was now very serious and my blood pressure was extremely low – even for me. As a quadriplegic I usually have a low blood pressure anyway – about 85/65 give or take five points. I asked for a small sip of water but was told I could have none because of the impending surgery.

Not being allowed any water – not even the tiniest sip – before surgery is a "rule" that I hear over and over and I really wonder how much validity there is to it. Was it something someone once said and it's been repeated so many times that it is now the rule? Nobody can explain to my satisfaction why drinking a couple of ounces of water would be harmful a couple of hours before surgery – especially if the patient is dehydrated and would absorb that water very quickly. One of the explanations I've been given is that there is a possibility for the water to back up into my throat and choke me while I am asleep from the anesthesia. I wonder what the percentage truly is of this happening.

A few hours later a couple of people came in the room and wheeled my bed down to the pre-operating area. The anesthesiologist came by and said that I would be given a general anesthetic. I asked him why he needed any anesthetic at all because they would be working on my leg and I have no feeling from my chest down.

The anesthesiologist paused for a minute with a strange look on his face and then answered that it was because my legs might spasm during surgery and the anesthetic would prevent that from happening. He also said that they were going to have some other medication on hand in case my blood pressure went up. I told him that drugs to lower my blood pressure were dangerous for me to take because I have autonomic dysreflexia. Since this is a condition that spinal cord injury people often have I assumed that as a medical doctor he understood what autonomic dysreflexia was.

Boy do I get in a lot of trouble when I "assume" things.

The anesthesiologist looked at me like I didn't know what I was talking about – he knew better, of course, because he went to medical school. He told me not to worry because they would monitor things very closely during surgery. I always get a little fearful when a doctor tells me not to worry.

I again told him not to give me anything to bring down my blood pressure unless my blood pressure gets so high that I am in danger of a heart attack or stroke. With that he just smiled – a little condescendingly in my opinion – and went away as they wheeled me into surgery.

In the operating room the surgeon again explained to me the procedure he would be performing. He told me that they will be placing a titanium rod in my femur after taking out some of the bone marrow and that if everything went well I could probably be out of the hospital in a couple days. I told him that was great news because I would like to get out of Minnesota and back home to Illinois, as soon as possible. As soon as the surgeon finished his explanation, the anesthesiologist put me to sleep.

The Event

The next thing I remembered was feeling extremely relaxed and euphoric at the same time. I wanted this blissful feeling to remain forever; just free my mind of everything, let go, and drift away. I barely perceived that something was intruding and upsetting the tranquil state I was in. I heard very faint sounds in the distance and I just wanted them to go away. I felt comfortable, with no worries and I wanted it to stay that way. But those sounds grew louder and then I recognized the sound of voices. I was thinking that if I ignored them they would go away and I could return to this unbelievably pleasurable feeling. Then I thought that if I could tell them to go away they would leave me alone and I could return to that wonderful comfort zone.

As I tried to understand what they were saying the voices got louder and angrier. I then realized I was coming out of anesthesia. I had not yet opened my eyes, but I could hear about a half a dozen people arguing loudly around me. I only heard fragments of the argument but they were saying that they would have to do something about my condition soon, and that they should probably inform another specialist doctor because whatever they were doing to me was not working.

When I opened my eyes I saw four people on one side of me, and three people on the other side of me. As soon as they noticed I had opened my eyes and was conscious they stopped arguing and seemed relieved.

One person asked me if I could talk but before I could answer that question someone else asked me what my name was. For a split-second I considered being a wise guy by giving them a bogus name. Two of my favorites are "Emo Zibinski" and "Dward Fartquart" but I thought better of it because this seemed like a serious situation. I answered by giving them my real name.

I was then asked how I felt. Again, I was tempted to be a wise ass by giving my usual response of "with my hands." Instead I just told them that I have felt better in my life but that I was okay. I then asked them if I could have something to drink. I was told that because of doctor's orders I could have nothing to eat or drink but could suck on some ice chips. I think I said, "To hell with the chips give me the whole ice cube." One person went to get me some ice chips and all but one of the others left the room.

The person who stayed behind told me that they were all very concerned about me. She asked me if I remembered anything about the event.

Event? What event? How could I remember the event if I was just waking up?

I asked how bad the event was. She told me that my blood pressure bottomed out – it dropped to 60/10. I really didn't understand what that rate of blood pressure meant. It didn't however sound like the event was a good thing and I thought it was better not to question her further.

I asked her what time it was and found out that I had been in the recovery room for the last three hours. Usually it only takes about an hour in recovery before they take me back to my room so I had no clue what was going on during all that time.

As one of the other people brought the ice chips, Edward came rushing in along with my brother, Bill, who came to be with me from his home in Rhinelander, Wisconsin. They were both very upset because they were not informed about what was going on with me the past three hours. The surgeon had told them that everything went well with the surgery and that I would be sent up to my hospital room within the hour. They could wait for me there. They went up to my hospital room and waited but after an hour they questioned the nurse on the floor about what was taking so long. But she couldn't understand why I wasn't back in my room yet, either.

The nurse called down to the recovery room and found out that I still had not regained consciousness so I would be there a little longer. After another hour, my brother was more than slightly ticked off so he called the recovery room himself. He was told that when I was better they would send me to the intensive care unit.

For the next hour or so Bill kept calling and they kept giving him the runaround so Edward and Bill came down to the recovery room and demanded to be let in. By that time I was just getting my ice chips. Bill spent about five minutes relating their story to me and then it was time to take me out of the recovery room. But instead of taking me back to my regular hospital room I was taken to the intensive care unit (ICU). Of course I asked why and of course they gave me the usual generic answer: it was strictly precautionary.

"I Don't Need No More Stinkin' Blood!"

When I arrived in the ICU they immediately started giving me a couple of units of blood. Again I asked why and was told that my blood pressure was low and the doctor had ordered a blood transfusion. I was now starting to feel uncomfortable with – and suspicious of – all that was going on. I was feeling well but it seemed they were doing a lot of things with me that were out of the norm for someone coming out of anesthesia after a fairly routine surgery.

I demanded to talk with my doctor. When I finally got him on the phone he told me that my lab tests showed that my hemoglobin level was below the normal range and they had to give me a couple units of blood to get it back up into the normal range. Gee, do you think being severely dehydrated and not being allowed to eat for the last few days might have something to do with my out of whack blood pressure or hemoglobin level?

The entire first evening in the ICU a blood pressure cuff was strapped to my arm and attached to a machine that checked my blood pressure every fifteen minutes. I was also given two units of blood. In the morning they took more blood to test in the lab to see if my hemoglobin level was up. It wasn't. I was told I was going to get two more units of blood early that afternoon.

I finally asked what a normal hemoglobin range was and what my current level was so I could monitor how far out of range I really was. Once I had this information I was able to confirm for myself that the tests showed I was still out of range so I allowed them to give me two more units of blood.

The blood pressure machine continued taking my blood pressure and it finally started going up. This was great. My doctor said he would not release me from the hospital until my blood pressure stabilized and my hemoglobin was within the normal range.

After the two units of blood given to me that afternoon they again took blood tests. The results showed that I was just below the lowest level of the normal range. The nurse came back and said that I would probably need a couple more units of blood. I told her 'no way' and I demanded to see or talk to my doctor again.

When my doctor came in I explained the situation from my point of view. I came in for a broken bone that was supposed to be a simple procedure. Fully expecting to be out and on my way home in a couple of days, I was now going on my fourth day and I hadn't even made it out of the ICU.

The doctor talked about wanting to get my hemoglobin levels up. I told him, yes, I knew what the lab results showed and that my current level was just below the bottom end of the range. I also said that I did not want to be transfused with any more blood and that my blood pressure, although still low, was pretty much normal for me as a quadriplegic.

The doctor did admit that I was making progress and I think he was a bit surprised that I seemed to know what I was talking about. He then said that, because my blood pressure was increasing and stabilizing, I could be transferred to a regular hospital room the next morning. He would then check the blood test results and let me know if he would recommend any more transfusions. I left it at that for the time being.

Enough Is Enough

The next morning I was transferred to a normal hospital room and my hemoglobin level was at the very low-end of the normal range. My condition was somewhat back to normal so I started pushing for my release. When the doctor came in he said that things were looking better and that if the situation was the same tomorrow morning he would release me to a nursing home in the city for six to eight weeks of recovery so he could monitor my situation.

I could not believe what I just heard.

Before surgery, the doctor told me that I would be out of the hospital in a few days but he never said a word about expecting me to go to a nursing home for six to eight weeks. I'd had enough and would have no more of this bullsh*t.

Once before I was sent to the nursing home wing of the hospital I was in after major surgery and received care so bad I wouldn't even have called it a medical institution. I know that it is hard for caregivers in a regular hospital to understand how to take care of a quadriplegic, but it is a whole different situation for a quadriplegic to go into a nursing home – especially for a short duration. Nursing home caregivers generally don't have a clue about what a quadriplegic is, much less knowing how to take care of one.

I told the doctor that I would get better care at home because of all the handicap modifications I made when I had my house built. I further told him there was no way I would be going into a nursing home for six to eight weeks – not here or anywhere else. I assured him that when I got back home I would have another bone surgeon follow-up on my fracture and relay my progress to him. I was ten hours from home and it was a long drive so I just wanted to get out of that hospital and back to more familiar surroundings.

The doctor said he would think about it and we could talk about it again the next day. Before he left the room I gave him the telephone number of the plastic surgeon who performed surgery on me the year before. He had visited my house and could tell this doctor about my living accommodations and set up.

The next morning the doctor came in and said that he had a good talk with my plastic surgeon, hearing all about the great living environment

I had at home. He then said he would release me as long as I promised him that I would follow up with a bone surgeon in my local area. He also said that his office called my local home care company and arranged a visiting nurse to come out for the next few weeks to check on my incision and take out the surgical staples after ten days. He was ready to sign the release papers so I could get dressed and get ready to go home.

Finally I would be free! I'd soon be on my way home with a titanium rod in my left femur that was much better than having my old brittle femur. What could be better?

The nurse came in to deliver my release papers and follow-up information. She said that people from physical therapy would come soon to help get me into my wheelchair. As soon as she left Edward started to get me dressed.

While putting on my underwear and pants Edward said that my right leg seemed to have more range of motion than usual. Someone from physical therapy had come in the day before to give me range-of-motion exercises to help stretch the muscles I haven't used in years. The therapy I received the day before should not have increased the motion on my right leg that much, if at all.

I didn't think having my fractured left femur fixed would have anything to do with my right leg so I asked Edward if it looked swollen. He said, "No." I then asked him if it looked red. He said, "No." So I said, "Let's just get me dressed and get the hell out of here."

Survival and Symmetry

After leaving the Minnesota hospital, our drive back home was without incident and I was glad to get into my own bed without all the commotion and hospital drama.

The next morning, the visiting health nurse came by to check in on me. Her orders were to simply check and monitor my incisions and take up the surgical staples in ten days.

While the nurse was there I asked her a hypothetical question. "What shape would a person be in if that person's blood pressure was 60/10?" She said that patient would probably be dead.

That was interesting.

219

After the home health nurse left I decided to call my cousin, who was also a nurse, and asked her the same hypothetical question. She said it was unlikely that the patient would be alive with a blood pressure of 60/10.

Had I barely survived another visit to a hospital? Was it just luck that saved me from being killed one more time in one of our great medical care facilities? Would my luck run out on me the next time I had to be hospitalized?

"Yes," I thought to myself. It looked like I survived because of luck rather than medical skill. I hoped I would not be going to another hospital for a very long time.

The next day a couple friends and I planned to go out for lunch. The doctor told me to get up in the wheelchair at least once every two days in order to avoid blood clots that sometimes occurred with bone fractures. As Edward started to dress me he, again, mentioned that my right leg seemed to have a lot more movement to it. We called Diane down to my room to take a look at it. As she moved my right thigh, we all could hear a crunchy crackling sound.

Yeah, you guessed it. Evidently my right femur was also broken when I was in Minnesota but because everybody was focused on the left femur no x-rays were taken on my right side. We immediately called for an ambulance service and I was transported to a hospital in the Chicago area.

When I got into the emergency room, the attending physician ordered x-rays to be taken on my right femur. Sure enough it was broken in half just like the left femur had been. So what are the chances that one person would break both femurs in half at the same time? I would imagine that the odds are pretty small. It looked like another operation was imminent.

By now I was searching for a bright side to all that had recently happened. So I decided that since I would now have two titanium femurs instead of just the one, I would never again have to worry about breaking the more brittle one. And besides, having rods in both femurs instead of just one sounded like good symmetry. Another plus side was that this time I was near my home and I counted on not having all the drama I had in the Minnesota hospital.

I was admitted to the hospital and told that I was scheduled for surgery the following morning around nine o'clock. I was also told not to drink or eat anything after midnight. Sound familiar?

I'm beginning to think this is a universal conspiracy in all U.S. hospitals.

I was up early the next morning to prepare for my nine o'clock surgery. Just about the time I should have been taken to the operating room, I was informed that surgery was being postponed until around three in the afternoon. Déjà vu! Was the drama starting all over again, or was this just a fluke?

About two o'clock in the afternoon someone came in and took my pre-operation EKG. The cardiologist read it about a half-hour later and I was informed that it was abnormal and the cardiologist would be up shortly to talk with me.

When the cardiologist arrived I told him that an abnormality showed up on my previous EKG but after being run through the numerous cardiac tests the results showed that my heart was normal. But I suppose doctors aren't trained to believe the patient and with all the medical suits nowadays they have to be very cautious. My previous cardiologist was on vacation so they could not get in touch with her to verify EKG results. They decided to give me the whole battery of cardiac tests over again.

Meanwhile the surgeon who was waiting to put a titanium rod in my right femur was waiting for me to be taken down to surgery. An hour later they were still conducting my cardiac tests, so the surgeon gave up and rescheduled the surgery for the next morning. Lo and behold, all my cardiac tests came back with the same results I told them it would. Everything was fine but it was now too late to get the surgeon back that day.

Once more I was told not to eat or drink after midnight.

Although I hadn't had much of an appetite since my stressful stay in Minnesota I did drink a lot of fluids since I'd been home. This time when I went to surgery I might be a little undernourished but at least I would be well hydrated.

The next morning I was taken down to pre-op and again I had an anesthesiologist telling me that I was going to have general anesthesia and they would be prepared with a drug if my blood pressure went too high. I told this anesthesiologist the same thing that I told the one in Minnesota – I had problems from autonomic dysreflexia and that he should be extremely careful before administering any drug that would make my blood pressure drop. This anesthesiologist seemed to be a lot more receptive to what I was saying, so I felt more confident as I was wheeled into the operating room.

The surgery went very well and I woke up in the post-op recovery room very soon after the surgery. All was well and at least this time everything was going according to plan. Until…

Hunger Pangs and Stomach Pumps

After waking up from surgery I was taken to the ICU as a precautionary measure and I was allowed to drink and eat as long as I could tolerate it. I was feeling very good and had a few glasses of water to drink. The water didn't present a problem so I ate a few saltine crackers. They didn't present a problem either so I was told I could eat something more substantial.

Edward was with me at the time and decided to go out around nine o'clock in the evening to get something to eat. I thought this was a good opportunity for me to also get some real nourishment. He was going to a delicatessen that we frequented so I asked him to bring me back some of their chicken soup, which was very good. I told him to have them throw in a matzo ball as well. I had tasted my very first matzo ball a few months before, liked it, and felt it would add a little bit of carbohydrate to the meal.

I then thought I could probably use something to help build up my blood because of the problem I had at the Minnesota hospital. The delicatessen was located near a great barbecued rib restaurant that had some appetizers that I thought would be beneficial. So I asked Edward to swing by the rib restaurant and pick me up some of their chicken liver pâté. I thought for sure that would help build up my blood.

Edward left, ate his meal, and came back with everything I asked for. I slugged down the chicken broth and ate the matzo ball, followed by a few crackers loaded with chicken liver pâté. My appetite was assuaged and I felt very satisfied… for about an hour.

After an hour or so I started to feel little uncomfortable and in about four hours I had an extreme case of heartburn. I asked the nurse for a couple of anti-acid tablets but she said I would need a doctor's order for that. I said fine, get one. She got the doctor's approval, which took about an hour, and then I had to wait for the pharmacy to deliver some to the floor, which took another hour.

They delivered one anti-acid tablet.

One.

I should have sent Edward out to the local drugstore to get a roll of Tums™. This was a good lesson for the next time I want something that can be purchased over-the-counter. I'll just send someone out to buy it before ever requesting one from the hospital staff.

At first the anti-acid tablet seemed to work and I felt increasingly more comfortable. But by morning when the doctors made their rounds I was having stomach acid backup into my esophagus. This is not a pleasant feeling and I mentioned it to the doctor. He put a stethoscope on my stomach and discovered that my stomach and intestines were not working. The general anesthetic put them to sleep and they were not waking up. I wonder if having general anesthesia two weeks in a row could have caused these complications.

The doctor then asked me what I had to eat since my surgery. After I told him about my previous night's self-assembled menu he just rolled his eyes and said they would have to pump out my stomach. I guess the matzo ball and chicken liver pâté was a little heavy for my first meal. Pumping my stomach did not sound good to me but I was willing to do anything to alleviate my distress.

The Big Sleep

As the nurses brought in the appropriate equipment to pump out my stomach the doctor said it would hurt a little bit while they were putting the stomach tube up through my nasal passage and down into my stomach. He said I would get used to the stomach tube in a little while. It did hurt while they were performing this procedure but as my stomach contents emptied I felt much better and I thanked the doctor for helping me out.

As the doctor started to leave my room I called him back and said he forgot to take up the tubing that went from my nose into my stomach. He informed me that they were going to leave it in as long as my stomach and intestines were still asleep and not working. I neither planned for nor expected this. The nasal tube was extremely uncomfortable and the tube going down my esophagus hurt my throat every time I swallowed.

I asked the doctor how long it would take before he thought my stomach would wake up and start to work again. He said that even though this sort of thing happens only occasionally that it might take a day or two. I just rolled my eyes. I couldn't imagine having to put up with this tube in my nose and throat for that long.

As long as the tube was in my stomach the doctor said I was not allowed to eat or drink – so much for getting nourishment in a hospital! The only nutrition I was getting was from my antibiotic IVs that had 5% dextrose in the solution, which was only around two hundred milliliters. I thought that they should probably put dextrose in the saline water solution I was getting as well because at least one liter of that IV solution was being hung three times a day. I mentioned this to my doctor and he said he would take care of it but I never did see a larger IV containing any dextrose. After working for so many years in the medical nutrition industry, I had read many studies showing how the lack of nutrition a patient receives in hospitals can cause patients to recuperate much slower. Here I was – a real life example – and there was nothing I could do about it.

After an excruciating two days with the tubing down my nose and throat I asked the doctor how much longer it would be before my stomach would wake up. All he could tell me was that sometimes it takes a little longer and it could be another day or two. By this time my throat was very raw and I was very conscious of it every time I swallowed.

Another two days passed and my stomach was still asleep.

I started to panic. It had been five days since my operation and four days since the tube was put into my stomach.

Would my stomach ever wake up? If it wouldn't wake up, then what would I do? Would I have to live with a feeding tube the rest of my life? Would I ever enjoy the taste of real food again? What would the rest of my life be like?

All of these questions and more raced around my brain. I asked one of the nurses that I truly trusted if this sort of situation could become permanent. She assured me that it would resolve itself and that I should be patient.

Patient.

Hmmm. I wonder if that's where the word 'patient' comes from; sick and injured people having to be patient.

At the end of the fifth day my regular physician came in and put a stethoscope to my stomach. He heard gurgling sounds. This was great news because it was the first sign my stomach was finally awake. I thought of that line from the old Frankenstein movie, "It's alive, it's alive!"

My utter joy was quickly dashed to smithereens when I was told the tube would not yet be coming out because the sounds were minimal. We'd have to wait. By the next day, my stomach gurgles were roaring! Thank God for gurgling stomachs. What a beautiful sound to my ears.

The stomach tube was removed late into the fifth day and I was allowed to have Jell-O®. "There's always room for Jell-O." It's the closest thing to real food I was able to have in four days and I was glad to have it.

The next morning I was allowed to leave the hospital. Actually, I pretty much forced the hospital to release me. In accordance with the "Patient's Bill of Rights" I exercised my right to refuse the medication and IVs they were trying to give me. I was given all kinds of medications relating to my blood pressure, diabetes, and to prevent potential pneumonia. I felt that, if they were going to keep on giving me medications that I never used when I was out of the hospital, I would never get out of there. I was in there to have a fractured femur fixed and not to have them mess around with other things that could result in potential health problems in the future.

I was certain that the sooner I could get home and back to my normal routines the sooner I would recover. Since I only take a couple pills for my diabetes, that's what I went back to taking. It took about two or three weeks before my digestive system straightened out but once that cleared up I returned to a normal life.

Boy, do I hate hospitals! *It's just one fine mess after another that the medical staff gets me into.*

I want to make it clear that I am not suggesting to anyone that you refuse medication being administered to get out of the hospital faster. What I am saying is that I have carefully monitored how my body acts and reacts to medications since my accident forty-four years ago. I have educated myself on what is normal and not normal for me.

I feel that everyone should educate themselves on their own health issues and understand their own body's workings. Make a point of researching what doctors are prescribing and why so you can ask questions and make an intelligent decision when medical personnel are going beyond reasonable treatment for your condition.

Although the doctors told me in both of my hospital stays that they were just being cautious and proactive, I think a lot of their precautionary treatment was to ensure they would not have to defend themselves

225

against a lawsuit. Unfortunately, our medical system has come to this. It seems that doctors need to prescribe every possible test available in order to prevent lawsuits. I don't blame them for taking these actions. If I were in their shoes, I would probably do the same.

CHAPTER 36

Three Rules To Live By as a Hospital Patient

During the last forty-four years, I have been a patient in various hospitals many times. During these times, there are many instances where the hospital personnel or procedures, not my injury, could have killed me. My advice to anyone who is entering the hospital as a patient is to follow these three rules:

Rule number one:

Any time a nurse brings you medication, an injection, or is about to hang an IV solution, make sure you ask the following three things:

1) What is the name of the medication, injection, or IV,

2) What is the medication, injection, or IV used for, and, most importantly,

3) Who is responsible for ordering the medication, injection, or IV?

If you are satisfied with the answer to all three of these questions, it is up to you whether or not you want to take the medication, injection, or IV. If you have any doubts about the answers you get to any of the three questions, call your physician and have him or her explain to your satisfaction that what is being prescribed will benefit you.

Remember, it's your body and not the physician's or the nurse's.

Rule number two:

Follow rule number one explicitly.

Rule number three:

Always obey rules number one and two.

Know Your Own Body

I can't stress how important it is to learn about and understand the medications prescribed for you. About a half dozen times during the last twenty years, I could've died because of medications that were not meant for me but for another patient, or that were meant for me but not the correct thing to give me because of my special conditions related to being a quadriplegic.

I really feel sorry for the patient who might not be able to intelligently ask questions about the medications they are given. I know it is difficult for a lot of people to do this, but the person who needs to have the greatest concern – and knowledge – about your health is you. Always question a new drug or medication you are prescribed and be sure you understand the appropriate dosage for each medication.

I once had a doctor prescribe a common vitamin that was supposed to promote healing. But I discovered that the dosage she prescribed was forty times the recommended daily dose for that vitamin. I called my wife and asked her to sign onto the Internet, look up the vitamin, and find out what the appropriate dosage was for it. She found out that the dosage the doctor wanted to give me had about twelve adverse side effects and could harm your kidneys, liver, and degrade your immune system.

When questioning the doctor about why such a high dosage was being prescribed, she told me that the higher dosage was always prescribed for people trying to heal tissue after surgery. She went on to tell me not to worry because the blood tests they routinely take would show any problems that might occur.

I then asked about all the side effects that could have a negative effect on my kidneys, liver, and immune system. She was very surprised that I knew of these and backtracked a little, deciding to set the dosage lower. She said her original dosage recommendation might have been too high once I told her the problems I had with constant and recurrent kidney stones. She was unaware I had any kidney problems whatsoever and didn't bother to ask, despite knowing about the potential side effects. This is just one example of how you need to be sure you know what people are prescribing and how it relates to your own personal situation.

In a previous chapter, I noted a situation where a doctor prescribed blood pressure medicine to be injected during the middle of the night, which would lower my blood pressure. Again, he did not understand that as a quadriplegic I typically had low blood pressure and that it was common for my blood pressure readings to vary widely within minutes. When the time came to give me an injection to lower my blood pressure, my blood pressure was already extremely low. I was very lucky to be awake and refuse the injection.

This example illustrates how doctors look at a symptom and then prescribe a solution, based on a general patient population. That is why it is so important when you enter a hospital to let them know everything that you know of that would be special to your specific condition. I do this every time I am admitted to the hospital. Unfortunately, the information I provide is often ignored or not even read once it is put into my hospital file.

Am I in Pain?

One of the most frequent things I contend with whenever I am in the hospital is not life threatening but just downright annoying. Every time a nurse comes in she asks me if I am in any pain. Since I cannot feel anything from the chest down I usually say, "No" but make it a point to mention why. "I'm not in any pain because I cannot feel three quarters of my body." Because I cannot feel pain does not mean that my body is not suffering in some area where I have no feeling.

One of the things I stress to the nursing staff and make sure is put into my hospital record is to be extra conscientious about removing any hard items that could inadvertently be left in my bed. Because I have no feeling I am unaware if I am lying on these objects. I can get a pressure sore within an hour of having one of these objects lodged under me.

I don't think I've had one hospital stay where I have not found hard syringe caps – or even empty syringes – in my bed and under my body that were supposed to be thrown away. To the nurses these are just little things that they tend to ignore, but these little things can quickly become a big problem for me. No matter how many times I tell them to be aware of this, they nod their heads to show they understand, but it happens over and over again. This is especially true during the late evening shift when there's not much light in the room and the nurse changes an IV or gives me an injection.

My Own Medications from Home

Another thing that I do when I enter a hospital is to bring along all my normal medications from home. There are two reasons for this. The first is so that these medications and dosages can be entered into the hospital records. The second is because after I talk with my regular doctor, I need to send these medications to the pharmacy to make sure they understand and approve of them before sending them back to me.

I send them to the pharmacy because I have my regular doctor inform the hospital pharmacy that I will be taking my own medication from home, using my normal medication schedule. This is usually very different from the hospital schedule because nurses make their medication rounds for all patients at prescribed times. Of course if there are any medications you normally take at home that have to be stopped during your hospital stay, you can have them taken home.

I can state with certainty that the hospital pharmacists are not too pleased to get this directive. Who ever heard of the patient taking his own medications? It can't be done! Yes it can. Don't let anyone tell you that it can't. I have taken my own medications with me for my last four hospital stays.

There's a valid reason for me to take my own medications. I'm a Type 2 diabetic and I am able to keep my blood sugar levels under control with two different oral diabetic medications. I use my own blood sugar monitoring device so that I have an accurate reading prior to my meals. I always take one dose of one medication but depending on the blood sugar level at the time the dosage for the second medication will vary between zero and three pills. I have been doing this for more than ten years and am able to keep my blood sugar levels under control.

Again, who is the best qualified for understanding your particular needs? You are. So why shouldn't you be allowed to control your medications in the hospital the way you do at home?

In the past there were times when the nurse's aide would take my blood sugar level after I had something to eat. This would screw up the results. When the nurse would come in with an insulin shot I would tell her that I just ate and that was why my blood sugar level reading was high. A few times the nurse refused to listen to me. What could a diabetic patient possibly know about blood sugar control? This became particularly tedious during one of my hospital stays and I finally decided I had enough of that kind of stuff going on. From then on I made sure I took my own blood sugar levels along with my own diabetic medications.

Continuity of Care

In most hospitals nowadays there is little or no continuity of care from day to day by the same nursing staff. It has been my experience that it is very rare to have the same nurse on one day, return on that shift the next day. This tends to be a real problem for me because I have to constantly reiterate information about my special needs. If it's only a two- or three-day stay in the hospital, it is not a problem but if my hospital stay is for a week or more, like most of mine are, this can become a major problem.

I have yet to find a solution to this problem. Maybe when I go into the hospital I should record my litany of special needs on a small voice recorder and then with each shift change make the nurse taking care of me listen to it. I wonder if that would work?

Patient's Bill of Rights

I believe that the majority of states, if not all of them, have a "Patient's Bill of Rights" policy. This allows patients to refuse any or all medications pertaining to their treatment. There were times when I had to argue with a nurse about not giving me a medication or injection that I knew would be very detrimental to my health. I finally had to confront her and let her know that I was aware of the "Patient's Bill of Rights" and that if she would not stop trying to administer the medication or injection I would inform the hospital administration of her actions.

Of my many stays in the hospital, I believe I only had to go this far once. A nurse proceeded to do whatever she was going to do despite my explicit demand that she stop. After informing the head of nursing the next morning, I am sure that the nurse who did not listen to me was now fully aware of what the "Patient's Bill of Rights" was all about. I hate being a bad ass, but when it comes to someone trying to do something that could possibly injure you, you have to speak up. It's your health at stake.

231

What You Can and Can't Control

Remember that you don't have a lot of control in a hospital so you must become an informed patient. Understand your medications. Ask questions. Make sure you're comfortable with the answers before you agree to take anything new or have something administered to you.

It's ultimately your responsibility to make sure you have the proper medical care. Doctors and nurses are human beings and can make mistakes just like the rest of us.

Part 4: Afterthoughts

This book wouldn't be complete without mentioning the vast differences between today's medical knowledge and care for spinal cord injuries versus what was known and available when I had my accident in the mid 1960s. There is both more help and more hope.

This section also gives me an opportunity to reflect on my personal accomplishments, trusting that it serves as a testament that anyone can reach his or her goals despite physical limitations.

CHAPTER 37

Then and Now

Looking back forty-four years, I can't believe all the changes that have taken place and medical advancements for spinal cord injuries. People who have spinal cord injuries now have a much better chance of not only surviving, but of walking again.

When I had my accident, the only thing that doctors knew to do was to place me in traction and hope my neck would heal as much as possible on its own. Today there are many ways to keep the area around the spinal injury from swelling immediately after the injury. This helps tremendously to minimize damage to the nerves and increases the potential for the nerves to regenerate.

Lifespan

After my accident in 1964, I was told that the normal lifespan of a quadriplegic was anywhere from six to ten years. This shortened survival rate is attributed to the many complications that can occur with serious urinary tract infections or blood clots due to poor blood circulation in the lower extremities.

Today however, these problems are minimized with a new group of antibiotics and a better understanding of how to treat quadriplegics.

I must be doing something right to have lived as a quadriplegic for more than four decades rather than the estimated six to ten years. There have been many times however when a urinary tract infection went septic and my life was in danger. Thank God, I have not had any problems related to blood clotting even though my circulatory system is not in the best of shape, with particularly poor circulation in my legs.

I was amused when I retired from the corporate world about ten years ago and asked someone in the human resources department to find out about my options for purchasing an annuity. The vice president of human resources said he had some good news and some bad news. The good news was that they could purchase an annuity relatively cheaply. The bad news, according to the actuarial tables, showed my life expectancy to be age sixty-two. I retired at age fifty-one and I'm now sixty-one. I guess I'll have to wait until next year to see if the tables were accurate.

Public Access

In 1964 there was very little focus in the public arena regarding people with spinal cord injuries. In fact there was very little focus in the public arena for anyone confined to a wheelchair.

It wasn't until the late sixties that communities started to set standards for public buildings to be accessible to wheelchairs as well as putting in ramps on their street curbs. This movement did not happen quickly but it did happen over the next twenty years. I often wonder if things started to change after so many Vietnam War veterans came back with spinal cord injuries and amputations. It's a shame it took a war for anybody to notice these relatively simple needs.

Restaurants

It was impossible to go out to a restaurant without calling ahead to make sure you could get into the building. Almost all restaurants had stairs, making it impossible to enter in a wheelchair, especially an electric wheelchair.

I remember often having to enter through the back of a restaurant where supplies were delivered, which was usually street level or ramped. I would then go through the kitchen to get to the dining room. (After seeing the conditions of some of the areas where food was prepared – even in some of the most famous and posh establishments throughout the country – I became a little wary of actually eating there.)

As buildings and restaurants began to install ramps, it opened up a whole new world for people in wheelchairs.

Public Bathrooms

There were no handicapped accessible bathrooms in public buildings. If I couldn't get around bathroom corners or get near a toilet I had problems emptying the urinary drainage bag that was strapped to my leg.

To empty it, I would roll my wheelchair as close as I could get to the toilet bowl and then the person I was with would roll up my pant leg until it was above the bottom of the drainage bag, and then lift my leg up and set my foot on the toilet seat. There was a valve located on the drainage bag tubing at the bottom of the bag that could then be turned into the open position so the bag could be drained. Once the leg bag was drained the valve would be closed, my leg would be put back on my foot pedal, and my pant leg rolled back down.

This was a relatively simple procedure if I could get near a toilet bowl. But if I couldn't, I always kept an empty coffee can with a lid in my vehicle so that if I had to have my urinary drainage bag emptied I could go out to the vehicle and empty it into the coffee can and then put the lid back on the can. When we got back home the coffee can was emptied and cleaned for the next trip.

Today, public bathrooms are equipped with handicap accessible stalls and hallways are wide enough to get to them.

Street Curbs

Towns did not have ramped street curbs so anyone using a wheelchair had to have somebody to tilt back the wheelchair, move forward to place the front wheels on the curb, and then lift and push the back of the wheelchair to get up the curb.

The first time I ever had to go over a curb in the wheelchair I remember thinking that, before my accident when I was able to walk, I never once gave any thought to getting up and down a street curb. In fact, I barely noticed them. It never occurred to me what a huge barrier curbs are to someone in a wheelchair.

Today nearly every sidewalk is built with crosswalks that slope to street level.

Parking

There were no handicapped parking areas when I had my accident. Now, every parking lot allots a certain number of spaces specifically for handicapped individuals to use.

I generally use an electric wheelchair to get around. So, for me, having a handicapped parking area close to a building or shopping mall is not as important as it would be to someone who would have to push a wheelchair around.

However, handicapped parking areas are still extremely important to me because of the extra amount of space on both sides of each handicapped parking spot. Once my handicapped van ramp is extended, the extra space gives me enough room to roll my wheelchair in and out of my vehicle. Without that extra space to maneuver a wheelchair around, my driver would have to back the van out of the parking area to a location where the ramp could be extended. Again, this is something that I never thought of when I was able to walk and drive a car.

While I'm on the subject I want to expound a bit on something that really ticks me off about the small blue-and-white handicapped parking stickers that people display in the front windshield of their cars. There are certainly a lot of people who use them and need them. But there are others who just abuse them.

As the baby boomer generation gets older and more and more elderly people have trouble walking, they need these type of stickers and rightly so. But there are people who get one of the stickers for the sole purpose of being able to park close to a building or shopping mall. All it takes is a prescription from a doctor to obtain one of these stickers and it seems that doctors hand them out like candy.

It really ticks me off when I see a car bearing a handicap sticker pull into a handicapped parking spot and the driver gets out and actually runs from the vehicle into the store. These people are handicapped all right, but not physically. These "mentally" handicapped people either don't realize what a hardship they can put on somebody else, or they just don't care about anyone but themselves.

Caregivers

When I started working and living on my own it was difficult to find qualified live-in caregivers. Now that the baby boomer generation is starting to reach its golden years, more and more businesses are tailoring their services to people who have trouble walking and are in need of assistance in their living environment.

With home health care agencies and placement firms that cater to those who need live-in help, I think finding a caregiver today is much easier. I guess the rest of the population is starting to catch up with me.

Schools and Careers

When I was ready to attend college, there were really only three major universities in the Midwest that offered special programs and had facilities to accommodate disabled students. Today, nearly every college is equipped to accommodate disabled individuals. This is a major plus for handicapped individuals, making it easier to get an education that, in most instances, will lead to a better future.

In today's technical age, there are many career opportunities open to people with disabilities. So many careers rely on computers now that a person doesn't have to become a specialist in programming them, but only needs the knowledge of how to interact with them by understanding the application in their field of endeavor. Just about every major industry or business has opportunities for people with disabilities.

Legislation

In a previous chapter of this book I described the problems I had trying to get a job even though I had a Master of Science degree. When the American Disabilities Act of 1990 was passed, it eliminated many of the discrimination issues associated with hiring disabled individuals and set standards for public access. It is now much easier for spinal cord injury people and other disabled individuals to compete for career opportunities as well as have greater accessibility in an office environment and when traveling.

Transportation

For me to get around easily, I had to purchase my own handicap van. At the time there was no place that rented handicapped accessible vans. Whenever I needed to travel to another part of the country for work, the company not only flew me to my destination, but also tried to locate a wheelchair accessible van that I could use during my stay. Years ago, there were only a few places in larger cities that had an available handicap van to rent.

It's probably only within the last ten or fifteen years that renting a handicap vehicle has become commonplace, and when I search the Internet today, I find literally hundreds of places that rent handicap vehicles.

In comparing how things were for me "then" to how things are for people "now" I'm pleased to see that it's a new and more welcoming world out there for people with disabilities. And as technology continues to advance more areas of opportunity will open up, providing all of us with increasingly better lives. Go for it!

CHAPTER 38

Final Reflections

Looking back at my more than four decades as a quadriplegic I feel a great sense of accomplishment and am very comfortable with my life. I wonder how many able-bodied people can say the same. I learned early on to set small goals that were attainable in order to reach larger goals. This philosophy, as well as trying to always see the positive side of any situation, has allowed me to be who I am today and accomplish the things I've accomplished in my life.

Educational Accomplishments

I met – and feel I exceeded – the educational goals I set for myself right after my accident. As I look back over my educational accomplishments they really started with that one little step of taking a couple of correspondence courses while I still lived at home in South Milwaukee. By the time I finished my formal education, I managed to receive four degrees:

1) An Associate degree from the Milwaukee Institute of Technology.
2) A Bachelor of Science degree from the University of Missouri in Columbia, majoring in physics.
3) A Master of Science degree from the University of Missouri in Columbia, majoring in physics.
4) A Master of Business Administration degree from Lake Forest College in Lake Forest, Illinois.

I was also fortunate enough to work with an astronomy professor on original research he was conducting in the field of cosmology and helped out by providing computer modeling for his research. When he published his original research he included my name as co-author on a couple of papers he presented at astronomy symposiums and that were also published in a well-respected international science journal.*

I certainly didn't imagine how much my educational path would contribute to my success in the business world. There is no way I could've predicted that my business career would be in the field of computers. A little thing like not wanting to use a slide rule because it was difficult for me to use led me to purchasing a book on computer programming. That one little book changed my life's career path.

Career Success

During my career of more than twenty years I worked in many areas of the computer field. I started at the very bottom level as a computer programmer and finished off my corporate involvement as a corporate vice president of information technology at Nestlé Clinical Nutrition. In that position I oversaw the computer operations in both the U.S. and Europe. Once out of the corporate world, I had my own computer consulting business until I was forced to close it down because of my health.

One of the accomplishments I am most proud of was being able to sponsor two employees, Carol and Laura, in a program offered by Chicago's DePaul University. Neither of them previously had the chance to get a college degree. The DePaul program allowed working adults to obtain a Bachelor of Arts degree by taking the equivalent number of credit hours that a normal student would have to take, but tailoring some of the courses to the educational experience one learns by working in a professional position on the job. A professional advisor – that would be me – designed part of each student's curricular program and an academic advisor on permanent staff with DePaul designed the other part. These student advisors met regularly to review the status of how well the student was doing as well as make any adjustments in the curriculum.

I was so proud of my two employees as they finished a very difficult program and were given their degrees during graduation ceremonies at DePaul. It felt good to be able to help someone get the education that so many people take for granted, and I hoped that this would provide each of them with opportunities for a better future.

With my continued career advancement I became financially independent. For more than twenty years, I contributed anywhere from twelve to twenty-five percent of my gross pay to my company's 401(k) and stock sharing plans.

I learned when I was young that I always spent whatever money I actually brought home in my paycheck. So having the company take money out of my gross pay for the 401(k) or stock-sharing plan before getting my paycheck was money I never saw. Over twenty years, this became quite a nest egg, especially when I was earning the salary as a director or vice president of the computer department. And, yes, I spent every dime I took home in my paycheck. I just didn't worry about what they were taking out of my gross pay. Fortunately, my wife did the same during her more than twenty-five year career.

Retirement Dreams

Just before I retired from the corporate world, Diane and I built a house overlooking a lake in northern Illinois. We had the developer design special blueprints that met all of my handicapped needs. The house was fully equipped for me to get around and live in easily. It has an elevator that goes up and down three stories, and my bedroom has an electric lift that moves back and forth on a track built into the ceiling. I use it every day to lift me out of the wheelchair and into bed and vice versa as well as getting me from my bed into my special bathroom where I have a large Jacuzzi bathtub.

All the doors in the house are thirty-six inches wide to allow for my wheelchair to easily get in and out of rooms. All fixtures for lights and doors are a little lower than normal with levers instead of doorknobs so that I can open and close doors myself. All entrance ways are sloped with no stairs to get up or down. Even though I don't drive, I have a handicap van with an automatic lift that folds down so that I can drive my electric chair into the van with me still sitting in it.

When I retired about seven years ago, I really wanted to spend a lot of time traveling around the United States and see all the marvelous sights this nation has to offer. I had several health-related issues that prevented my traveling by plane or train. The handicap van was a great option and worked for a while until I had a serious skin breakdown on one of my trips while I was three days from home. I knew from that day forward I had to find a better alternative if I still wanted to travel.

If you've read the chapter entitled *Rocky Mountain Low*, you know that I finally found a solution. I recently ordered an RV motor home from Winnebago Industries that has been modified to include a wheelchair lift for entry and exit, and a lift and track system installed in the ceiling of the back bedroom so that I can be transferred in and out of bed easily. I also put in a hospital bed in the back bedroom that has an alternating pressure mattress to prevent pressure sores. This way, if I ever have medical problems when I am far away from home I can stay in the hospital bed while we travel. Life is still an adventure and I can't wait to see what kind of trouble I can get my friends into with this vehicle.

Personal Satisfaction

I can't close this chapter without reflecting on all the family members and friends who have inspired me and been with me during good times and bad times. Without them, this book could not have been written, and because of them I thought our escapades were worth relating to others. They all serve as the main characters in this book. My part was just getting them into trouble.

My life has come a long way since I was seventeen years old, strapped into a circle bed, and concerned that I would never be able to earn a living or live relatively independently, without my family's assistance. Yes, there were many times that I was discouraged and many times that I thought the obstacles were too great to overcome. But I always thought that, if I could just get over this one last obstacle, things would get better – and they usually did.

People talk of change as if it were easy. It isn't! Change is difficult. Change is taking a risk; leaving a comfortable environment and moving into a situation that is unknown and scary. I made many changes throughout my lifetime, not because I wanted to but because I had to. And, after making so many changes along the way, I came to realize one thing about change. Once the change is made and it is successful, it then becomes the next comfortable environment.

Yes, there are times when change is not what you really want, but then it is that much easier to make the next change. After a few major changes in life, it can actually become exhilarating and you begin to wonder what new experiences await by taking that risk.

I am very satisfied with my life and I don't take each passing day for granted. In fact the last line of the last paragraph of the last chapter of this book doesn't say, "The End." I have many more adventures planned for the coming years, and I continue to look forward to what the future might have in store for me.

Barnes, Ronnie C. and Prondzinski, Robert: "A Comparative Study of Brans-Dicke and General Relativistic Cosmologies in Terms of Observationally Measurable Quantities", *Astrophysics and Space Science,* Vol. 16, Number 3 (June 1972): 499-504

ADDENDUM

For What It's Worth

As I look back after writing this book, I realize how much has changed during my forty-four years as a quadriplegic and how many more options are available to make living and traveling easier. The technologies available today provide far greater opportunities for someone like me to become as independent as they can and live a very successful and productive life.

I thought it would be of benefit to share a few of the things I learned and some of the products I use that contribute significantly to my ability to live a more independent life. Hopefully this information will prevent having to reinvent the wheel, so to speak, if you are someone – or if you know someone – who has suffered a spinal cord injury.

Transportation

Purchasing a handicap van:

One of the most important pieces of equipment I have is my handicap van. Being able to travel anywhere out of the home provides a great deal of independence. Even though I could probably outfit my handicap van with hand controls to drive, I have chosen not to. I always have a caregiver or friend around to do the driving so I have no need to drive myself. When I researched the possibility of driving myself early on in my life I found that the insurance at that time was just too great. Keeping the driver's seat and controls standard makes it a lot easier for a normal

245

person to drive. When I purchased insurance on my vehicle, I made sure that the agent knew I would not be driving. I had to name one or two people who would be the primary drivers and the insurance rates were then based upon those two drivers.

Just after my accident I used a regular car to get around in, but it was difficult getting in and out and I had to rely on the driver to place my wheelchair in the trunk. This was almost impossible if I used an electric wheelchair. Purchasing a handicap van really increased my independence for traveling and taking vacations.

I have had three handicap vans over the years and have found that my current van, a Chrysler Entervan, is nearly maintenance-free and the most comfortable to drive in. If I ever need to get another one, I will go to the same company, Braun Corporation. The company specializes in providing excellent vehicles for the handicapped. To find one in your area, the Braun Corporation has a list of dealers on its website at: http://www.braunmobility.com

The basic maintenance on my vehicle is performed by my local Chrysler dealership, while the maintenance on the handicap modifications are performed by the dealership I bought the Entervan from. One of the most important aspects to owning a handicap van is to make sure you have a good qualified dealer that can service and perform maintenance on the handicap modifications made to your van. You might get a better price from a dealer, but if that dealer doesn't provide adequate maintenance service, you would probably be better off purchasing from another dealership. Make sure you ask for references and talk to some of the dealer's customers who take their vans in for servicing. If the dealer does not provide you with any references that should raise a red flag.

I have encountered a few very bad maintenance places in the past and I now make it a practice to talk with some of the customers to make sure they are extremely satisfied with the work that is performed. If you're not satisfied with the service you receive, don't be afraid to move your business elsewhere.

Handicap van rentals:

When I used to travel by airplane, I always made sure I had a handicap rental van waiting for me at the airport. Many companies in North

America have handicap vans available for rent. If you travel by airplane or train it is fairly easy to arrange for a handicap van that meets your specific needs ready and waiting for you when you arrive at the airport or train station. When the trip is over, the van can be left at the airport and the rental company will pick it up later. If the rental company doesn't provide this service check to see if there is more than one to deal with at your destination location.

I have often dealt with a company called Wheelchair Getaways and have always been satisfied with their service. The company has 450 handicap van rental dealers throughout the United States and Canada and I have personally rented vehicles from them in about half a dozen states. Their web page is: http://www.wheelchairgetaways.com.

Public transportation:

In most city and suburban localities public transportation is available for the disabled. Buses are usually well equipped for people in wheelchairs and they have priority for seating. There are also special buses that will pick you up in front of your house if you can't get to a local bus stop. You have to call ahead and schedule these rides but it's a small inconvenience for getting that type of door-to-door service. In some cases you need to get a special pass to use the pickup service but that is often only a formality. Many local trains are also equipped with cars that have wheelchair access.

I am most familiar with the public transportation in the Chicago area. I live a long way from central Chicago in one of the northern areas close to the Wisconsin border and find it very easy to catch a train to the downtown station and then take a wheelchair accessible bus anywhere in the Chicago area. I was amazed and impressed by how well Chicago's public transportation is geared to the disabled traveler. I found that if I can get to the train station, I am able to travel alone anywhere in the Chicago area.

I am guessing that most of the major metropolitan cities have very similar public transportation capabilities for the disabled. Call or visit your city's web site for more information about public transportation in your area. There is a lot of information available if you simply take the time to look for it and I urge you to do it. I think a lot of people are amazed to discover that this type of transportation is well systemized and stress free.

Traveling by airplane:

I gave up on traveling by airplane a few years ago. Because of my increasing problems with pressure sores, it became more and more difficult for me to travel this way. In my experience, airplane travel for the handicapped has not improved much in the last forty-four years. In some instances, such as the current extensive process for security checks, it's even worse.

If you have to travel by airplane and are in a wheelchair here are some tips that might help:

- When purchasing tickets through a travel agency or directly from the airline make sure that the airline knows that you are in a wheelchair and need to be helped in and out of the airplane. Do not use online web sites to purchase your tickets because they usually have no capabilities to include your special needs. If you deal through a travel agency make sure they talk with someone at the airline directly. When you receive your tickets verify that your requests have been noted. I believe some airlines indicate right on the ticket that there are special needs required for this passenger.

- Make sure you are pre-assigned an aisle seat and that it is located as close as possible to the door you will be using to enter the airplane. The airline will know this information. In most cases you'll be lifted into a portable aisle chair and moved to your assigned seat. It is much easier on everybody if you are close to the entrance and exit door.

- Make sure you arrive at least a few hours before the scheduled flight. A person in a wheelchair is usually the first one on the airplane and the last one off. When you reserve your tickets the agent will remind you to arrive early so you are in front of everybody else waiting to board the plane. Because of the additional security in recent years I have spent quite a bit of time getting my wheelchair checked out before I could even get near the boarding area.

- Always stay in your wheelchair until you are sitting in front of the open airplane door. There are two reasons for this. First, when you are checking in at the boarding pass station make sure the person at that station puts the appropriate wheelchair baggage tags on the wheelchair in a location where they will not fall off. Second, since you will probably be lifted into a narrow aisle chair and carried to your seat, if you're in your wheelchair at the entry door of the airplane you have less distance to travel while sitting on this uncomfortable and very tipsy aisle chair.

- Make sure that if you need to be lifted out of your wheelchair and put into one of the narrow aisle chairs to be carried on board you have the appropriate manpower to do so. Mention this to the boarding station personnel repeatedly so that when they are ready to board you they actually have the people necessary to get you boarded. I am 6'1" and weigh about 250 pounds, which is a lot of dead weight to lift. Once you are lifted onto the aisle chair, make sure you are strapped in properly to minimize the chance of falling out of it. The more safety precautions you take the better. You don't want to end up going to the hospital instead of your destination because of a mishap.

- Make sure when you get out of your wheelchair that the baggage personnel use the airport's elevator to take the wheelchair down to the level where it will be put into the baggage compartment. Also make sure that when you arrive at your destination you tell the flight attendants to direct the baggage handlers to bring your wheelchair up the elevator and then to the airplane exit door. You have to let the flight attendant know that it is imperative they bring the wheelchair up this way. Whenever I flew somewhere, more than half the time airline personnel tried carrying the wheelchair up and down the stairs connected to the telescope tube near the airplane door. I have had many wheelchairs wrecked and bent out of shape by people trying to get a wheelchair up and down the stairs. This is especially true if you are using an electric wheelchair.

- Before the plane departs, ask the flight attendant to check with the baggage handlers to make sure that your wheelchair has been loaded aboard the plane on which you are traveling. You don't want to arrive at your destination without your wheelchair.

- If you are traveling with an electric wheelchair you need to make sure that you have the recommended and authorized battery that the airline is allowed to put in the baggage compartment of the airplane. You should be able to get that information when you call to make ticket reservations. Once I went to the airport with what I was told was an approved gel cell battery that could be put on a plane, but when I arrived at the airport I was told that the particular brand was not on the airline's approved list. It was a tremendous hassle to try to resolve the issue. They finally put my electric gel cell battery in a special airtight container so that it could be put in the baggage compartment of the airplane. This is not as much of a problem now as it was in the past when electric wheelchairs contained acid batteries.

- If you use a urinary drainage bag attached to your leg, you can use one of the "sick bags" available on the airplane if necessary to empty it in while in the air. I found them to be very leak proof – at least they were when I used to fly, and they can be carried to and disposed of in the bathroom.

These tips won't guarantee that you'll have a smooth plane trip but they might help anticipate and alleviate a few of the problems you could encounter. Beyond that, all I can do is wish you a lot of luck!

Traveling by train:

I have never traveled across the country by train but have extensively researched the possibilities of doing so. I thought it would be great to travel on Amtrak to a destination city and then rent a handicap van to get around the area.

Amtrak advertises its ability to accommodate handicap individuals in wheelchairs. At the time I was looking into it, they also offered their handicap accessible rooms at a discount. It seemed like a great idea until I saw the dimensions of some of the floor plans in the brochures, which looked very small.

However, I noticed that the room size also depends on the train you would travel on. The trains on the East Coast had smaller room dimensions than the ones traveling to the West Coast. Amtrak does have a special phone number to call to make reservations if you're handicapped. If you are thinking of traveling by train, I would recommend going to one of Amtrak's stations to actually see what the train's handicap accommodations are like. I was invited to do just that by the Amtrak people at Union Station here in Chicago and if I ever decide to take a trip by train, I'll take them up on their offer.

RV motor homes:

If you like to travel and see the country by driving and camping you are pretty much out of luck trying to rent anything. As of this writing California, Florida and, I believe, New York each have a few RV rental places that have some motor homes equipped for the handicapped. I hope that as the aging baby boomer generation increases demand for motor home travel, the RV rental business on a whole will accommodate the need for handicap accessible motor homes.

If you can afford it, a handicapped equipped RV motor home is a fantastic way to travel. Unfortunately it is also expensive because it has to be purchased. Because of my own personal problems with travel this is the only way I felt I would be able to spend my retirement years traveling around our beautiful country.

I researched about fifteen RV motor home and motor coach companies, contacted four, and only found one that would modify and outfit an RV with handicap modifications during the manufacturing process. The other three manufacturers' dealerships I contacted recommended that I buy one of their standard units and then take it somewhere for modifications. That sounded a little absurd to me.

Winnebago Industries was the only RV manufacturer I found that has a special department to work with you on designing an RV to meet your special needs. Talk directly with the people in their special accessibility department at Winnebago Industries before you select a dealer. If you visit the company's web site don't be discouraged by the advertised prices. Dealerships are more than willing to negotiate, and may be willing to pass along special handicap modifications at dealer cost depending on what they are. If you do select a dealer, talk with some of their customers and ask about their experiences with the dealership.

There are a large number of specialized Winnebago RV clubs around the country and by going to their web sites you can contact some of the members to ask questions about the various dealerships. Word gets around that community about which dealerships to avoid and which ones are exceptional to deal with. Winnebago Industries is itself an excellent company to deal with.

The company website is: http://www.winnebagoind.com/products/commercial/ability

Travel

Portable patient lifts:

A portable patient lift, that I also call a body lift, can be used while traveling as well as in the home to lift you in and out of bed. Since I already have a ceiling mounted patient lift at home I use a portable patient lift when I travel and stay in hotels.

I have had a couple of different models over the last ten years and the one I currently use is far better than my previous one. It is truly portable and fits in the back of my handicap van without taking up a lot of room. This lift will also fit easily into the trunk of a car. It weighs only about fifty pounds, which is less than half the weight of my previous one. It unfolds and folds up in less than two minutes. My previous one had to be disassembled into three parts and then put back together, a twenty-minute process each time.

Both of the lifts were electrically controlled to go up and down using batteries that could be recharged over and over again. Electric-powered lifts are helpful for your caregiver, too, so that the caregiver doesn't have to manually crank the lift up and down.

Although my current lift cost quite a bit more than my previous one it was well worth it to me and my caregiver because of the ease of use and its light weight for portability. The lift I currently own is the MoLift Smart. You can find more information about this lift on the company's web site at: http://www.moliftinc.com.

Hotel accommodations:

Almost all hotels have handicap accessible rooms but their level of accessibility can differ greatly.

All of the handicap rooms I have been in have well thought out handicap accessible bathrooms but sometimes other little details are overlooked. For instance, because I use a portable patient lift to get me in and out of the bed in the hotel room I need to make sure the bed is standing on legs rather than being encased by a wooden border around the bottom. This seems like a small thing but it becomes a major problem when you need to push the base of the portable patient lift under it.

The patient lift needs approximately three or four inches of clearance so that the base can be pushed under the bed and positions you correctly over the bed to be lowered down onto the mattress. If there is a board all around the bottom of the bed the patient lift does not work very well. I usually carry four, four-inch high wooden blocks in the back of my van just in case I have to prop up the hotel bed.

I stay at many of the major hotel chains and it is relatively random as to whether the beds have boards under them or not. Before reserving a room I always call the specific hotel I would like to book a room with and asked them to check to see if their handicap room beds have boards around them or not.

One hotel chain I found that has a good percentage of their locations with handicap room beds accessible for a patient lift is the Hampton Inn. When I talked to one of the hotel managers and expressed that I was pleasantly surprised that they took this into their consideration I was informed that all the Hampton Inn handicap room beds were supposed to be that way. I then sent e-mails to a few of the Hampton Inn chief executives, thanked them, and told them how pleased I was to hear of their policy.

One of the executives thanked me for my e-mail and said that if I ever did find one of their rooms that had boards instead of legs on the bed I was to e-mail her and let her know. During my subsequent travels I found only a couple of Hampton Inns that still had boards around the bottom of the bed and I e-mailed her each time. I was glad to have someone interested and welcome feedback on my experience while at the hotel. It never hurts to mention some of these little things to local staff and corporate personnel so that others will understand and try to remedy the situation.

Housing

For the first thirty-four years after my accident I lived in a variety of college dormitories, apartments, and houses that in many respects were not handicap-friendly. During those years, I accumulated a long wish list of items that I would include in my perfect house if I ever built one. Just prior to my retirement Diane and I built that dream house and for the last ten years my living accommodations have been the most comfortable I have ever had. But you don't have to build a house from the ground up to add special conveniences. Many of the items that were incorporated into the plans when our house was built were based on modifications I had incorporated into the existing houses I lived in before.

Here's how we made our new house more handicap friendly:

- There are no stairs between the driveway and house entrance. The concrete is ramped so the wheelchair doesn't have to get up or over stairs. The same holds true for the openings in both my main floor patio and my walkout basement patio. The patios have four-foot wide sliding glass doors.

- All the hallways are wide enough to accommodate the width of the wheelchair as well as wide enough to accommodate ninety degree turns the wheelchair has to make to get into other rooms or hallways.

- All doorways are a minimum of thirty-six inches wide to accommodate the width of a wheelchair.

- All doors have latches on them instead of doorknobs. Since I cannot use my fingers to grip anything I can at least push down on a latch to make the door open. Also, all these door latches are at a level that I can reach easily. We also chose to install hollow interior doors so that they are much lighter to open and close.

- All light switches are at a level I can reach easily.

- I have a fully adjustable hospital bed in my bedroom. If you have a caregiver who needs to get you dressed and positioned in bed a hospital bed that can move up and down becomes a necessity. Without being able to raise and lower the bed height, the caregiver could develop severe back problems if he or she has to take care of you by bending down too far.

- My hospital bed has an alternating pressure mattress that is designed to prevent pressure sores from forming while lying in bed for long periods of time. Due to pressure sore problems I had more than twenty years ago from sleeping on a foam rubber mattress, I switched to an alternating pressure mattress. For the last twenty years I have not had one skin breakdown from lying in bed for extended periods.

- My bathroom has a Jacuzzi bathtub with water jets that can circulate the water while I am taking a bath. This is not only relaxing, but I was told therapeutic for the skin as well. The one thing I would do differently if I had a chance to do it over again would be to raise the bathtub a few feet off the floor. It is very difficult at times for my caregiver to kneel on the bathroom floor to help me wash. The Jacuzzi web site is: http://www.jacuzzi.com/

- My bathroom has a sink that I can get under with a wheelchair and faucets with large levers so I can control the hot and cold water.

- A patient lift is one of the most important things to consider in any living environment. It saves a lot of wear and tear on your body as well as your caregivers. I have a patient lift that moves back and forth in a track built into the ceiling of my bedroom and bathroom, which are adjacent to one another.

The ceiling track that the lift moves in is a straight track that goes the entire length of my bedroom, through a doorway between the bedroom and bathroom, and the entire length of the bathroom. The wall between the bedroom and bathroom has a four-foot wide double door so that when I am in the lift traveling from my bed to the bathtub there is enough space for me to pass through without bumping into the wall. I park my electric wheelchair about four feet from the right side of my bed and transfer in and out of it using this lift.

I can also transfer in and out of the bathtub using this lift. If you are going to use a lift of this type to get in and out of a bathtub, make sure that the hand controls on the lift are not electric. There are lifts available that have vacuum hand controls so that you do not have to worry about getting electrocuted if the hand controls fall into the water. There are hundreds of companies that can provide a variety of patient lifts to suit your needs. Your local medical supply company can provide you with information about patient lifts, or just Google "patient lifts" on the Internet.

- My house has a three-story small elevator that will fit my electric wheelchair and me. My wife has her bedroom on the second story of the house, and I have my bedroom in a fully furnished walkout basement that has an extra-tall ceiling. That pretty much makes it mandatory for me to have the elevator. Although elevators can be retrofitted into pre-existing homes, it is much better to have one designed in if you're building a home from scratch.

Elevators are expensive. The three-story elevator costs around $25,000. If you ever think about getting an elevator, make sure that the brand you buy has been around for a long time and you have a dealer that can fix it if something goes wrong. Elevators require quite a bit of maintenance and an elevator maintenance agreement is a yearly expense.

- Make sure your bed is located so there is a way to get out of the house when you're lying on a stretcher or gurney. If at some time you need paramedics to take you out of the house, you need a good way to exit. Unfortunately, this happened to me and when I was put on a stretcher I had to be taken out of my basement. The elevator was not large enough for the gurney and the paramedics didn't want to walk up the basement stairs with the collapsed gurney because they thought it would be too difficult – even though that was my emergency plan of evacuation when I built the house.

Fortunately, our house has a walkout basement with large sliding doors leading to the back patio. Unfortunately, there are steep hills on the sides of the house and it was difficult for the paramedics to get me up the hill. They had to walk on wet grass and between pine trees before they could get me to the top of the hill and into the ambulance. I am remedying that situation by putting a sidewalk on one side of the house that goes from my driveway down to my basement patio area.

- When I am alone downstairs, I communicate with others in the house using four methods. Two of the methods are by computer and the other two are by using other equipment.

When my computer is running, I can send a message to a printer on another floor or sign on to Yahoo messenger to talk with or send instant text messages to my wife, who's logged on to another computer in our house. We have a local-area network in my home so that we can share printers and log onto each other's computers.

If my computer is down and I am in bed I use a doorbell chime that can be purchased at any home improvement store. They are relatively inexpensive and we bought two units. We have one set of chimes placed on the main floor and the other set of chimes placed on the second floor where my wife's bedroom is located. The chime doorbell ringer is attached to a string that is attached to one of my bed rails. I usually keep the doorbell ringer on top of my blanket at night so that if there's an emergency I can ring the chimes of both of the other floors.

We also have an intercom system throughout the house and outdoors. The intercoms are all placed at a level I can reach and I only need to push a button to talk to other locations of the house.

Wheelchairs and Wheelchair Cushions

I have owned many different wheelchairs over the years and each year the manufacturers come up with new models and features so I'm not going to recommend any specific wheelchair. Each person's wheelchair and cushion needs are different. But I would recommend is that you go to a wheelchair "seating clinic" in your area to have a professional determine what is best for you.

257

I would bet that most people purchase their wheelchairs through their medical supply company without first trying out the wheelchair or cushion. They look through a catalog of recommended products for both wheelchairs and cushions and the salesperson takes measurements and fills out a form to be sent to the manufacture with the order.

At a seating clinic you actually get to try various wheelchair styles and cushions while a professional therapist evaluates whether or not that combination is appropriate for you. Clinics also have engineers on hand to modify and design special changes to the wheelchair or seating arrangement that does not come standard on a wheelchair.

I have made many visits to the Rehabilitation Institute of Chicago's Seating Clinic to be fitted for an appropriate wheelchair and cushion combination. One of the ways the seating clinic can determine whether you have an appropriate cushion is to sit you on a pressure-mapping device. The pressure-mapping device is just a thin pad laid on top of your cushion while you sit in the wheelchair. A computer cable is then attached to the pressure-mapping device.

When the pressure-mapping software is brought up on the computer, you and the therapist can see where your pressure points are and whether or not they could cause you problems. As you move or shift your weight in the wheelchair you can see the changes in the pressure points. If you have problems with pressure sores I would highly recommend going to a seating clinic and have a pressure map done.

Although you may not be in the Chicago area, I'm sure that there are many other rehabilitation centers that can provide this service. I am including the web site URL for the Rehabilitation Institute of Chicago so that you can at least contact their seating clinic to find out more information about a possible similar clinic in your area. Make sure you talk to someone in the seating clinic directly. The Rehabilitation Institute of Chicago's web site is: http://www.ric.org/

I also recommend you always have a backup wheelchair. When you get a new wheelchair make sure you keep your old one to use as a spare. Without a spare wheelchair that you're familiar with you could get stuck with a loaner from the medical supply company you deal with that will not work well for you.

Make sure that the medical supply company you use has a good reliable wheelchair repair maintenance service department. Since getting around in a wheelchair is a good part of your life, you don't want to be without one for long periods of time. It doesn't hurt to ask if you could talk to some of the clients the wheelchair service department has serviced. It won't take more than a time or two of having your wheelchair serviced before you know whether or not you can count on good quality service. Don't be afraid to change your medical supply company if you are dissatisfied with their maintenance service. The maintenance of the wheelchair is much more important than the initial price of the wheelchair.

A warning about wheelchair air cushions: I have had wheelchair cushions that fill with air for many years and I found them to be relatively reliable. There is one problem that can occur which I found out about recently (see anecdote *Rocky Mountain Low*) that I feel I should at least mention.

If you're traveling around the country where there is a significant change in elevation between your starting point and ending destination you need to be aware that a wheelchair air cushion will expand as you go higher in elevation and contract as you go lower in elevation. If you are unaware that this process occurs you could be in for a rude awakening when you get out of your wheelchair and find you have the start of a pressure sore. The manufacturer of your air cushion should be able to provide you with some guidelines relative to elevation changes.

Computers

I don't think I could really function without a computer. My computer allows me to access the outside world by myself. It allows me to communicate with people by phone or e-mail. It keeps me entertained because I can watch television through it, listened to all my music CDs, and control a videotape player, a DVD player, and a satellite TV receiver. It also provides me with a way to do work.

I do a lot of writing with the word processor, create many spreadsheets to keep track of our finances and other items, create databases containing various inventories and phone numbers, store and view our family pictures, monitor and change our investments, view the current and future weather forecasts, and search the Internet for all kinds of information.

In my furnished walkout basement I have two computers. There is one in my office and one in my bedroom. Both of these computers have a computer monitor attached to a swivel arm mount connected to the wall. I have found these swivel arms extraordinarily helpful to move the monitor into a position that is easy to view. I purchased these swivel arms through a company called Innovative Office Products. You can view their products at the following web site: http://www.lcdarms.com.

On my office computer I use a keyboard to input information. When I'm sitting in a wheelchair at my computer desk I have a pencil wedged between my two fingers and the inside of one hand. Gravity helps with my arm movement so I have learned to type on the keyboard using this method. I can actually type this way relatively fast. I use a mouse pad that is fixed to my computer desk so it cannot move. The mouse pad has a small rectangular area in the middle. When I touch the pencil to its surface and move it around it moves the cursor on the computer screen. When I have the cursor positioned where I want it, I click the appropriate mouse pad button with the pencil.

I have a little different setup in my bedroom. I have a computer that has a monitor attached to a swivel arm that can be positioned over my bed for easy viewing when I'm lying on my back. There is a microphone taped to the bottom of the monitor so that I can speak to the computer using a software package called Dragon NaturallySpeaking™.

Dragon NaturallySpeaking is a fantastic product I cannot say enough about. It is a speech-recognition package that allows me to talk to the computer and have the computer do anything that I could have done by typing on a keyboard. This type of speech recognition technology has been around for a while but I feel it is finally being perfected. Five or six years ago the product worked fairly well. But, with all the enhancements made in Dragon NaturallySpeaking, and the faster computer processors that have been introduced during the last two years, the speech-recognition product is extremely accurate and easy to use.

I can now enter information into the computer much faster than I could ever do using a keyboard and probably a lot faster than normal people can type.

Dragon NaturallySpeaking is available from a company called Nuance. There are many versions of this product available on Amazon.com. The prices range from $30 to $920. I have found that the $87 Standard version is more than adequate for most people and if you've never tried it I would highly recommend it. The web site for the Dragon Naturally-Speaking company is: http://www.nuance.com/naturallyspeaking.

For my base software products I use Windows XP and Microsoft Office. Microsoft Office contains: Word, Excel, Access, PowerPoint, and Internet Explorer applications. These applications are very easy to use with Dragon NaturallySpeaking, and any other applications that you might use could be adapted to work with the software. The Microsoft web site is: http://www.microsoft.com.

I find it very handy to have a TV card in my computer so that I can watch TV, videotapes, and DVDs through my computer monitor. The TV card I have is from a company called Hauppauge and their basic product is called WinTV. They make many types of Win-TV cards and you can get one to fill many different needs. The Win-TV cards start at around $100 dollars. The Hauppauge web site is: http://www.hauppauge.com/index.htm.

I used to have a telephone card in my computer that was connected to our main phone line in the house but I found that using a product called Yahoo! Messenger is much easier to use and the sound is much clearer. There are similar messenger products from other vendors that you might also want to research.

The basic Yahoo! Messenger is a free product and great if you are going to use it to communicate with other friends who have computers. You can also purchase additional functions such as receiving outside telephone calls and making telephone calls to normal landlines for a very nominal expense. If you make a call to a normal land line you are charged around a penny a minute and can have your own personal telephone number that anybody can call for around $2.50 a month. This product can be downloaded for free from the following web site: http://voice.yahoo.com.

My wife and I have purchased computers from a few of the major computer vendors over the years but currently we use Dell equipment. We have found them to be very reliable. The computers we purchased have a lot of processing speed, memory, and disk storage space. Again, the improved capacity of the computer equipment is one of the reasons that Dragon NaturallySpeaking is so much better than it used to be a few years ago. The Dell web site is: http://www.dell.com.

Finding a caregiver

It was often difficult for me to find a qualified and reliable caregiver. If you live in a neighborhood around a college there is a good chance you could hire in a student or two for room and board. Otherwise, there are now quite a few organizations focused on home health care. With the baby boomer generation getting older home health care is becoming a major business. These organizations can provide various levels of care. They can send you a person to help out part-time or full-time. They also can provide personnel with different levels of caregiver skills based on your specific needs. To find home health care organizations you can Google the Internet for "home health care", "assisted living", or "caregivers" and add the city you're interested in finding listings for. For instance, to find caregivers in the Chicago area, in the search box on Google you would type in: caregivers+Chicago.

Alcoholic beverages

I have a real problem drinking alcohol because of what it does to my digestive system. But I did eventually find a few options that work most of the time. Actually I found three drinks that seem to have dastardly effects on my digestive system only occasionally. It took years of trial and error (mostly error) to find alcoholic drinks I could somewhat tolerate. I still drink alcohol only very occasionally because my solutions are definitely not foolproof. Below I've listed three drinks that I have had success with in case there are others reading this who have similar digestive problems and want to give them a try.

1) The only wine I seem to be able to tolerate is Carlo Rossi's Paisano. It is a red table wine that I usually can pick up in gallon size jugs. It is also very inexpensive. Some of my friends indulge in expensive wines, but I am more than satisfied with my cheap bottle from Carlo.

2) Another drink I can tolerate is often called a Snowshoe. This drink is mixed with equal parts of vodka and peppermint schnapps. I never could stand the taste of vodka but somehow the peppermint schnapps makes it one of the smoothest drinks I ever tasted, especially after having two of them. You

can drink it straight or over ice. I usually start with one and a half ounces of each in a glass of ice. After two drinks I usually forget the ice.

3) I really never cared for the taste of regular beer (a sacrilege for a Milwaukee-born boy) but I once tried a mixed drink called a red beer in a small bar in upper Wisconsin that I really liked. A red beer is equal parts beer and tomato juice. I guess I liked it so much because of the tomato juice. If you have never tried it I would highly recommend it. Once in awhile I substitute the tomato juice with V8 juice and if you like your drinks a little more spicy you can mix it with Bloody Mary mix. If you use a Bloody Mary mix I would recommend that you use a little less mix and a little more beer. If you can get your hands on Del Monte Foods Snap-E Tom™ tomato and chili cocktail, I find it to be the perfect mixer to spice up your beer. Hey, don't knock it if you haven't tried it! However I never drink more than what can be mixed up with two twelve-ounce bottles of beer.

Product Disclaimer:

The specific products and web sites I mention in this chapter are some of the products I currently use and I present them for your information only. New and improved products and services are introduced to the market every year so I encourage you to conduct your own research to compare options and offerings that might benefit your living situation. The opinions expressed here are mine alone. I have not received any gifts or monetary compensation from these companies in exchange for mentioning their products in this book. I have spent many years using and testing products and services that bettered my life and thought that you might benefit from some of my experiences.

Photographs

Circle Bed Photos Courtesy of Jim Hemauer

Jim Hemauer, a native of Plymouth, Wisconsin, sustained a C 3-4 spinal cord injury in 1970 at the age of 15 in a swimming accident. Thanks to the unwavering support from family and friends, Jim went on to build an

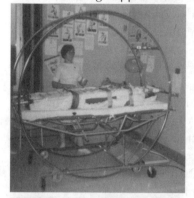

independent life for himself. He earned a Bachelor's degree from the University of Wisconsin-Oshkosh and a Masters degree from Arizona State University.

Jim is currently an Assistant Director within the Department of Educational Development at Arizona State University and oversees the Disability Resource Center. He resides in Tempe, Arizona and shares personal, insightful stories of his own life's journey on his web site at:

http://www.public.asu.edu/~gimpy.

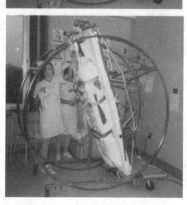

Tenodesis Splint

Jaeco Orthopedic F-21F

Tenodesis Splint is a device used to grasp objects by C6-C7 quadriplegics who lack finger movement but retain the ability to extend their wrist. The device straps onto the user's forearm, hand, and fingers. When the user extends the wrist (back of hand toward forearm), digits 1-3 are pushed together in a grasping motion.

Reprinted with the permission of Jaeco Orthopedic.

http://www.jaeco-orthopedic.com

Contact: info@jaeco-orthopedic.com

Sliderule

Reprinted with permission of Eric Marcotte. For more information and examples of slide rules, visit:

http://www.sliderule.ca

ANOTHER *fine* MESS
you've gotten us into

The Life and Adventures of a Quad

IS AVAILABLE AT:

www.finemessadventure.com

www.amazon.com

In select bookstores

Do you have a question for Bob?
You can email him via the
www.finemessadventure.com website.